Archibald Wright Murray

Wonders in the Western Isles

Being a Narrative of the Commencement and Progress of Mission Work in Western

Polynesia

Archibald Wright Murray

Wonders in the Western Isles
Being a Narrative of the Commencement and Progress of Mission Work in Western Polynesia

ISBN/EAN: 9783337412883

Printed in Europe, USA, Canada, Australia, Japan

Cover: Foto ©Andreas Hilbeck / pixelio.de

More available books at **www.hansebooks.com**

WONDERS
IN THE
WESTERN ISLES

BEING A NARRATIVE OF THE
COMMENCEMENT AND PROGRESS
OF
Mission Work in Western Polynesia.

BY THE
Rev. A. W. MURRAY,
FORTY YEARS A MISSIONARY IN POLYNESIA AND NEW GUINEA IN CONNECTION WITH
THE LONDON MISSIONARY SOCIETY.

"That which we have seen and heard declare we unto you."—1 *John* i. 3.

LONDON:
PRINTED BY YATES AND ALEXANDER,
7, SYMONDS INN, CHANCERY LANE, W.C.

1874.

CONTENTS.

CHAP.		PAGE
I.—GENERAL VIEW OF THE PRINCIPAL GROUPS AND ISLANDS IN THE PACIFIC		1
II.—FOTUNA		9
III.—ANEITEUM		16
IV.—ANEITEUM—*continued*		48
V.—ANEITEUM—*continued*		83
VI.—TANNA		123
VII.—ERAMANGA		153
VIII.—NIUA		188
IX.—VATE, OR SANDWICH ISLAND		192
X.—NEW CALEDONIA AND THE ISLE OF PINES		235
XI.—MARE, or NENGONE		262
XII.—LIFU		285
XIII.—NIUE, OR SAVAGE ISLAND		313

LIST OF ILLUSTRATIONS.

	PAGE
A View of Tahiti	*Frontispiece.*
A Chief of Aneiteum	5
Natives of Fotuna	11
Mission Station, Aneiteum	17
Aneiteumese Heathen Village	27
Effects of a Hurricane	38
Native Mother and Child	41
The Harbour of Aneiteum	49
A Group of Natives (Papuans)	59
The Island of Borabora	69
Yeapai, an Aneiteumese Chief and a Christian	79
Island Scenery	92
Natives of Aneiteum carrying Timber to Build a Church	99
An Island Chapel	109
Missionaries landing	118
Going off to the Missionary ship	126
Murderous attack of Natives	137
Sketch of Natives and their Home	154
South Sea Fishers	162
The "John Williams," Missionary Ship	173
Scene of the Massacre of Williams and Harris, Dillon's Bay	185
Island of Upolu	193
A View in Rarotonga, one of the Hervey Group	205
Raiatea.—House of the late Rev. J. Vivian	217
General View of Aneiteum	227
A Native House	241
Mission Printing Office, Leulumoenga	249
The Mission Settlement at Borabora	259
Society Islands	268
Welcoming a Missionary	275
Island of Lifu	286
A Missionary Meeting in Polynesia	295
Launching a Missionary Boat	305
A Chapel at Taha	314
A Group of Natives	320
Papeeto Bay, Tahiti	326
Reception by Savage Islanders	331
Rev. John Green's Island Home	337
Queen Pomare's Palace, Tahiti	341
The Island of Fotuna	344

WONDERS
IN THE
WESTERN ISLES.

CHAPTER I.

GENERAL VIEW OF THE PRINCIPAL GROUPS AND ISLANDS IN THE PACIFIC.

THE islands of the Pacific consist of two great divisions, designated Eastern and Western Polynesia. These designations, though indicating the geographical positions of the islands, do not rest merely on local grounds, but have also reference to the fact that the two divisions are peopled by races totally distinct. New Zealand indeed is an exception. Though locally included in Western Polynesia, it must, on the more important ground of oneness of people, be considered as belonging to the eastern division.

Eastern Polynesia embraces all the islands from the Marquesas on the east, to Horne's Island on the west; and from the Sandwich Islands on the north, to New Zealand on the south. All the tribes that inhabit the numerous islands and groups scattered over this immense region are evidently one people. The marks of identity, such as oneness of language, the prevalence of substantially the same manners and customs, the employment of the same terms to designate the Supreme Power, similarity in colour and appearance, and agreement in their traditions, are so plain that they cannot be mistaken. Those who have had the best opportunities of forming a judgment are all but unanimous that their origin is Malayan. It does not comport with our design to attempt the discussion of this subject, nor would it answer any very important end.

The other great division of Polynesia embraces all the islands and groups, from the Figis on the east, to New Caledonia on the west, and from about 23° south lat. to the large islands in the neighbourhood of New Guinea on the north.

These islands, as already intimated, are peopled by tribes altogether distinct from those of Eastern Polynesia. A few of these, indeed, are found among them, but they consist, not of aboriginal inhabitants, but of parties, or descendants of parties, who have lost their way at sea, or been carried out of their track by contrary winds.

Of late years, another name has been adopted to distinguish the northern part of Western Polynesia from the southern, viz., *Mikronesia*. The islands embraced in this division are generally, as the name imports, small, but they are very numerous, and are scattered over an immense region, extending from the meridian of longitude about 50° in a north-westerly direction, and from lat. 3° S. to 21° N.; the islands are many hundreds in number, and have a population estimated at 200,000. American missionaries are successfully employed in planting the Gospel in Mikronesia.

The aboriginal inhabitants of the islands of Western Polynesia differ widely among themselves, as we shall hereafter see. They have so much in common, however, that a general name, that of Papuan, and more recently that of Melanesian, has been employed to designate them. Another term, viz., Negrillo, has been adopted by ethnologists to distinguish the races inhabiting the New Hebrides and other islands from the Figians and from the purely Negro race. The Mikronesians are not included in the above designations. Respecting them our information is scanty and imperfect. In reference to Eastern Polynesia, it is a fact on which the Christian's heart dwells with the most delightful satisfaction, that all the principal groups have long been the spheres of successful missionary operations. More than half a century has now passed away since the *Duff* bore the first missionaries, sent forth by the London Missionary Society, to the shores of Tahiti. On that island the grand experiment was made; there the problem, Are missions to the heathen practicable? was solved. After a long season of apparently fruitless suffering and toil, which severely tried, almost overcame the faith and patience of both missionaries and their supporters, God was pleased to affix the seal of His approbation to their efforts. He made bare His own gracious and all-powerful arm in the sight of the heathen, and in the sight of an intensely interested few among His own people. Effects followed such as had not been witnessed since the primitive ages of Christianity. A nation was born in a day. A system of idolatry and superstition, the growth of unnumbered ages, was swept away with a rapidity and completeness which confounded adversaries and assured friends. The pure and holy religion of the Bible became the religion of Tahiti, and that island was thenceforth a centre whence the light went forth to surrounding islands and groups, far and wide; and now we have the high satisfaction of seeing all the principal groups of Eastern Polynesia more or less Christianized.

The Sandwich Islands, in the extreme north, and New Zealand in the south, the largest of all the groups, have long been under Christian culture, and most delightful results have been realized. The Hervey group, the Samoan group, and the Friendly Islands, are themselves all the spheres of successful missionary labour, and each is becoming a centre whence the light and blessings of the Gospel are being extended to other islands and groups. Thus there is ground to hope that at no very distant day the whole of Eastern Polynesia will be brought under the influence of the Gospel, and the friends of Christian missions are supplied with ample encouragement.

But it is to Western Polynesia that we intend to devote

the following pages; and, by way of introducing the notices we are about to offer of the efforts that have been made towards the evangelization of that region, we may furnish our readers with a brief general description of the group which will first engage our attention, viz. :—

THE NEW HEBRIDES,

and of the first efforts made towards introducing the Gospel to that group.

The New Hebrides are situated between latitude 14° 29′ N. and 20° 4′ S.; and longitude 166° 41′ and 170° 21′ E. They extend about 400 hundred miles, N.N.W. and S.S.E. The northern island was discovered by Quiros in 1606. He regarded it as a part of the Southern continent which at that time was supposed to exist. The group was visited by Bougainville in 1768. Besides ascertaining that the land was not connected, but composed of islands, he did but little; and it was reserved for our own great navigator, Cook, to complete the discovery. He visited it in 1774, discovered all the southern islands, and more or less fully explored the whole of it. He gave it the designation it now bears. It is remarkable that a group so extensive, and possessing resources so great, should have continued so long comparatively unknown. This has been owing, doubtless, chiefly to the savage character of the inhabitants; and, when these are brought into a state which shall render it safe for foreign visitors to approach their shores, the islands will, in all probability, speedily be laid open to the world, and their resources made available to the purposes for which they are adapted. With the exception of the Figis and New Zealand, there is no group in the South Pacific that will bear comparison with the New Hebrides. In extent, population, and resources, they have no other rival. There are no fewer than *thirty* inhabited islands, two of which are about two hundred miles in circumference. Besides these, there are a number of inhabited islands, in the immediate vicinity of the larger

A CHIEF OF ANEITEUM.

ones, of which no notice is takes in geographical works, and which have no place on any chart. The names of the principal islands of the group, proceeding from the north in a south-easterly direction, are, Espiritu Santo, the largest island of the group; Malicolo, the next in size; Bartholomew's; Leper's Island; Aurora; Pentecost; Ambrym, or Chinambrym, as the natives call it; Apee; Paum Islands, two in number; the Pyramid; the Monument, so named because of its shape; Two Hills; Shepherd's Isles, five in number; Three Hills; Montague; Hinchinbrook; Vate, or Sandwich Island; Eramanga; Niua; Tana; Fotuna, and Aneiteum. All these islands are inhabited, some of them thickly so for heathen lands. Of course we can only guess at the population. It is very probable that it may not be less than one hundred and fifty thousand. The Islands of the New Hebrides are, so far as our knowledge goes, all of volcanic origin. They resemble in their general appearance the islands of Eastern Polynesia. In beauty and fruitfulness they are not a whit behind the finest of these. Some of them, Ambrym for example, are perfect gems. The writer has seen many beautiful islands, both in Eastern and Western Polynesia, but one more lovely than the island just named he never beheld.

A little more than thirty years have passed since the initiatory step towards the evangelization of the New Hebrides was taken; the circumstances were such as to render the event for ever memorable. The large-hearted, generous Williams had long looked wistfully towards Western Polynesia, and longed to impart to its benighted tribes the blessings of the Gospel.

He had succeeded, by the help of God, in obtaining the necessary means for carrying into execution his long-cherished project. Glowing with ardent zeal, and sanguine of success, he embarked on his glorious enterprise. Fervent prayers and wishes followed him, and high hopes were entertained as to the results. Nor shall these hopes fail; but how different the manner of their realization from that which man had conceived!" "Not by might nor by power, but by My Spirit saith the Lord of hosts." "The Lord seeth not as man seeth." Williams did succeed. He was instrumental in kindling a fire which will never be extinguished; in commencing a work the progress of which will never be stayed till the light of the knowledge of the glory of God fill every island and group as the waters cover the seas. But the Lord our God is a jealous God; He will not give His glory to another; He will hide pride from man, and will so arrange His dispensations as to lead His people to have their eyes directed to Him instead of the agents whom He is pleased to employ. And many a painful lesson does it require to effect this end, but it must be taught at whatever cost.

On the 19th day of November, 1839, Christian teachers were placed on the island of Tana; on the following day Mr. Williams proceeded to Eramanga. We know what followed. His work was done; the gracious Master granted him so far the desire of his heart as to permit him to view the land, and take possession of it in His name; and, that being done, He took him to Himself. The removal of this honoured servant of God led to no interruption in the enterprise which he was privileged to begin. Others were ready to take up the work where he had laid it down; and by the help of Him who orders and disposes all, it has been carried on with the most blessed results.

We shall now proceed, in a series of sketches, to notice the commencement and progress of Missionary work on the different islands that have been brought under Christian culture, with a view to stimulate and encourage the friends of Christian missions in the prosecution of the work which their Lord and Master has solemnly enjoined them to perform.

CHAPTER II.

"Your labour is not in vain in the Lord."—1 *Cor.* xv. 58.

FOTUNA.

WE shall take up the different islands that are to come sucessively under our notice in their geographical order, beginning at the east, and proceeding towards the west. The most easterly island of the New Hebrides is the small island whose name stands at the head of this chapter. This island is not of great importance in itself, nor as compared with many other islands of the group to which it belongs, but in a missionary point of view there are circumstances of interest connected with it. It has a population of about 1,000 souls, and has been the scene of the labours of Christian teachers, some of whom have sealed their testimony with their blood. On this lone isle of the ocean martyr-blood has flowed, so that it can never cease to be regarded with tender interest by the followers of Christ.

The island consists of one high bluff mountain, a "massive square block of land," as Captain Erskine calls it, with narrow valleys, or ravines, in which are found the habitable and fertile spots. Captain Cook estimated its circumference at about fifteen miles.

Fotuna is peopled by a race speaking a dialect of the Eastern Polynesian language. With this exception, they seem to have little in common with the Eastern Polynesians. Their general appearance, as also their habits and customs, would, on the contrary, rather identify them with the Western tribes. They are, indeed, superior to any other race found in the southern group of the New Hebrides, although essentially one with these. The probability is, that at a remote period there were two distinct races on the island, the one Melanesian, the other Malayan. In process of time an amalgamation took place, and the result is the present somewhat mongrel people, with the remarkable peculiarity of their speaking a language totally different from what is found on any of the neighbouring islands, except the small island of Niua.

Fotuna is the native name of Horne's Island, which is the most westerly island of Eastern Polynesia, and quite in the track of the prevailing easterly trade winds; so that a party losing their way at sea would be quite likely to make Fotuna, which, as already stated, is the most easterly island of the New Hebrides. Our knowledge of the people of Fotuna is as yet very imperfect; the probability is, that their state is similar to that of the neighbouring islanders. They are a fierce, savage-looking people, and have proved themselves to be as cruel as their appearance indicates. They are evidently a people of superior capabilities.

It was in 1841 that the first attempt was made to introduce the Gospel to this island. Mr. Williams had touched at the island, and had held intercourse with some of the natives, as he passed, a day or two before his death. This had, to some extent, prepared the way for us, as Mr. Williams had given presents, and so far prepossessed the people in our favour.

We made the island in the brig *Camden* on 29th March, 1841, and the same day succeeded in placing two teachers upon it. Their names were Apolo, from Tutuila, and Samuela, from Upolu. Apolo was unmarried, and Samuela had left his wife and family at home, until it might be ascertained how far it would be advisable for females to be placed on such islands in the state in which they then were.

They had a very encouraging reception, and after visiting the neighbouring island of Aneiteum, with a principal chief of Fotuna, named Kotiama, on board, we returned to the island, and were happy to find all going on well, and the prospects very promising. Such

NATIVES OF FOTUNA.

was the commencement of our connection with this people,
And not only was the commencement auspicious, but
everything continued to go on encouragingly for a long
period. The newly-formed stations on that and other
islands were visited in the *Camden*, by Messrs. Buzacott
and Slatyer, in 1842. Samuela's wife and daughter were
taken to him, and all seemed encouraging, and so continued
until about February or March, 1843. The next visit to
the island was made by Dr. Turner and the writer, in the
John Williams, in the month of April, 1845. We were not
without anxiety when we approached the island on that
occasion, especially as so long a time had elapsed since
the former visit; but we were not prepared for what had
actually occurred. We did not expect that the little light
which had begun to glimmer amid the thick darkness, and
to give promise of approaching day, had been quenched
in blood; yet so it was. The whole mission party had
been murdered by the misguided people whose salvation
they sought. As nearly as we could ascertain, the affair
took place about February or March, 1843. An epidemic
was raging on the island at the time. The people entertaining the notion, common in Western Polynesia, that disease
and death are caused by men, supposed that the disease
was in some way connected with the teachers and the new
religion; and, under the influence of that supposition,
they determined to put the whole party to death. On the
morning of the massacre, the teachers had gone into the
bush to visit their plantations. They were accompanied
by the daughter of Samuela. His wife remained at home
alone. The savages waylaid them, and murdered Apolo
and the girl as they were on their way home, after which
they proceeded to the place where they had been at work.
Here they found Samuela, who was immediately killed.
They then made their way to the mission premises, and
surrounded the house in which was the remaining member
of the little party, all unconscious of what had occurred.
Alas! what a terrible situation was hers! A wretch,

named Nasaua, the leader of the party, entered the house and asked her to become his wife. From this proposal she recoiled. She offered him property, but instead of receiving it, he raised a shout, the signal of an attack which sealed her doom. There was a rush into the house, and the deed was done. The savages wound up the dreadful tragedy by dividing among themselves the little property which had belonged to the teachers, burning the house, and apportioning two of the bodies among the different districts of the island. The body of one of the teachers, and that of the girl, were not cooked, but cut in pieces and thrown into the sea, probably as an offering to the gods. Thus terminated the lives and labours of these witnesses for Christ.

A long dreary period followed their death. When the island was visited on the occasion to which we are now referring, namely, in April, 1845, all our efforts to obtain intercourse with the people were unsuccessful; and it was not until 1853 that we were able to resume missionary operations. At that date the work had taken such decided hold on the adjacent island of Aneiteum, that evangelists from thence were ready to become the messengers of mercy to their benighted neighbours; and, on the arrival there of the *John Williams*, in October, there were providential indications which seemed clearly to intimate that the time to reoccupy Fotuna had come. An important chief, together with a number of people, had been for several months on Aneiteum; there they had learned something of Christianity, and had witnessed its effects among a people similar to themselves. They had become decidedly disposed to receive Christian instruction, had renounced heathenism, and avowed themselves Christians. We found them waiting, in the hope that the mission ship would take them home accompanied by Christian teachers. Teachers, moreover, were waiting, ready to go with them. Thus our way seemed clear. The esteemed brethren on Aneiteum, Messrs. Geddie and Inglis, had selected two natives of that island, Waihit and Josefa, who were considered suitable for the important embassy; and, on the 26th of October, they were landed on the island, together with the chief and party. The going forth of these men as evangelists was an interesting event, as they were the first who had so gone forth in Western Polynesia. It opened a new door of hope for these extended regions, and was exceedingly cheering to those who had been taking a part in the arduous struggle that had been in progress for the previous fourteen years.

Messrs. Drummond and Harbutt, who visited the island as a deputation from the Samoan Mission in June, 1857, remark, after stating that the teachers had been in great peril, and that only three or four individuals had renounced heathenism—"The night here is still dark, no ray of light shooting up behind these dark mountains indicates the approach of the morning star." Dr. Turner, who visited the island, as a deputation from the Samoan Mission, in 1859, in company with Mr. Inglis of the Aneiteum Mission, writes as follows:—"Since last year the teacher's house at Ipeke has been burned. The teacher was blamed as the cause of disease. A person died, and the friends sought revenge in burning the house." And again—"A few at each of the three stations are nominally Christians, but it is still 'the night of toil on that heathen shore.' Not long ago the brother of the chief Kotiama died. Some parties were blamed as having caused his death by witchcraft, and six of them were forthwith killed, namely, three men and three women. More would probably have been sacrificed, but they fled to sea, and escaped to Aneiteum. It was the same Kotiama that consented to the massacre of our teachers a number of years ago. He is friendly again, and it is hoped that he will ere long receive a teacher to his settlement. We arranged to leave another Aneiteum teacher here, and also an Aitutaki teacher, named Ru, and his wife. The chiefs and people expressed their satisfaction."

CHAPTER III.

ANEITEUM.

"The dark places of the earth are full of the habitations of cruelty."
Psalm lxxiv. 20.

"ON the day of prosperity be joyful, and in the day of adversity consider: God hath set the one over against the other." Even so it is: with wise and beautiful adaptation does God set one thing over against another, so as to secure, in the highest degree, the safety and usefulness of those whom He honours to advance the interests of His kingdom. Man requires to be restrained and checked on the one hand, that he may be preserved from undue, or perhaps rather misplaced, confidence; and he needs to be stimulated and encouraged on the other, lest he sink into despondency and become unfitted for active service. Hence, checks and encouragements are wisely and mercifully blended. Of this we have had abundant and striking illustrations in Western Polynesia.

Witness the island that has just passed under review as an instance of the former; and that to which this chapter is devoted as strikingly illustrating both views. Further illustrations equally marked we shall meet with as we proceed in the case of other islands.

Before coming to the missionary history of Aneiteum, we may take a glance at the island itself,—its extent, population, and other matters of interest connected with it. It was discovered by Captain Cook, in 1774, and by him named Matam, a name by which, except in missionary circles, it is still generally known. It is the most southerly island of the New Hebrides. It lies in south lat. 20°, and

THE MISSION CHAPEL. THE CHIEF'S HOUSE. MR. GEDDIE'S STUDY. DWELLING HOUSE.
MISSION STATION, ANEITEUM.

east long. 170°. It is forty miles in circumference, and has a population of 3,600. It is lofty, some of its mountains rising to the height of 3,000 feet. Its general character is mountainous, but it has a considerable amount of good agricultural land. It is well wooded and watered. Large quantities of Kauri pine are found of excellent quality, and a great variety of other wood, which might be turned to valuable account. But the chief distinction of Aneiteum, among the islands of the southern division of the New Hebrides group, consists in its harbour. This is of a very superior character. It is spacious, and sheltered from all points except the west, to which it opens. It is easy of ingress and egress, the entrance being wide and free from obstruction. Anchorage for vessels of any size is found at a convenient depth of water, and with good bottom, and the circumstances must be very extraordinary that would endanger any vessel properly secured. A considerable number of vessels have of late years resorted to the island. For several years the average number was forty—not forty different vessels, for the same vessel would, in some cases, anchor two, three, or more times during the course of the year.

The island of Aneiteum is seen from a great distance; some say sixty miles. It is a beautiful island. Hill and valley, mountains of every shape and size, intersected by deep ravines, cultivated spots, and barren tracts, covered with scrub, or entirely without vegetation, diversify the scene and give it a lively and picturesque appearance.

But Aneiteum has of late years come to be distinguished by riches more to be prized, and beauties more enduring than any that mere natural advantages can confer. Comparatively, it is a gem on which the eye of the Christian rests with a satisfaction which words cannot adequately express.

Let us try briefly to trace those movements which, under the guiding hand and by the blessing of Him, from whom all good comes, have raised Aneiteum to the distinguished position which it at present holds among the isles of the sea. It was during the third voyage of the *Camden* to Western Polynesia that Christian teachers were introduced to Aneiteum. On that occasion the writer was privileged to make his first acquaintance with a department of missionary work in which he has since been permitted to have a considerable share; a department than which none is more important or more thoroughly congenial to the missionary's heart. Vividly was this feeling realized on the morning of March the 30th, 1841, when we approached Aneiteum. We had succeeded, on the preceding day, in introducing teachers to the adjacent island of Fotuna. There we had experienced comparatively little difficulty, as on that island a dialect of the Eastern Polynesian language is spoken; but how were we to manage at Aneiteum, the language of which was utterly unintelligible to us? We had made the best provision against this difficulty of which our circumstances admitted, having brought with us the chief Kotiama, from Fotuna, to act as our interpreter.

An odd character, indeed, was Kotiama to bring on such a mission—himself a heathen, and afterwards concerned in the murder of his own teachers, and, alas! a heathen to this day. He was of essential service to us, however, as without him there is no likelihood that we should have succeeded in the object of our visit. When we drew near the island, canoes came off towards the ship; but the natives would by no means come on board. The reason of their shyness we could only conjecture at the time, but it has since been explained. Only three vessels had visited the island before us. Cook, though he discovered the island, had no intercourse with it. The first of these vessels was seen by the natives off a place called Umetch, on the opposite side of the island to that on which we were. All was amazement and consternation at the sight of the wonderful object. What could the great moving mass be? The sage conclusion reached was that it was a

Natmas, spirit or god; and the next thing to be considered was, how the unwelcome visitor was to be either frightened away or induced to depart quietly. The first plan was resorted to. Large shells, which they were accustomed to blow in order to scare away unfriendly natmases, were brought, and the poor Aneiteumese blew away with might and main, but all to no purpose. The terrible natmas continued to draw nearer and nearer. The conciliating plan was now had recourse to. Offerings were brought. Yams, cocoa-nuts, etc., etc., were collected and piled up in a heap on the shore. Now it was evident that the right expedient had been hit upon; a boat was sent from the ship, which carried off what had been collected, and so confirmed the people in their conjecture, only they concluded now that, whereas they had thought at first that the vessel was itself a single natmas, it was filled with natmases. Having taken on board the food collected by the people the vessel departed, and so ended the first visit of foreigners to the island of Aneiteum.

The second visit had a different issue. A vessel called at a place named Anauiae, about four miles to the east of the harbour, and put a man on shore; most probably the poor man was ill, or perhaps he may have been guilty of some improper conduct on board. However that may be, he was turned on shore, and left to the mercy of the savages. They stripped off his clothes, probably to satisfy themselves as to whether he was really a natmas or a being made up of flesh, blood, and bones, like themselves. The result was fatal to the poor man. They allowed him to live a short time, and then killed and cooked him.

The next visit was that of a brig named the *Alpha*. The object of this visit seems to have been commercial. It was in March, 1830, and the part of the island visited was the same as that at which we first had intercourse with the people. On board the vessel were a number of natives of Rotumah and Tahiti. These were sent on shore to cut sandal-wood. All went on smoothly for a time, the natives appearing friendly, and assisting in the cutting of the wood. One morning, however, the Tahitian and Rotumah men were surprised, while at breakfast, by being attacked by the natives with showers of spears. Several were wounded, and two afterwards died. Five of the natives were killed in the affray. The disturbance seems to have arisen from a Rotumah man having stolen some sugarcane from the natives. Our visit was the next; hence the distrust and apprehension which the people manifested.

All our efforts to induce the natives to come on board being unsuccessful, a boat was lowered, and Captain Morgan and myself went in close to shore. After a while one character of note ventured near enough to our boat to receive from my hands a string of beads. Snatching the treasure, at the risk of his life, as he seemed to think, he immediately backed astern; but the scale was turned. His venture had succeeded—and having succeeded once, he might a second time; hence distrust soon gave place to confidence, and we were in a fair way to gain our object. The bold fellow who received the beads was Iata, the chief of the district off which we were. I have seen many a heathen of a deeply degraded and savage character, but a more finished savage, to all appearance, and, as we afterwards found, in reality, I never saw. He realized most fully the idea one forms of the ferocious and bloodthirsty savage. And yet this man received and protected the messengers of peace. We shall meet with him again in the course of our narrative. In the meanwhile we proceed with our account. We made known our object as well as we could through Kotiama. The teachers intended for the island went on shore, and on their return they expressed themselves satisfied with the prospects, and were willing to remain. The reception they met with was interesting and encouraging. Large numbers of people were congregated on the beach. They expressed their pacific and friendly disposition by waving green boughs. Thus they welcomed to their shores the messengers of salvation, and the initiatory step was taken towards the wonderful revolution which has since been effected. " Who hath despised the day of small things ? "

Having introduced the teachers to their sphere of labour, let us now take a glance at their future charge. What was their character? What their condition? The people of Aneiteum are rather an inferior race. They are generally small of stature, and, on the whole, unprepossessing in their appearance. They are a mixed race. Some have woolly hair and a negro expression of countenance, while others have straight hair, and exhibit Eastern Polynesian features and colour. And this agrees with a tradition that at a very remote period a canoe came to their island from Savaiki (Savaii, the largest island of the Samoan group), and that the people that were in it became amalgamated with the natives; and it agrees, moreover, with the fact that several purely Samoan words *Aneiteumised* are found in the language.

The Aneiteumese did not *tattoo* their bodies, as is common among all the eastern tribes, but used paint, and adorned themselves with a profusion of what they regarded as ornaments. The men wore nothing worthy of the name of clothing; the women were decently covered. They had nothing deserving the name of manufactures, except perhaps their clubs and spears, and these were inferior. Their canoes were exceedingly poor, as were also their houses. The men wore their hair long, after the Tanese fashion; the women had theirs cropped short.

As to the moral and social state of this people, it had reached about as low a point as men can well reach; this will come out more fully as we proceed. In the meantime we merely glance at it. They were "hateful, and hating one another." War, murder, cannibalism, the strangling of widows, the murder of orphan children, polygamy, and the consequent oppression and degradation of the female sex; these, and such like, were the characteristics of the Aneiteumese when "the dayspring from on high" opened upon their dark and cheerless shores. And add to this that they lived under the most abject bondage to their natmases, of whom they were in constant dread.

The principal deity of the Aneiteumese was *Nugerain*, a personage held in such veneration that his name must not be pronounced except by official characters of the highest degree of sacredness. To Nugerain was ascribed the origin of the island. On a certain day he went out to fish (strange employment for a god!) and as he carried on his fishing operations, his hook got fast to some unknown object, and he hauled away till, lo! he brought up Aneiteum. It is a matter of conjecture with the Aneiteumese as to the state in which the island was when it was drawn up from the great deep; whether composed, as it now is of mountain, hill, and valley, and clothed with vegetation, or otherwise. They ascribe their origin to Nugerain; but how they were produced they cannot tell. They have a dim and vague tradition of the fall, to the effect that on a certain occasion Nugerain, who was furnished with a shell like a tortoise, cast his shell and left it behind him when he went to some distant part. During his absence his children pierced the said shell with the stalk of the cocoa-nut leaf, and burned it with fire, and on account of this the race were doomed to die. But for this they would have lived for ever.

In addition to Nugerain, the Aneiteumese had a host of minor deities, who they say are his progeny. He was the great father and creator. The inferior deities were designated according to the places and things where or in which they were supposed to reside, and over which they exercised control. They were called gods of the sea and gods of the land; gods of the mountain and gods of the valleys; gods of war and gods of peace; disease-making gods; storm-producing gods, etc., etc. Among the gods of the Aneiteumese, the sun and moon, especially the latter, held a distinguished place. They are represented as husband and wife. They originally dwelt on the earth, somewhere away in the east; but in process of time the sun went up into the heavens, and told the moon to follow, and she obeyed. They have a daughter, named Sina, a very curious coincidence with the Samoan tradition about their women in the moon, whom they call Sina. To the moon distinguished honours were paid. The natives were wont to assemble and dance before her, and sing songs in her praise. On certain occasions a small figure was dressed up to represent her, which was danced about and honoured as her representative. Offerings were also made to her as to other deities. These consisted of cooked food, and kava prepared for drinking, which were placed on altars constructed of wood. These altars were situated in sacred groves. Occasionally, small temples of rude construction were found in these groves. The offerings were presented by sacred characters only. Animals do not seem to have been offered in sacrifice. The fat of pigs, indeed, was offered to the gods, and at one place on the island, Anelecauhat, where there was a god of peculiar sanctity, and where Nohoat, the principal chief of the island, resided, the shoulder of a pig was occasionally offered. First-fruits were offered to the gods, and on occasions of feasts no one tasted the food until a part had been presented to the gods by a priest. When that was done, and the priest had eaten a portion of the food, it was pronounced to be no longer sacred, and the hungry multitudes were at liberty to feast upon it without stint.

Prayers accompanied the offerings that the gods would be propitious and prosper the people in their undertakings. Nothing of importance was entered upon without acknowledging the gods and seeking their assistance and blessing. Thus were the Aneiteumese, like the Athenians of old, "in all things too superstitious." And to compare small things with great, the number of their deities and sacred objects rivalled those of ancient Athens. Sacred stones, sacred places, and sacred objects were without number; and the poor Aneiteumese were in constant danger of offending the patrons or proprietors of these. What between the fear of incurring the displeasure of some among the multitude of spiritual beings, who, as they thought, "walked the earth unseen (not always 'unseen'), both when they waked and when they slept;" or of being surprised by the spear or the club of the assassin, they led a most unenviable life. They were accustomed to sleep with their clubs and spears by their pillows. They were emphatically all their lifetime subject to a most harassing bondage through fear of death. *Human* sacrifices were sometimes offered, though, from all that appears, not frequently. On one occasion a young man, who was about to be slain, in order to secure, as the deluded people thought, a plentiful crop of bread fruit, fled to Mr. Geddie for protection. But what were their prospects for the future? What, we mean, according to their own belief? Gloomy enough, and grovelling enough. They believed in a future state, which they called Imai. This state consisted of two divisions: the one a sensual paradise, supplied with all kinds of food, and everything calculated to minister sensual delight; the other a most miserable place, where the wretched beings that are doomed to it live upon the vilest refuse, and are tormented by being dragged over sharp stones, and having the ears and the cartilage of the nose pierced by a sharp instrument. The classes that went to the place of misery do not appear to have been numerous; the chief were the *stingy*, and murderers, properly so called. Stinginess is reckoned of all sins the greatest at Aneiteum; and generosity reckons among the cardinal virtues. Hence the fondness for public feasts, as furnishing occasions for display, and securing the reputation which is so much coveted. The poor people would starve themselves for months, saving their food for an anticipated feast, or it may be, giving

ANEITEUMESE HEATHEN VILLAGE.

their best to a *pig*, and living on rubbish themselves, in order to have the praise of making the largest contribution of food, or turning out the largest and finest hog.

Such is a glimpse of what the Aneiteumese were in their heathen state. Let us now endeavour to trace, as far as our materials will allow, the progress of those movements which have led to the deliverance of so many of them out of the miserable bondage in which they were held, and their introduction into the glorious liberty of the children of God.

The teachers were landed on the north side of the island, at a place called Ipece, adjoining Aname, which has been the station of the Rev. John Inglis since he settled on the island in 1852. The names of the teachers were Tavita and Fuataiese. They were both natives of Samoa, and were from the church at Sapapalii, Savaii, then under the care of the Rev. Charles Hardie. The post they were called to occupy was indeed a trying one. Their lives were safe, however, and they were enabled to struggle on amid all the dangers and discouragements by which they were surrounded; but neither was permitted to see any decided fruit of his labours, one having died at an early stage of the mission, and the other having returned to Samoa.

In the month of April, 1845, it was again the writer's privilege to visit the island in company with Dr. Turner. Between that time and the first landing of the teachers, it had been once visited. Mr. Buzacott, of Rarotonga, and Mr. Slatyer, of Samoa, had visited it. At the time of our visit, it was still "the day of small things." The teachers whom we then found on the island, Apolo and Simeona, reported that a few months before a large number of the people had been accustomed to attend the services, but that of late the greater part had drawn back, influenced, as they said, by a suspicion that the teachers were abandoned, and would not again be visited. A few, however, remained steadfast. Among these, the most hopeful was a man named Wumra. For some months before our visit he had regularly worshipped God in his family, kept the Sabbath; and availed himself of all the opportunities that were within his reach of increasing his acquaintance with the Word of God. To all appearances the grace of God had touched his heart.

By his assistance and that of the teachers we were enabled to take a step during this visit which led to the commencement of a station at Anelecauhat, in the bay which forms the harbour already described. We visited this place in company with Nohoat, its chief, who had come round to the ship and had expressed his willingness to receive teachers. Nohoat made a considerable figure in the after history of the mission, as we shall see by and by. At the time referred to, though he zealously aided us in the accomplishment of our object, he had no proper conception of what that object was. The supposed temporal advantages were then all he looked at, nor did his view of these rise very high. To get from the ship a pig with "long ears" was the all-absorbing desire of Nohoat; and ever and anon, as we passed along in the boat, Nohoat's hands would be lifted up to the side of his head, to remind us of his desire to get the pig with long ears. There seemed no room in Nohoat's mind for any other subject. However, we gained our object, and located two teachers, Simeona—whom we removed from Ipece, as being experienced—and Poti, who was newly arrived. Another teacher, named Apaisa, just arrived from Samoa, we left with Apolo at Ipece. Wumra wished very much to go with us to Samoa, that he might enjoy greater advantages for becoming acquainted with the Word of God than he could in his own dark land; and perhaps another consideration had weight with him: the decided stand which he had taken on the side of Christianity had enraged his savage countrymen, and his life, in consequence, was in danger. We thought the wish reasonable, and agreed to take him and his wife, in the hope that to do so would be for their own good and the good of the mission; a hope which, in both these respects, was realized.

We are unable to furnish a minute account of the labours and trials of the teachers during the early years of the mission. Their trials were many and great, and, not seldom, their lives were in imminent peril; yet they were preserved, and enabled to struggle on till brighter days dawned. Before that, however, the mission was brought to the very verge of extinction. Reverses which had taken place on Tanna had led to the suspension of that mission, and all the teachers had fled to Aneiteum. They, with the Aneiteum teachers, were a large company, about fifteen individuals, including the wives and families of those who were married. Food was scarce at the time on Aneiteum; hence, to have such a large company to support was felt by the Aneiteumese to be an intolerable burden. Accounts from Tanna also increased their dissatisfaction, and emboldened them in their opposition to the teachers and the Gospel. At length their indignation rose to such a pitch that they determined to kill the teachers, and on two different occasions all was arranged, and bands of men went, headed by Iata, for this express purpose. Each time their courage failed, and He who holds all hearts in His hand suffered them not to do His servants any harm. Their sufferings, however, from want of food, disease, and other causes, were very severe; and, moreover, their work was quite at a stand. Such was the state of affairs when the Rev. W. Gill of Rarotonga, and the Rev. H. Nisbet, of Samoa, visited the island. Their visit was made in September, 1846, and at that time the teachers presented a united request to be removed. The missionaries acceded to their request, and all were received on board, and the island was virtually given up. The teachers who had been stationed at Anelecauhat had left their station, we know not for what reason, probably for want of food, and had joined their brethren at Ipece. Before finally quitting the island, it was thought advisable to visit the harbour, Little or no hope seems to have been entertained of doing anything there; this, however, was the turning-point of the mission's history. While the *John Williams* lay at anchor in the harbour, Mr. Nisbet dropped a remark to the teacher Simeona to the following effect: "What a pity it is to leave this fine place without a teacher, and let go our hold upon the island! What would you think of staying and giving it another trial?" Simeona replied that he would not mind staying if another could be got to stay with him. Just as this conversation was going on, Pita, another Samoan teacher, who had had considerable experience, joined them. The question of remaining was proposed to him. He expressed himself willing to stay, and the thing was settled. Thus the door was kept open, the reason for which we shall soon see. Not only the future of Aneiteum, but the whole of the New Hebrides group, and other lands far remote, were to be affected to an incalculable extent by these apparently fortuitous and unimportant occurrences. The day was at hand when the Aneiteum mission was to be taken up by more effective agents.

How wonderful are the ways of God! Far away, in a very distant region of the earth, a train of remarkable movements had for a length of time been in progress, fraught with consequences of incalculable magnitude, not only to Aneiteum, but to the whole of Western Polynesia, and the country itself where they took their rise. In that country the future missionary of Aneiteum was being prepared, and was being led to take the necessary steps for accomplishing the work to which God had called him. Like Hans Egede, in another age and country, with whom originated those deeply-interesting missions to Greenland, of the labourers connected with which Cowper so beautifully says:—

> "Fired with a zeal peculiar they defy
> The rage and rigour of a Polar sky;
> And plant successfully sweet Sharon's Rose
> On icy plains, and 'mid eternal snows."

Like Hans Egede, John Geddie left his pleasant home and a people loving and beloved, among whom he had laboured for eight years, and cast himself and his family adrift on the wide world, and went forth not knowing whither he went.

Mr. Geddie was a minister of the United Presbyterian Church, Nova Scotia. He was happily settled on Prince Edward's Island, and labouring successfully in his Master's work. But the Master had other work for him to do. A more prominent and distinguished career was marked out for him: and irrepressible yearnings were kindled in his heart, which impelled him onward towards his destination. His feelings and convictions were fully shared by his noble, large-hearted wife; and, in spite of difficulties, great and formidable enough, one would have thought, to have daunted the stoutest heart and shaken the firmest purpose, they determined "to leave home, and friends, and native land," and go where Providence might direct to make known to the benighted heathen the glorious Gospel of the Grace of God. They left home without any definite information as to where they were to labour; but He who had moved their spirits, and "by His love's constraining power" had thrust them forth, had chosen out their inheritance for them.

It was in the month of October, 1847, that Mr. and Mrs. Geddie and their two children arrived at Samoa, having come *viâ* the United States and the Sandwich Islands. Two dear children had been removed by death just prior to their leaving Nova Scotia. They came with instructions to be guided by the advice of the missionary brethren in Samoa as to the selection of a field of labour. After a residence of about eight months in Samoa, they sailed in the *John Williams* for Western Polynesia, accompanied by the Rev. G. Turner and the Rev. H. Nisbet, as a deputation from the Samoan Mission; and the Rev. Thomas Powell, appointed to labour in connection with Mr. Geddie, on the field to which Providence might direct.

All the fields at that time under culture by native teachers were visited and their claims considered; and the decision to which the brethren were led was, that Aneiteum was the most inviting. It is hardly necessary to remark that the subsequent history of the mission has clearly shown that the decision was right. Aneiteum has proved to be, as we expected, the key to the group to which it belongs.

It was on the 29th May, 1848, that Messrs. Geddie and Powell, and a young man who had come as a teacher, settled with their families on Aneiteum. They took up their abode together, at Anelecauhat. The missionary party had a very cool reception from the natives of Aneiteum. The intercourse they had had with foreigners prior to the arrival of the missionaries had not been such as to encourage them to expect any good from the residence of white men on their shores. They apprehended, as one of the consequences of such residence, that they would be deprived of their land; and when they knew that it was decided that the missionaries should remain among them, they took counsel together, and proposed to their chief, Nohoat, to oppose their landing. Nohoat replied that he would not oppose their landing, and added that, if the missionaries took their lands, they must just retire to the bush. In after days Nohoat acknowledged that he told the people they might steal from the missionaries, and annoy them in any way they pleased, suggesting that in that case they would soon get tired and leave. "Only," said he, "don't kill them, for if you do that you will get me into trouble."

The missionaries were satisfied with very humble accommodations at the outset of their labours. A small plastered cottage belonging to the teachers was given up to them, and the frame of a small house, which Mr. Geddie had brought from Samoa, was soon erected and fitted up. A small place of worship was added; and this, with a servant's house, completed the first missionary premises at Anelecauhat.

Only a few weeks had passed when the missionaries opened their commission, and began to speak to the Aneiteumese, in their own language, the wonderful works of God. They itinerated on the Sabbath, and addressed small groups, as they were able to collect them. Two services were regularly conducted in the chapel, but very few attended. It was necessary to "Go out into the highways and hedges, and compel them to come in." The natives generally behaved with decency when being addressed. The time for active opposition and hostility had not yet arrived. Sometimes a question would be asked, which the missionaries found difficulty in answering. "How is it"—said the natives, one day, after listening to an address—"how is it, if these things you tell us be true, that we have never heard of them before?" A solemn question for those on whom it devolves to carry out the great commission.

On making a tour of the island, the brethren found that it was divided into five districts, each district being under the authority of a principal chief. At each of these districts they were able to place a teacher. Thus the island was well supplied with labourers; and everything wore as encouraging an aspect as under the circumstances could be expected. The vessel had had a promising launch, and a fair start, but storms were gathering.

A change took place in the conduct of the natives. Hitherto, scarcely anything had been stolen from the missionaries; now the natives commenced stealing from them in right earnest. It was a common way to show their displeasure to steal, and it is still the practice on the neighbouring island of Tanna. The services were almost deserted, and those who did attend looked sullen and angry. The missionaries were totally at a loss to account for the altered conduct of the people. At length the problem was solved. A man named Nathaua, who claimed to have dominion over the sea, went to the teacher, Simeona, and told him that the people were very much enraged with the missionaries, and that they were talking of burning their houses and driving them from the island. The missionaries lost no time in inquiring into the cause of the displeasure of the people. The following grave misdemeanours were laid to their charge. First, they had taken cocoa-nuts from trees on their *own* land, whereas the cocoa-nuts were all under a *tabu* for a great feast which was at hand. The missionaries pleaded ignorance of the tabu, but agreed to respect it for the future, though it seemed rather hard that it should be extended to trees growing on land which they had purchased and paid for. Missionaries, however, must not stand stiffly on their rights under such circumstances, so they wisely yielded. Secondly, the missionaries had taken coral from the reef to make lime for their buildings. The Natmases, who were supposed to have their residences near the mission premises, had smelt the burning of the coral, and were very angry at the natives for allowing it to be taken, and, to punish them for their undutiful conduct, had made the fish scarce. The missionaries told them, of course, who it is that reigns over sea and land, and all that is therein; they agreed, however, not to take any more coral, only begging that they might be allowed to burn a kiln which was already prepared, and which was necessary to complete works that were in hand. To this the natives agreed, and so the second charge was disposed of. The third charge was, that whereas a small hill behind the mission premises was the residence of some important Natmases, and the path by which the said Natmases were accustomed to pass from the mountain to the sea lay through a piece of ground on which the chapel was being erected, and, as the missionaries were about to put a fence round the chapel, the path would be obstructed, the Natmases would be angry, and would punish the natives with sickness and death in consequence. The missionaries replied that the contemplated offence was a sin of ignorance, the man from whom they bought the land not having told them anything about the path of the Natmases. This the man admitted, and the matter was amicably settled by the missionaries agreeing to leave the path open. Thus all the charges were satisfactorily met, and a good understanding was again established between the missionaries and the natives.

Shortly after the above occurrences a curious circumstance occurred. Three men were reported to be possessed with Natmases. The missionaries hastened to the spot where the scene was transpiring, in order to witness it. It was nearly a mile distant, however, so they were too late. The Natmases had taken their departure before their arrival.

The following account of the affair was given. A battle had been fought that evening between the Natmases of the sea and those of the land, in which the demons of the sea had been completely routed. These had been angry with the natives for worshipping Jehovah and neglecting them, and had determined to be revenged. Those on shore had compassion on the people, and decided to espouse their cause: hence the battle; and three of the victorious party had come to make known to the natives the joyful tidings of their deliverance from the destruction which, unknown to them, had been impending. Messrs. Geddie and Powell suspected that the whole was a trick of the sacred men to strengthen the system of deceit and imposture to which they owed their importance and influence. No doubt, however, it was firmly believed by the bulk of the people.

In the month of February, 1849, a severe hurricane swept over the island, occasioning great destruction of cocoa-nuts, bread-fruit, etc., etc., and this calamity had wellnigh led to another, which might have been of more serious consequence. The natives in the district of Anelecauhat were enraged on account of the destruction of food, and other evils produced by the storm, and they determined to be revenged on the chief of a neighbouring

SEVERE HURRICANE.

district, named Thua, who had the credit of being a sort of Jupiter in a small way, a maker of thunder, lightning, and storms. War was declared against the said chief, and preparations were immediately made. On the day when the engagement was to have taken place, the missionaries

EFFECTS OF A HURRICANE.

hastened to the scene of action. They found the hostile parties assembled, and confronting each other a short distance apart. They were shouting, and yelling, and throwing themselves into various attitudes of defiance, in truly savage style. The brethren had great difficulty in getting a hearing—those bent on war endeavouring to drown their voices by yelling, or to take off the force of what they said by ridicule and bad language. The issue was, that they succeeded, through Nohoat, in effecting a reconciliation; and returned home, thanking God, who had enabled them successfully to perform the part of peace-makers.

In the following month there was another severe hurricane. From that no serious consequences appear to have arisen affecting the interests of the mission. But it was not long without troubles. The son of the chief of Umetch, one of the principal districts of the island, died. The teacher had removed to Anelecauhat, to remain there for a time, on account of illness, and the people took advantage of his absence to burn his house and property. This was done agreeably to a native custom, to commemorate and honour the death of the child, and with the same view two women were strangled. The destruction of life and property was the usual mode of expressing sorrow and honouring the departed, when persons of consequence died. About the same time, Mr. Geddie and a boat's crew narrowly escaped falling into the hands of a hostile party who had laid a plot to attack them. Happily, they had timely warning, and by leaving Ipece, where they were at the time, at midnight, and standing out to sea, they eluded the vigilance of their enemies. Providentially, the boat was anchored on the night in question. Had it been dragged up on the beach as usual, it would have been impossible to have got it into the water without being discovered by the natives, who were on the look out; and, in that case, Mr. Geddie and party must have fallen into their hands.

In addition to other trials and interruptions, the missionaries suffered from attacks of fever and ague—the disease incidental to certain localities on almost all the islands of the New Hebrides. Mr. Powell especially had a very severe attack of illness, which brought him very low. He was mercifully restored, and when the writer visited the island, in company with Mr. Hardie, in September, 1849, both the families were well. We found the brethren and their devoted partners labouring on in their self-denying work, in circumstances as encouraging, perhaps, as could reasonably be expected, considering the short time that had elapsed since the commencement of their mission. Some progress had, no doubt, been made, though no decided indications of success were yet apparent. Many things had come to the knowledge of the missionaries, evincing the fearful degradation of the people, and the cruel and revolting customs to which they were addicted. Of these, perhaps, none was more shocking than the practice of *strangling widows*, which universally prevailed. At the time of our visit the brethren knew certainly of ELEVEN cases of strangling that had occurred during their residence, which had extended over a little more than twelve months, and how many more had shared the same fate it is impossible to conjecture. The natives generally endeavour to conceal such things from the missionaries, as they soon find out that they are abhorrent to them. It was quite accidental that we came to know of the eleventh case. While the *John Williams* was at anchor, we were going on shore one day in company with Mr. Geddie, when we met a canoe, in which was a man with his body all bedaubed with some black substance, the native mode of expressing grief. This led to inquiry, and we ascertained that the man was mourning the recent death of some relative.

This practice had a strange hold upon the people. They clung to it with most determined pertinacity; and the fact that the strangler was the woman's own son, if she had a son old enough; if not, her brother, if she had a brother; or, if she had neither son nor brother, her next of kin, was not the least revolting thing connected with the practice. In some cases it was done by a *daughter!* There is a woman now living in Mr. Geddie's district who

NATIVE MOTHER AND CHILD.

strangled her mother. And the thing *must* be done, according to the notions entertained by the deluded people; else the whole family, and especially the son or other relative on whom it devolved to do the deed, would incur lasting disgrace.

During our early visits to the island, an old woman was a very rare sight. I remember one being pointed out as having been rescued by the teachers from the hands of her murderers. She is still alive, and is a very useful and consistent member of Mr. Geddie's church. But the teachers very rarely succeeded in their efforts, as not only the relations opposed them, but the woman herself was bent upon being put to death. Such is the strange power which systems of heathen superstition exert over their votaries!

The following extract from a letter of Mr. Powell, under date August, 1849, will convey a vivid impression of the mad infatuation with which the deluded people clung to this horrid practice:—

"All the heathen customs are still practised here. *Eight* women, to our knowledge, have been *strangled* during our residence. How many more it is impossible to say. The last I attempted, though in vain, to save. Soon after I came here there was a native very ill; the poor creature was reduced to a skeleton. I found him lying outside his hut; his wife, an interesting young woman, was by his side. I administered a little medicine, with the design of abating the severity of his sufferings, but not with any hope of his final recovery. In prospect of his decease, I requested Iata, the chief of the village, to forbid the strangling of the wife, and he faithfully promised to do so; but it resulted as I feared. About noon of the 23rd ultimo, our attention was suddenly arrested by the commencement of the *death wail*. We knew whence it proceeded, and anxiety filled our minds for the safety of the poor widow. I hastened to the spot. The corpse was lying in the open air, surrounded by a number of women, who were rubbing it with broken leaves, and at the same time wailing in the most piteous manner. Tears were pouring down their cheeks; many of them were pulling their hair in seeming excess of grief; while so deafening were their lamentations and their shrieks, that I could not stand near them. I looked anxiously around for the poor widow, but she was not there; and I hastened to a house where I hoped to find her, but the search was vain. I returned to the place of weeping, and there she sat. I said, 'This woman must not be strangled!' and several women joined me, and said, 'Oh no, do not let her be strangled!' I commenced leading her away; but immediately several young men (her relations) seized her, and attempted to lead her in another direction. One of these men pushed me aside, and held up his club in a threatening attitude; and by this time, another of her relations, a powerful young man, had seized her by the necklace, and commenced strangling her therewith, as the proper instrument had been taken off her neck. I made an attempt to interrupt the murderer; but he tried to kick me, and pushed me aside with one hand, while he held his victim with the other. Meanwhile, several were standing around with uplifted clubs, and one especially behind me, ready to prevent effectually any interference on my part. I called aloud for the chief to come and forbid it, but in vain; and prudence dictated that I must stand aside, and allow the fearful scene to proceed, the particulars of which are too shocking to describe."

The above is but a specimen of what frequently occurred in the early days of the mission when the teachers or missionaries interposed to rescue poor creatures doomed to death. To do this was indeed a thankless as well as a dangerous task. There is a woman living now at Anelecauhat who was saved by Mrs. Geddie's instrumentality, the particulars of whose deliverance are worth recording. Mr. Geddie had left home, having gone with Mr. Sunder-

land and the writer, on a missionary voyage among the
neighbouring islands. The woman's husband was in a
dying state for a fortnight; and, during the whole of that
time, Mrs. Geddie was kept in a state of intense excitement,
as it was necessary to be constantly on the alert. The
man might die at any moment, and in a few moments more
the woman would be murdered. She had a son and
daughter, both Christians, and they joined heart and soul
with Mrs. Geddie in efforts to save their mother. With
intense anxiety they watched the progress of events, and
kept Mrs. Geddie and the Christian people about her informed of all that was going on. Frequently, at dead of
night, she was aroused, and had to collect her party and
send them off to the scene of anxiety. In this case, as in
most others, the woman was bent on her own destruction.
She had a brother living a short distance from her own
house. To him she fled, thinking that by so doing, she
would make sure of having the deed accomplished, as soon
as the death wail for her husband arose. The Christian
party got information of this movement; and Waihit, a
relative of the woman, and a powerful man, went and
seized her, and brought her away on his back. She
rewarded him by savagely biting his shoulder, as he was
carrying her along. He kept his hold, however, and
succeeded in bringing her to her own home. Mrs. Geddie,
almost worn out with excitement and want of sleep, applied
to the captain of a vessel that was at anchor in the harbour
at the time for assistance. He came with a party of men
and was joined by Mr. Underwood, the head of a sandal-
wood establishment on the island, with whom also was a
band of men. They went and brought away the woman by
force. Mr. Underwood proposed to take her to his own
house, and have her watched; to this Mrs. Geddie as-
sented: but unhappily, the woman managed to make her
escape, and hid herself in an outhouse near where her
husband was, intending, no doubt, to strangle herself when
the death wail should be raised. This led to another

midnight summons to Mrs. Geddie, who had retired to rest with an easy mind, in the persuasion that all was right. The Samoan teachers who were within reach, and the Christian party, were hastily collected, and they reached the scene of death in time. They found the deluded woman in the outhouse mentioned above, kindled a fire, and surrounded her. The death of the husband took place that night, and they watched her till the morning, by which time the body of the husband had beeen thrown into the sea—the native mode of burial—and she was no longer in danger. And what was Mrs. Geddie's recompense for all her efforts? Will the reader credit it? A scolding from the woman herself. She came to Mrs. Geddie some time after with her child on her back, and accosted her as follows:—" Why did you save my life, and not let me be strangled when my husband died? Who is to provide food for me and this child?" pointing to the child on her back. The food was a matter of no difficulty, as Mrs. Geddie told her, as she was strong and able to work. She lived, however, to see and feel differently, though she is not a decided Christian. She has thanked Mrs. Geddie again and again for her self-denying efforts on her behalf.

The avowed reason for strangling wives was that their souls might accompany those of their husbands to the world of spirits. Married women were accustomed, from the time of their marriage, to wear about their necks the cord with which they were to be strangled on the death of their husbands, as wives in Christian lands wear the marriage ring! What an idea, to carry about continually the badge of a violent death! But such is heathenism. It is emphatically the *shadow* of death, and where the shadow is, of course the substance is at hand. Blessed Gospel! that sheds on man's otherwise gloomy path the light of immortality.

But to return from our long digression. We found on our visit that the young man formerly mentioned as having come to the island as a teacher, had withdrawn from the mission, and subsequently left the island. Mr. Powell also left, and returned with us to Samoa, where he has continued to labour up to the present. Thus Mr. Geddie was left to pursue his work with only native assistants, that is, natives of Samoa. Most faithfully and perseveringly did he and his devoted wife struggle on through storm and calm. They did endure hardness as good soldiers of Jesus Christ, and all was borne in a spirit which it was refreshing to behold. The writer speaks what he *knows* and testifies what he has *seen;* not to exalt mortals, but to magnify the grace of God which was in them, and to advance the interests of that holy cause with which they are identified.

CHAPTER IV.

ANEITEUM—*Continued.*

"Persecuted, but not forsaken; cast down, but not destroyed."
2 *Cor.* iv. 9.

AS we have already remarked, no decided success had yet appeared. The night, however, was fast wearing away, and the morning was drawing on. Only a few months after our visit the dawn appeared. In December, 1849, Mr. Geddie wrote as follows:—"Perhaps I am sanguine, but I do think that God has given some measure of countenance to our labours. I think that I can discern some faint rays of light beginning to arise over the horizon of darkness in which these poor islanders have from time immemorial been enveloped. . . . I do hope that the spirit of God has begun to breathe upon the dry bones, and that the symptoms of animation will at no distant day appear." The good man was right; the "faint rays of light" were the harbingers of day; the "Spirit had begun to breathe upon the dry bones." The next tidings from the island, dated May, 1850, bore evidence growingly decisive of this. "At this station (Anelecauhat), our usual attendance on Sabbath is from thirty to forty. Several of our natives observe family worship regularly; our Friday meeting (a select class) numbers about ten members, who are very decided in favour of the new religion. Three of the natives whom I have under instruction occasionally itinerate on the Sabbath day, and promise to become useful auxiliaries in the work. On the north side of the island, several villages have simultaneously applied for Christian instruction." Thus

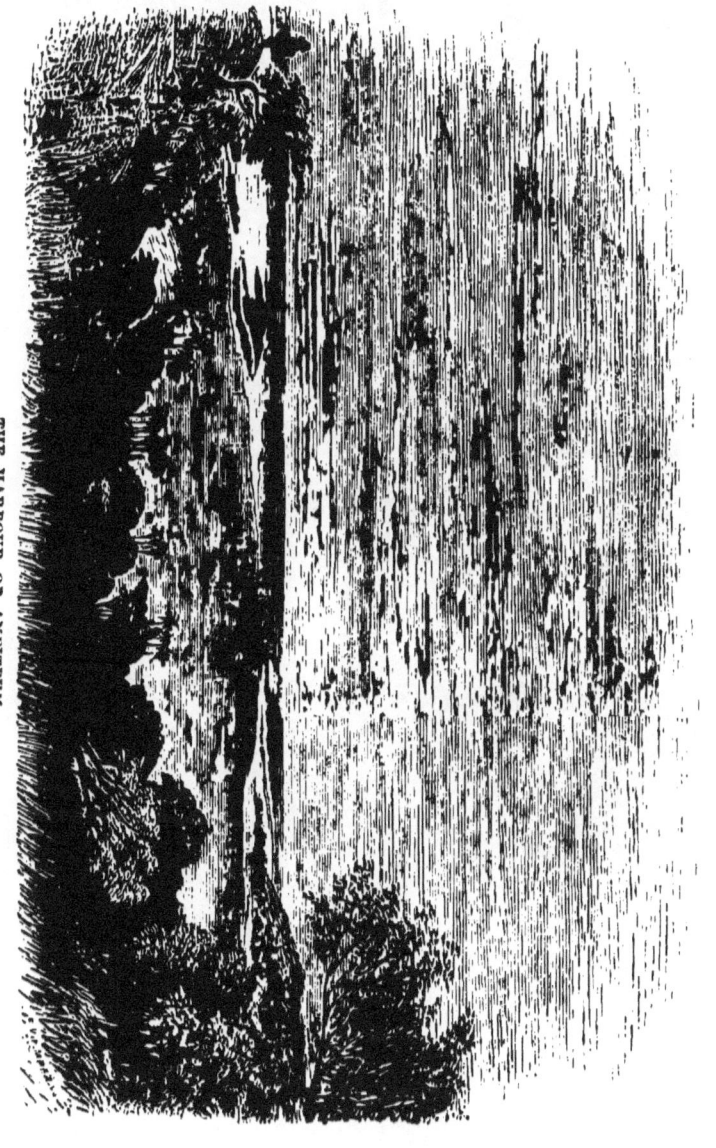

THE HARBOUR OF ANEITEUM.

was the light slowly spreading, and the "symptoms of animation" gradually appearing.

In the same month in which the letter was dated, from which the above extract is taken, a small book was published. It was a little thing in itself—an elementary school-book—but interesting, as being the first book that had been printed on the island.

Deeds of blood still continued to pollute the shores of Aneiteum, though the Gospel had evidently begun to take hold of some hearts. The following account of an unsuccessful attempt made by Mr. Geddie to save a poor doomed woman will be read with melancholy interest:—

"I have just made an ineffectual attempt to save a poor woman from being strangled. I heard in the morning that her husband was dying, and immediately repaired to the spot. About forty or fifty were assembled around the dying man. I saw from the scowling looks of many present that I was not a welcome visitor. I inquired for the wife of the dying man, but could get no satisfaction. Some said he had none; others said that she was at a distant village; and some few in whom I thought I could confide told me that she was present. But there was so much wailing among the women, that I could not tell who the victim was. I told the natives what I had come for, and laid before them as well as I could the wickedness of strangling. A portion of them showed many symptoms of displeasure at my presence; and others, more courteous, endeavoured to persuade me to leave, saying the man would not die on that day; but I felt assured that all were bent on the bloody deed. As the man was evidently dying, I was determined to remain on the spot till I should see the issue. In the course of the day the man died. As soon as life was extinct, the body was laid out on a mat, and a spear and club placed by its side; also, the small noose which is used in throwing the spear was placed on the forefinger of the right hand. The whole was then bound up together and a large stone was tied to the feet. While these operations were going on, the corpse was surrounded by women wailing in the most hideous manner, and I thought the widow must be one of the number. I waited till I saw the body carried out to the shore, and laid on a canoe to be conveyed to its watery grave. I now began to cherish a hope that the widow's life would be spared, as the strangling is always done as soon as the husband dies, and usually on the spot; but what was my grief when I was afterwards told that the poor woman had, on account of my presence, been conveyed to another village, more than a mile distant, and strangled there. I saw her body, from my own widow, conveyed to the spot where her husband's body had been deposited, and thrown into the sea. The cruel practice of strangling prevails to an awful extent on this island. It is not confined to widows. I have known of two women being strangled on occasion of the death of a child; and when chiefs die, several persons are put to death."

Shortly after the above occurrence, other sad events of a kindred character took place. A poor woman, driven to desperation by the brutal conduct of her husband, put an end to her miserable existence by committing suicide; and, sad to say, a young lad and a girl were murdered as a Nābatū—offering, or sacrifice—on the occasion.

But the influences were gathering strength which were, ere a great while, to sweep these abominations from Aneiteum. Of this the following occurrence affords pleasing and interesting evidence:—

Mr. Geddie heard that a married man was dying, and knowing well what would follow his death, if the people were left to themselves, he hastened to the place where the man was—about a mile from his own house. He found a number of people assembled, among whom were the relatives of the woman, waiting to perform the horrid deed. Mr. Geddie had a very ungracious reception. He was not daunted, however, but spoke to the people plainly of their wickedness, and begged them to desist from their purpose. Evening drew on, and the man was still alive. Mr. Geddie went home, intending to return shortly, and leaving trustworthy persons to watch movements in his absence. He had been but a short time home, when the death wail announced that the man was gone. He was off again instantly, and had the high satisfaction to find that those he had left had succeeded in saving the woman. As soon as the man had expired, the stranglers were about to commence their bloody work, when Waihit, who had joined the Christian party only a few months before, and who up to this point had sat a silent spectator, thus addressed the Christians who were present: "Let us not be fainthearted; we must prevent this deed; let us take courage, and be strong." Then turning to the heathen party, he said, "If you kill that woman, we will kill you." Those addressed knew the character of Waihit too well to venture to oppose such a speech from him, so they desisted. But the difficulty did not end here. The woman herself was bent on being strangled, and cried out that, if her relations would not kill her, she would run to the bush and strangle herself. To prevent her carrying out this threat, Waihit took his station at the door of the house, and talked kindly and soothingly to her. The Christian party remained all night for security's sake; though there is little or no risk after the body of the husband has been cast into the sea, which, ordinarily, is immediately after death. In half an hour from the time that life is extinct, when the parties lived near the sea, all the proceedings would be completed, including the strangling of the widow, and the bodies deposited in their watery tomb. And the notion seemed to be that, unless the deaths of the husband and wife were so near together as to allow of the bodies being cast into the sea about the same time, the souls would not be able to set out in company on their journey to the world of spirits; and thus the object of strangling the woman would not be secured. Hence the safety of the woman when any considerable interval elapsed.

We leave the reader to form his own judgment respecting the course adopted by Waihit. In the result we can only rejoice. Before we proceed further we may as well give a little information respecting Waihit, as he is one of the most remarkable characters that appear in the history of the Aneiteum mission. In the days of heathenism there was not a more important man on the island, among the class to which he belonged, than Waihit. He was a *Natimi itaup*, or sacred man. The sacred men were supposed to possess supernatural powers within a prescribed limit. Waihit was ruler of the sea in the district of Anelecauhat. There was, perhaps, no man more dreaded on the island. He was a man of a determined will, and a cruel and ferocious disposition. Mr. and Mrs. Geddie were often sorely pained by his savage treatment of his wife; and it was to them a matter of surprise that she was not murdered outright. On one occasion Mr. Geddie had to attend as doctor a poor woman whose arm he had broken by a blow of his club for some trifling offence,— a breach of some *tabu*, most likely, through mistake. And it was out of his hands that the teachers rescued the woman, Nathieri, mentioned before, when she was half strangled. He was the operator on the occasion.

We cannot enter minutely into the history of his conversion. The transition was gradual; and the blessed result was, that Waihit was brought out of darkness into light, and became as marked a man in the kingdom of light and peace as he had been in the kingdom of darkness. No sooner had he experienced the effects of Divine truth himself, than he longed to go forth and tell to others the wonderful tale which had produced so happy a deliverance. Great was the opposition he had to encounter, and not small the danger to which he was exposed. This he had foreseen, and he had counted the cost; so that insults from parties who would have trembled before him in his savage days were meekly borne; and threatenings, and sometimes spears hurled at him, when he went to speak of Christ to his benighted countrymen, were met in a spirit of dauntless courage. None of these things moved him. An illustration or two may be given. One day, a heathen, a forward young man, perhaps sent by his elders, went and tore down the inclosure before his house; a deed which, a few months before, would surely have cost him his life. On a certain Sabbath, he went to Umetch, a place about six miles from Anelecauhat, to talk to his countrymen about the Word of God. There had just been a severe storm, which had done great damage among the bread-fruit and cocoa-nut trees, and among the plantations. The foolish people blamed Waihit for having caused the storm, and surrounded him with their clubs, in great wrath, threatening to take his life. He escaped, however, out of their hands; and, on the following Sabbath, nothing would satisfy him but to visit them again, though Mr. Geddie advised him to wait till their anger should have subsided. He urged the matter so much, that Mr. Geddie reluctantly consented. He went, and was well received, and a very favourable impression was made upon the people. When a church was formed in Aneiteum, Waihit was one of the twelve who composed it; and when Aneiteum was in a position to send out evangelists to the dark islands in its neighbourhood, Waihit was one of two that led the way. He, and a young man named Josefa, went to Fotuna, where he has laboured zealously and faithfully till the present day. But we are anticipating our narrative.

In August, 1850, two years from the time the missionaries landed, Mr. Geddie wrote as follows:—"Our average attendance on Sabbath, during the first year was ten; during the second year, forty-five. Should we progress in the same ratio, there is reason to hope for a brighter day at no distant period. During the past year many have given up their heathenish customs, and are earnestly inquiring the way to be saved."

A short time after the above date, serious danger again

threatened the Christian party. Some cases of sickness had occurred among the heathen; these were supposed to be caused by the Natmases, because of the indignities done to them by the Christians. The heathen determined to be revenged; and one Sabbath evening a messenger was sent to inform the Christians that they were to be attacked next morning. All was alarm and consternation. Mr. Geddie's advice was sought as to the course that should be adopted. Mr. Geddie replied, that he could give no advice till he had seen the chief of the hostile party. He went at once to Nohoat, and asked whether what he had heard was true. Nohoat replied that it was, and that he was determined to have the lives of two persons, whom he named, next day; but he added, Mr. Geddie need give himself no concern, because the mission premises were not to be molested. Mr. Geddie replied, that the Christian party and he were one, and that he would regard an attack upon them as directed against the mission, and used all the arguments he could think of to dissuade the chief from his purpose. Nothing, however, seemed to move him. Pointing to his heart he said, "I know that this heart of mine is bad;" and pointing to the fire he said, "I know that if I am killed I shall be burned in the great fire, but I don't care, I will have revenge." The case seemed hopeless, and Mr. Geddie was at his wits' end, when an argument occurred to him which happily had the desired effect. Nohoat had come to attach great value to Mr. Geddie's medicines, having often experienced their efficacy; it added to his importance to have Mr. Geddie residing in his territory, and sundry temporal advantages accrued from that. Hence, when Mr. Geddie told him, in a decided tone, that if he lifted a weapon against any Christian native, he would, when the *John Williams* arrived, leave his district, and go to some other part where the people wished to know the Word of God, and that those natives who had abandoned heathenism, and wished to leave his persecuting land, would be taken to some other, where they could worship God without molestation, he was moved, and after a great deal of talk, he agreed to abandon his design, or, rather, agreed to change it from a war of blows to a war of words. Mr. Geddie, fearing that the scolding which the chief intended to give to the Christian party might end in blows, proposed that all weapons should be left at home. Nohoat consented at once that the spears should be left, but said they must take their clubs. "No," said Mr. Geddie, "all weapons must be left." To this, however, the chief would not consent; and as the club was considered rather as a defensive than an offensive weapon, Mr. Geddie did not further insist on its being left. He told Nohoat that he would rely on his word as a chief, and leave him with the assurance that there should be no fighting. The chief gave him his hand, and assured him that he would not deceive him.

When Mr. Geddie reached home he found the Christian party assembled, waiting for him. Before telling them the result of his interview with the chief, he asked them to what decision they had come. Waihit replied, "Our word is peace; we know that it is sinful to fight, and we are not afraid to die for the cause of God." There was a noble reply from one who had himself, not a great many months before, been a dark-minded, ferocious savage, and one of the bitterest opponents of Christianity! There was "the lion changed into the lamb, the vulture to the dove." Mr. Geddie was greatly surprised and delighted with the spirit manifested by the Christians, and remarks upon it as follows: "I began to feel for the first time, with some degree of confidence, as if a sacred flame had been kindled on this island which the waters of opposition and persecution will not quench."

After communicating to the Christians the result of his interview with the chief, Mr. Geddie urged them, when they met their enemies, to display nothing but kindness and gentleness towards them, and, when reviled, not to revile again. All was concluded with prayer. The Christians first united with Mr. Geddie's family, and then, at his suggestion, retired to pray among themselves. On the following morning the parties met; the heathen painted and decorated, or rather disfigured, in heathen style for the occasion; the Christian party clothed, and in their right mind. The chief took his stand between the two parties, and commenced his harangue at the top of his voice, and in a very wrathful tone. He went on for nearly two hours railing against the Christians, enumerating all the grievances he could think of, the sum and substance of all being their abandoning heathenism, and disregarding practices and injunctions therewith connected; in consequence of which, he said, some were sick already, and he might be sick himself. The Christians bore all meekly, only occasionally interposing a word designed to repel such charges as they thought it worth while to notice. And so the war of words, being all on one side, soon came to an end. "A soft answer turneth away wrath." The assembly broke up when the chief had finished his speech, the more peaceably disposed among the heathen being glad that the matter had so ended, others being grieved and mortified on that account.

After the above affair, which took place towards the close of 1850, the Christian and heathen parties were more distinctly marked than they had formerly been; the latter standing entirely aloof from schools and services, and manifesting a more decided and determined spirit of opposition. In January, 1851, a heathen used his wife so badly for attending the services that she was driven to desperation, fled into the bush, and attempted suicide. She was found suspended before life was extinct, and was rescued. Suicide was a common refuge for oppressed wives on Aneiteum in the days of heathenism. In February, a man named Vakki, who had joined the Christian party but a few months before, had his house burnt, his clothes stolen, and all his plantations destroyed, and

A GROUP OF NATIVES.
(PAPUANS.)

stones and spears thrown at himself, for the great crime of eating some of the fruit of his own trees without presenting the first-fruits to the Natmases. Vakki was not sufficiently under the dominion of Christian principle to bear all this quietly, so he retaliated by destroying the taro plantation of one of his heathen persecutors. It is a marvellous thing, however, that this was a solitary instance on the part of the Christians. Mr. Geddie remarks on it: "This is the only instance in which our Chistian natives have retaliated on their heathen countrymen." He further remarks: "Almost all our natives have suffered more or less from their heathen countrymen. They have been called at a very early period to suffer for conscience' sake. They have displayed in general a forbearance under their trials which could scarcely have been expected. It is not their practice to revile again, but to pray for those who revile, and persecute, and despitefully use them."

While the opposition of the heathen was going on, Wumra was rather suddenly taken away from evil present and to come. He, there is good reason to believe, died in the Lord, and was gathered into the heavenly garner the first sheaf of a glorious harvest; the first fruit to God from Western Polynesia. The heathen gloried. Wumra's death was surely a judgment from the Natmases for the many indignities they had suffered from him; and severe were the taunts which the Christians had to bear. Loudly and bitterly the heathen continued to talk, not only against their Christian countrymen, but against Mr. Geddie; going the length of threatening his life. The instigators of the persecution were the chiefs and sacred men. Most, if not all, the chiefs were also sacred men; thus their influence was sure to suffer in proportion as Christianity spread. Mr. Geddie remarks: "The chiefs except Waihit, have all along stood aloof from us, and the more they understand, the more they oppose. The man who follows Jesus on this island must, at least for a time, expect to take up his cross, and exercise much self-denial." Some sacred men, who were not civil chiefs, had at this time (March, 1851) joined the Christian party. "Thank God," says Mr. Geddie, "some have made the sacrifice. Among the little party who have joined us there is one bread-fruit maker, one inmop maker (the horse-chestnut), and one fish maker, and others by the grace of God, will follow." What strange conceits the heathen in their blindness entertain! The idea of men endowed with reason and understanding seriously arrogating to themselves the above powers, seems almost incredible. But there are no bounds to human folly.

About this time an incident occurred which is important, as showing that Christianity was taking a deeper and deeper hold of the community, and influencing more and more public opinion—an immemorial custom was set aside. A woman whose husband was a Christian, and who had herself joined the Christian party a few weeks before had fallen from a cocoa-nut tree, and died of the injuries which she had received. Her husband had her body conveyed to the mission premises, and intimated his wish to have it buried, instead of thrown into the sea. Mr. Geddie had selected a suitable spot, and set some lads to work to dig a grave, and was superintending their operations, when a messenger arrived, requesting him to hasten home, as the woman's relatives, who were all heathen, had come, greatly excited, demanding her body, to throw into the sea. Mr. Geddie found his yard filled with men armed with spears and clubs and talking in a very angry manner. They charged the death of the woman upon Christianity, and demanded that the body should be given up to them. The Christians were disposed to take a stand, and contend the point. Waihit addressed the heathen in a kind but determined strain, telling them that they were not content with ruining the soul, but they wished to destroy the body also. In the meanwhile, Mr. Geddie got some cloth, and set the women who were present to do up the body in it, and place it on a mat in the yard in the presence of all. After a while Mr. Geddie interposed with a conciliatory speech, telling the heathen that it was a matter of no consequence to the woman what was done with her body, as the soul was gone, and only the body remained; and though he hated the custom of throwing the dead into the sea, as a heathenish practice, they might do as they pleased: the body was there before them, and if they chose to throw it into the sea, no one would oppose them; but if, on the contrary, they would give it up to him and the Christians, they would carry it to the grave, which was already prepared. The heathen now quarrelled among themselves, part of them being inclined to give up the body, and part being violently opposed. One man, named Naurita, a brother of Waihit's, behaved in a most savage manner, flourishing his club, uttering the most abusive and threatening language against the Christians, and demanding that the body should be thrown into the sea. Mr. Geddie says, "I never saw such a specimen of savage fury as this man exhibited." His brother, Waihit, endeavoured in vain to quiet him, but at length he succeeded in getting him outside the premises, when he became quiet. Mr. Geddie now requested the heathen party to consult quietly as to what they would do. They could not agree among themselves as to what part of the sea the body should be taken to— whose canoe should be employed in conveying it out to sea —who should go and seek a canoe, etc. By this time night was drawing on, and the heathen were getting tired, and wished to go home, so one of them jumped up and proposed that they should all go, and leave the Christians to do with the body what they pleased; and upon this they all retired outside the fence. Mr. Geddie, fearing after-troubles to the Christians, addressed the heathen, telling them it was with them to say what should be done with the body. Several replied, "Bury." He then asked, "Is this the wish of all?" There was no opposition; even Naurita was silent. So the body was borne to the grave, the heathens themselves accompanying it along with the Christians. A short service was conducted, the body was laid in the grave, and thus the first Christian burial took place on Aneiteum.

The difficulty in the above affair was greater than it might otherwise have been, as the body was that of a woman. Women, as we have seen, ranked very low on Aneiteum; and in the present case, the woman, by being buried in the earth, instead of thrown into the sea, had an honour conferred upon her which belonged exclusively to the highest chiefs. *Natimariths*, that is, chiefs of the highest rank, were not thrown into the sea. In their case a shallow grave was dug in a house, in which the body was placed, and covered with earth except the head and face. In this house the people were accustomed to assemble daily "to take care," as they termed it, of their chief till the flesh was all consumed from the head and face, when the skull was removed, and placed on a tree as an object of worship.

The death of this woman, like that of Wumra, was regarded by the heathen as a judgment from the Natmases, and occasioned great excitement. Nohoat accosted Mr. Geddie in an angry and abrupt manner, telling him that Christianity was a lie, and demanding to know how, if it were not so, Wumra, the very first man who had embraced it, had died, and now this woman had also died; and added, what of course was untrue, that there was no death among them before the introduction of Christianity. When Mr. Geddie had replied to these statements in a manner which silenced the chiefs, he said, "The Natmases were becoming so enraged on account of Christianity, that he expected there would soon be neither bread-fruit, nor cocoa-nuts, nor taro; and then what would they eat?" Mr. Geddie replied, directing poor, dark-minded Nohoat to Him who sendeth rain from heaven and fruitful seasons, and telling him how he might obtain the forgiveness of his sins, deliverance from all the evils he feared, and a better life than the poor one to which he so fondly clung.

In the midst of all this turmoil, Kuku, a Rarotongan teacher, a good, faithful man, who had for some time shared in the labours and trials of the mission, was taken to his rest. He died of fever and ague. His death was rather sudden, but he seemed prepared. He expressed a wish to die, and to exchange the sorrow of this suffering world for the joys of heaven. He was a young man, and spent but a few years in the mission to which he had devoted himself, but his work was done, and the end of life was secured.

"That life is long which answers life's great end."

Mr. Geddie mourned much the death of Kuku; he says of him, "He was a pious man, and devoted to his work, and had he been spared would have been a useful man."

At the close of this month, March, 1851, poor Waihit was called to pass through a sharp trial. He lost a child —an only child—a boy about fourteen months old, to whom he was fondly attached. He was in great affliction, and went to Mr. Geddie, begging him to tell him something that would comfort him. Mr. Geddie set before him the grounds of consolation which the Gospel supplies to bereaved parents, and related to him the case of David, when in circumstances similar to his own. Waihit listened eagerly, and drank in with avidity the consolation. The idea of a happy meeting with his child beyond the grave was balm to his bleeding heart. Afterwards, Mr. Geddie went and visited him in his own house, and found him quite composed, and engaged in unfolding to his heathen countrymen the life and immortality which the Gospel brings to light. "I shall go to him," he again and again repeated; "I shall go to him, but he shall not return to me." This scene must have been confounding to the heathen, and was well fitted to check their disposition to glory over the Christians on account of the deaths that had recently taken place among them. They would talk, however, and continue to plot mischief. Nohoat made a statement, occasioned by the death of Waihit's child, to the effect that formerly a great many children had died on Tanna, on account of Christianity, but the people there killed one teacher and drove the others away, and then death ceased among them. The remark was eagerly caught at, and it seemed the best policy to do as the people of Tanna had done. The news was soon abroad that the Christian party was to be attacked. Mr. Geddie wished to go to Nohoat, but to this the Christians were opposed, probably being apprehensive for his safety. They chose two of their own number, and sent them as a deputation to wait upon the chief. The result was satisfactory. Nohoat assured them that they should not be molested. Amid this continued excitement Mr. and Mrs. Geddie sighed for and anticipated the joyful day when their harrassed and persecuted flock should sit every man under his vine and fig tree, none making them afraid. That time was not far distant, though many dangers had yet to be encountered, and many difficulties to be overcome.

On the 24th April, 1851, Mr. Geddie wrote as follows: "Our prospects begin to brighten a little. We have been sowing in tears for several months, but we have some reason to hope that we have not sown in vain. Some of our natives are apparently in a thoughtful state, and I have had some applications for baptism. A man notorious for his opposition to Christianity has, a few weeks ago, placed himself under instruction. His name is Nimtinjauphas. He says he is tired of the old system, and wishes to learn the truth. This man is one of the greatest sacred men in the district, and I believe has lived by the superstitions of his people. If he should hold on well, he will be an important accession to us." Others of the heathen party were at this time inclined, perhaps decided, to join the Christians, but they were waiting till a feast which was at hand should be over. There was so much heathenism mixed up with their feasts, that those who avowed themselves Christians could take no part in them.

In August of the same year Mr. and Mrs. Geddie and their adherents were cheered by a visit from Bishop Selwyn, of New Zealand. The Bishop remained a few days, and did everything in his power to assist Mr. and Mrs. Geddie and to encourage the Christians and teachers. The Aneiteum mission, and, indeed, all our missions in Western Polynesia, owe much to Bishop Selwyn for his visits, and the many kind and generous deeds he has performed with a view to promote the comfort of the missionaries and the success of their labours.

While signs of promise were thus multiplying and indicating the near approach of brighter days, works of darkness and cruelty continued to be practised among the heathen. Under date August 15th, 1851, Mr. Geddie wrote: "The horrid practice of strangling is still carried on to a fearful extent. There have been much sickness and several deaths among the natives of late, and many poor women have fallen a sacrifice to a most revolting and barbarous superstition. In one case three women were strangled on the occasion of one man's death. I have always made it a practice to interfere when I have known that life was in danger, though in many instances my interference has been in vain. Knowing with what abhorrence we regard the practice of strangling, every effort is made to conceal it from our knowledge till interference is too late. Often the first intimation of a man's illness is the information of his death and that of his wife. A few mornings ago, as we sat at breakfast, a dead body, slung upon a long pole, and borne by a number of people, was carried past our door. In a few minutes another body, carried in a similar manner, made its appearance." These were the bodies of a man and his wife, the former having died, and the latter having been strangled. They had been brought from the interior of the island by an inland tribe to be buried in the sea. On this occasion the Christian party, being now sufficiently numerous and influential to venture on such a step, made a great stir. They seized the murderer, an old man, and thoroughly frightened him, and made him promise never to be guilty of such a deed again. When inquiry was made for the murderer he started off at his utmost speed, making his way inland, but he was soon overtaken and caught. He was greatly terrified; he seemed to apprehend that he was going to share the fate of the poor woman whom he had murdered. The natives were inclined to handle him severely, but at Mr. Geddie's intercession they somewhat reluctantly set him at liberty. As soon as he was released he made off as fast as he could run.

The following is a cheering and *instructive* statement; highly instructive, especially to missionaries. It is under date August 23rd, 1851. "Of late several natives have professed to forsake their heathen superstitions, and desire Christian instruction. Among the number is Kapaio, a brother of Nohoat, a thorough savage, and notorious for his wickedness. He is a virulent hater of all white men, and has hitherto been very much opposed to the cause. To the surprise of all he has lately commenced attending religious services. In a conversation which he lately had with Mrs. Geddie, he said that when we first came to this land he regarded us as liars, and, along with others, had stolen our property, and done many other bad things towards us, but that he had narrowly watched our conduct, which was so different from their own, that he was now convinced of the truth of our religion and of the falsity of his own." Well may Mr. Geddie add—"How exact ought all Christians to be in their outward conduct! Of all others, missionaries ought to be living epistles of Christ, known and read of all men."

Among the many dangers to which Mr. Geddie was exposed during the early years of his missionary life, perhaps none was ever more imminent than that which arose from the deadly hatred which for a long time was cherished against him by Kapaio. He confessed, after he became a Christian, that for many months he was on the watch for an opportunity of taking Mr. Geddie's life. It seems a wonder that he did not succeed, for he lived not more than half a mile from Mr. Geddie's residence. At the time, however, when his enmity was at its height, Mr. Geddie, knowing that his life was in danger from various parties, was not in the habit of going far beyond his own premises. This was the case for about two years,

THE ISLAND OF BORABORA.

and terminated with the attempt to burn his house, which brought matters to a crisis, and revealed the relative strength and influence of the heathen and Christian parties in such a way as gave the latter the ascendency from that time forward. Kapaio, seeing that he was not likely to find an opportunity of accomplishing his object by waiting at a distance, determined on another plan. He came several evenings after dark to Mr. Geddie's:

6*

garden armed with his club, and hid himself under a bush, in the hope that Mr. Geddie would go outside the house. He was a strong, powerful man, and one well-directed blow from him would have been sufficient. Mr. Geddie went outside one night, and passed close by the bush under which Kapaio was concealed. Now the critical moment had come; the long-desired opportunity was found. Kapaio grasped at his club that he might spring upon his victim and fell him to the ground; but, lo! his hands forgot their cunning—they are powerless—a strange sensation comes over him—and all thoughts of injuring the man of God are at an end. Perhaps his own conscience was the sole *agent* employed in arresting his murderous aim, and expelling the thoughts of murder from his heart. But who can fail to mark the gracious hand of the Keeper of Israel in securing the safety of his servant? *His* eye was upon him, and he effectually interposed for his deliverance.

Kapaio was a member of the church for about six years before his death, which took place early in the year 1861.

As we trace the history of the mission at this time, it becomes more and more evident that heathenism was losing ground, and that Christianity was taking a deeper and deeper hold. Mr. Geddie was startled one morning by the son of Nohoat coming to him in haste, with the exciting intelligence that his brother, a child, was dying, and that his father had declared that, as soon as the child died, his mother should be strangled. The lad who brought the intelligence was a scholar in Mr. Geddie's school. Mr. Geddie started immediately in search of the chief, and, having found him working at his taro plantation, asked if the report he had heard was true? The chief replied that it was. Mr. Geddie spoke strongly to him of the wickedness of his intention, and reminded him of the many promises he had made to him to discourage the horrid practice of strangling women. He attempted to vindicate the intended proceedings on the ground that the mother was the cause of the child's illness. Mr. Geddie, finding reasoning useless, cut the matter short by telling the chief that he should take his wife and child home with him, and that he would be glad to see him to visit them whenever he pleased. This was a bold step, and would not, we apprehend, have been deemed advisable a few months earlier, but by this time heathenism was to some extent losing its hold upon the mind of Nohoat. Mr. Geddie went to Nohoat's house and told his wife to come with him. She hesitated, but Mr. Geddie insisted, as did also her own son and some other natives who were present. When the party had nearly reached Mr. Geddie's house, they saw the chief running after them. He called to his wife to return; instead of this, however, the party quickened their pace, and got inside Mr. Geddie's yard before the chief came up to them. He appeared greatly enraged, and ordered his wife to go back with him. Mr. Geddie and his party succeeded in getting him quieted down, and his wife and child remained under Mr. Geddie's care. Two days afterwards the child died. Nohoat was inconsolable. He mourned as those who have no hope. He pressed the lifeless body to his bosom, rolled himself on the earth, and cried out in bitterness of soul. He made eager inquiries of Mr. Geddie as to what he thought about the soul of the child, and appeared comforted when Mr. Geddie told him his belief that all children dying before they reach the age of accountability are safe. Mr. Geddie asked him how he wished the body of his child disposed of—whether thrown into the sea, or buried in the earth. His mind seemed to revolt at the idea of having his beloved child thrown into the sea, and he requested that it should be buried. There was no more talk of strangling the mother, and there seems reason to believe that the event was blessed to the father.

About the close of August the feast referred to in a preceding page came off. It was a great occasion among the heathen. They assembled in very large numbers from different parts of the island; and the thought occurred to them that the opportunity was a good one to strike a decisive blow at Christianity. It was continually making inroads upon their system; and they were becoming more and more concerned as to the ultimate issue. The Christian party was still small and uninfluential compared with themselves, and they did not see why, on the present occasion, they might not, by one decisive stroke, put an end to the mischief. They were more inclined to this at the time referred to, and were more indignant at the Christians, inasmuch as the chief Topoe, who was to receive the feast in return for one he had given about twelve months before, had declared his intention to embrace Christianity as soon as this was over; and, moreover, he had urged those who had the preparation of this to make the arrangements with all possible speed, in order that his way might be clear to abandon heathenism; and he had intimated that he would not countenance any heathen practices on the occasion. Topoe was a brother-in-law of Nohoat, and next to him the most important man in the district. Thus to lose him was a serious matter; and the prospect of this, together with his conduct on the present occasion, had put the heathen in very ill humour, and the consequence was a determination to bring the matter to a crisis. Accordingly preparations were made, and an attack resolved upon. Of this the Christians were apprised. They were in great consternation, and the question as to what course they should adopt was anxiously discussed. They determined to assemble on the mission premises and hold themselves in readiness to defend themselves if attacked. Mr. Geddie made every inquiry in order to ascertain the real intentions of the heathen, and the more he investigated the matter the more was he convinced that the danger was real; and no doubt a vast majority of the heathen would, in as far as inclination was concerned, have fallen upon the Christians with a hearty good-will. Their counsels were divided, however. As the feast drew near, some of them became faint-hearted, and a few came and joined the Christian party with the intention, in case of a battle, to fight for them. But what decided the matter, was the course adopted by Topoe. In the midst of the excitement he abandoned the heathen, and with several hundred followers went and openly joined the Christians—determined to make common cause with them. This was a terribly mortifying blow to the heathen: they relinquished their intention, and the missionary and his people had again to bless Him who had heard their cry and delivered them out of the hand of those that were stronger than they.

Very soon after this, there were more and highly important accessions to the Christian cause. Under date September 1st, Mr. Geddie writes:—"We have had many accessions of late. Several who promised to join us after the feast in August have been true to their word. Among the number who have joined us is Naurita, the brother of Waihit, who behaved so badly on a former occasion." Since that time, he had speared a native boy, who died of the wound, and had himself been speared in return, and now he was a cripple in consequence. In October, Mr. Geddie writes:—" Nohoat, the chief, has been regular in his attendance on the public ordinances of religion for several weeks. He professes a desire for religious instruction; and, at his own request, I send a native every evening to conduct family worship."

While these things were taking place, the heathen continued their decided but futile efforts to arrest the progress of the mighty movement which now threatened at no distant day to embrace the whole island. On the 9th October, Mr. Geddie writes:—"A party of our natives went out to-day to visit a heathen village named Utchia. They were attacked with stones and spears, and obliged to flee for their lives. They brought home six or seven spears which had been thrown at them."

A little later in the same month, a teacher's house was

burned on the opposite side of the island, at a place near Ipece. A woman who professed Christianity died. Her husband was also a Christian. Her relatives ascribed her death to Christianity; and her brother vented his rage by burning the house of the teacher and the house of the woman's husband. This man manifested a very becoming spirit under his trial. He told Mr. Geddie that "the death of his wife had not weakened his heart to the Word of God, but that it was more strong for that than ever." He spoke of meeting his wife again in another and better world.

The life and immortality which the Gospel brings to light seemed to console the old man's heart.

In November of this year, 1851, *the* crisis came. To this things had been tending for many months, like the houses of Saul and David of old, the one was continually becoming stronger and stronger, and the other weaker and weaker. It was evident one or other must soon be in the ascendant.

In these circumstances, the heathen, aided and abetted by some white men who were resident on the island, determined to resort to an atrocious expedient. The time chosen was opportune. A party, including all the men of importance in Anelecauhat, except Nohoat, who was not yet sufficiently decided to go on such an embassy, had left home in order to make a tour of the island. The object was to hold friendly conversation with the heathen, and endeavour to induce them to embrace Christianity. They left on Monday, the 24th of November. Mr. Geddie remained behind to repair his boat, and prepare for the journey, intending to follow on the Tuesday. The heathen party was by this time so much weakened in the district of Anelecauhat, that Mr. Geddie did not think there was any risk in his leaving home. All unconscious of danger the mission family retired to rest. A little after midnight Mrs. Geddie was aroused by the sound and smell of fire, and on looking up she saw that the roof of the house was in a blaze. She gave the alarm, and Mr.

Geddie ran to awake the natives, who were in two buildings close by. Mrs. Geddie escaped with the two children from the burning house. Mr. Geddie, with the help of his domestics and Mrs. Geddie's school girls, succeeded in getting the fire under. The sea was near and the night was calm. Had it been otherwise it would have been impossible to have saved the house, and the probability is, that the whole of the mission premises would have been destroyed. It was at once ascertained that the burning of the house had been the work of an incendiary. The brand with which the house had been fired was found, and a quantity of combustible material which had been brought in order to ensure the business being effectually done. Mr. Geddie sent for Nohoat, who, when he came and saw the mischief that had been done, burst into tears. The tidings spread rapidly, though it was the dead of night, and the house was soon filled with men, women, and children. Mr. Geddie now learned that, on the preceding day, a party of the heathen, who were known to be hostile, had been seen in earnest conference with a foreigner, who was at that time at the head of the foreign residents, and in the afternoon it had been whispered that Mr. Geddie's house was to be burnt. But it appeared so unlikely that the heathen, who had dwindled down to a small and uninfluential party, would attempt such a thing, that no attention was given to it. We refer to the heathen in the district of Anelcauhat, for they were still a great majority in most other parts of the island.

On the day following, Nohoat set himself at once to collect information as to the origination and perpetration of the deed. He ascertained that five persons had been engaged in it, and obtained the names of three of them. He learned, moreover, that the people of two heathen villages were concerned in the business; the one had engaged to burn Mr. Geddie's house, and the other to burn the chapel. All was vigilance, now, on the part of the Christians. The men were divided into watches, and kept guard all night for some time; nor was this unnecessary, as two men were seen making their way for the chapel, no doubt with bad intentions, as they fled when they found they were discovered. In this extremity, Nohoat behaved nobly. For two months he slept every night in Mr. Geddie's house. He seemed determined that Mr. Geddie should not be in danger without his sharing the danger. Thus did He, whose eye is ever upon His people, graciously raise up friends, and provide for their safety in all their perils. No weapon that was formed against them prospered. "The heathen raged, and the people imagined a vain thing." Each successive plot ended in confusion. The cause of the heathen lost ground continually, while the Word of God grew and multiplied. On the present occasion Mr. Geddie had great difficulty in saving the incendiaries from being very roughly handled. The party who had gone to make a tour of the island heard of the affair on the morning of the day after it had occurred, and immediately returned. They came in a body to the mission premises, and when they saw what had been done, many of them could not speak, but burst into tears. Mr. Geddie encouraged them, telling them they must bear patiently the efforts of Satan to hinder the progress of the cause of God, and that no doubt those who had been guilty of that base deed would one day be ashamed of it. In the afternoon of the same day a scene occurred which one blushes to record. Of that scene Mr. Geddie writes: "I was walking home with Mrs. Geddie, when I looked round and saw ―――― and ―――― coming towards me with all haste. The former came up to me, pale and trembling with rage, carrying a large pistol. He addressed me in a very rude and boisterous manner, and spoke to Mrs. Geddie in a way that is scarcely credible. I did not feel angry at the man, for his position was such as to excite any other feelings than those of anger. It was evident, from the strain of his talk, that we had been too successful among the natives, and won too much of their confidence for him. He told me that he intended in a few weeks to look out another island, and that I should then have the island to myself. I will not soil my paper by recording the conversation that took place, nor have I any desire to keep it in remembrance. The natives were alarmed when they saw the state of excitement in which the man approached me; and the chief was going to order the natives to seize and disarm him, but others adopted a more prudent course. Several of them came round us, and Waihit came partly between us in a way that I, at the time, thought intrusive, but the whole was afterwards explained. The natives had planned, if they saw him lay his hand on the pistol, to seize him at once. I thought the pistol had been brought for fear of the natives; they thought it had been brought on my account. When ——— and his companion had gone, the natives, old and young, male and female, crowded round Mrs. Geddie and myself, expressing their sympathy for the trials we were called to endure in their dark land."

The Christian party determined not to pass this matter lightly by, so a general meeting was summoned of both parties; and "on the morning of the 27th," continues Mr. Geddie, "the day fixed for the meeting, the people came together from all quarters, and took up their positions.

"All the chiefs of any importance on this side of the island were among the Christian party. I spoke to the chief and people, and entreated them on no account to have any fighting, but to say what they had to say in a calm and inoffensive manner. About 10 A.M. the two parties assembled. The heathen party had sent inland, and got the people of the interior to join them. Both parties were armed with clubs and spears, and some of the heathen had pistols furnished them by their foreign abettors. The heathen party were very much frightened, and expected, according to their own customs, to be attacked at once. They would not come within speaking distance of our people, so some of the chiefs went forward and told them they had nothing to apprehend, as the Christian party had no intention of fighting, but wished only to talk to them about the burning of the house. All parties sat down now on the grass, and were engaged in conversation till three o'clock in the afternoon."

All passed off quietly and hopefully. The heathen acknowledged that their conduct in setting fire to Mr. Geddie's house at midnight was base and cowardly. It was contrary to their own custom: for, barbarous and cruel though they be, it is their uniform practice, when they design to attack, or in any way injure their enemies, to give them due notice; and, besides, they do not injure women and children in their wars. Hence the part they had acted was contrary to all *their* ideas of honourable warfare. They promised, moreover, that Mr. and Mrs. Geddie should not be again molested. The case of Mr. Geddie's two children seemed to affect the friendly natives more than anything else. "If," said Nohoat to Mr. Geddie, after the meeting was over, "Lucy and Elizabeth had been burnt, and my *coat* (a military coat which he kept in Mr. Geddie's house) had been burnt, we would not have listened to your word for peace; there would have been many persons killed to-day."

Thus happily ended this disgraceful business. The missionary, his family, and the Christian party, sustained no serious injury, and the cause of truth gained greatly. To it we may apply that remarkable declaration of inspired truth which is so often verified in the history of our world, "Surely the wrath of man shall praise thee: the remainder of wrath shalt thou restrain." So it emphatically was in the above case.

The following statement contrasts pleasantly with the scene that has just passed before us. "Jukai," writes Mr. Geddie, "the chief of a small village, has just died. He had been ill for some time, and three days ago he was

HAPPY DEATH OF A CONVERT. 79

brought to a neighbour's house, where I might attend on him. He was a great sufferer during his illness, but his mind was composed and peaceful. When he was near death all the Christian party assembled, and I believe they were in the act of prayer when he breathed his last. A little before his death, Waihit asked him what his hope

YEAPI, AN ANEITEUMESE CHIEF AND A CHRISTIAN.

was now in the hour of death; he replied, 'I rest on Jesus only.' The man's calmness in death, and hopes beyond, have made a great impression on our people, and also on such of the heathen as were present when he died. In the days of heathenism all was darkness and uncertainty;

now, life and immortality are brought to light by the Gospel. On the day of his death, the people of his village (that is, the heathen part of them) burnt his house, killed his pigs, cut down his cocoa-nut trees, and destroyed his taro. This is always done by the heathen on occasion of the death of any one of importance. It is also customary, on the death of a chief, to have a sham fight, which sometimes ends seriously; but in the present case this was dispensed with."

A painful occurrence marks the close of this eventful year. Hitherto, though life had often been in imminent danger, no one had actually fallen a sacrifice to heathen superstition and cruelty. Now, however, the heathen were permitted to shed Christian blood on Aneiteum.

The people of Anauunse, who were bitterly opposed to Christianity, sent a message to the Christian party at a place called Aneito, near Ipece, to the effect that they wished to cultivate friendly relations with them, and proposing, according to native fashion, an exchange of presents. Their sincerity was not doubted, and the people of Aneito sent a party of four young men with the present. When the young men reached the place, they saw some movements which awakened their suspicions; but an Anauunse man who was with them, probably the same that had taken the message to them, told them not to be afraid, but just to go and sit down in the chief's yard, and no one would molest them. Nalakiang, the chief, was out of the way. The man now left them, telling them that he would soon be back. Before leaving, they observed him enter the house, and take out a spear and a club. In a short time a number of armed men came and surrounded the inclosure where the young men were. It was now evident that evil was determined against them, and that their only chance of escape was in flight. They made a rush through the circle. Two of them took to the bush, and escaped; the other two ran to the seaside and along the shore, pursued by their savage countrymen. Waiwai, the lad who was killed, was first overtaken and struck. His companion, looking round and seeing his danger, ran back, and, throwing his arms around him, andeavoured to shield him from the blows of his murderers, and, in so doing, received some blows himself. Poor Waiwai was killed in his arms. The generous young man, who had jeopardized his own life to save his friend, now said, "You have killed him; kill me also." This they would not do, as he had some heathen relations in the place whom they did not wish to offend. The spirited youth asked some of them to let him have a canoe in which to carry home the body of his murdered friend, to have it buried. This request was treated with ridicule. The young man now tried to carry off the body on his back; the savages, however, took it from him, and bore it away in triumph to the oven.

Referring to this case, Mr. Geddie remarks, "From all that I can learn from the natives, I am decidedly of opinion that the death of this young man is to be ascribed more to a feeling of opposition to the cause of God in their dark land, than to any ancient grudge among the natives themselves. A fearful responsibility attaches to those through whose instigations the late excitement against the cause has been occasioned, and which has led to consequences so disastrous. The heathen around us, who have been revelling in the flesh of the martyred young man, now exclaim in triumph that Christianity is false. The body has been cut up and distributed, and devoured, and they consider that its resurrection is impossible. They mock like the Athenians of old. God will yet arise and vindicate His own cause in this benighted land, notwithstanding the formidable opposition with which it has now to contend."

Yes; God did arise and vindicate His own cause. While the opposition was at its height, God was powerfully at work. While the enemy came in as a flood, the Spirit of the Lord was lifting up a standard against him.

Under date December 20th, Mr. Geddie writes: "Superstition declines fast, even among the heathen. There has of late been a great destruction of sacred groves in this district. Those who have embraced Christianity are now cultivating spots which from time immemorial have been sacred to natmases. The time is not distant when it will be difficult to find traces of the ancient system of worship in this district. Sacred stones, which were supposed to be inhabited by natmases, are now despised by many of the natives. They may be found strewn about the settlement in every direction. Not a few study what indignity they can show to them. Offerings to the natmases have in a great measure ceased, wholly of course among those who avow themselves Christians; and the heathen themselves are becoming ashamed of them."

Thus were the idols being abolished, and the true God exalted. Even Nohoat had got the length of eating sacred food, a thing which, a few months before, no earthly consideration would have induced him to do. And so closed this eventful year, the most eventful, exciting, and perilous, perhaps, through which the Aneiteum mission had passed. Enemies, perceiving that their cause was becoming desperate, had striven with increasing vigilance and perseverance to check the progress of Christianity—indeed, to uproot and destroy it; but all their efforts had been vain. Silently, but surely, its omnipotent energies continued to operate. Enemies raged, and plotted, and strove in vain: "He that sitteth in the heavens did laugh; the Lord had them in derision." Each successive effort ended in their own confusion, and tended only to serve the interest of the cause they sought to destroy.

CHAPTER V.

ANEITEUM—*Continued.*

" The darkness is past, and the true light now shineth."—1 *John* ii. 8.
" Now thanks be unto God, which always causeth us to triumph in Christ."
2 *Cor.* ii. 14.

WE now enter upon what may be regarded as a new era in the history of the Aneiteum mission. Great difficulties were yet to be encountered, and sharp trials to be passed through; but heathenism had received a deadly blow, and its abettors, both native and foreign, were in a great measure powerless. The crisis was past. It was no longer night, nor even dim twilight; morning—bright joyous morning!—giving promise of a glorious day, had opened upon Aneiteum. The progress of the day we are now briefly to trace.

During the month of January, 1852, the leading foreign opponent of the mission took his departure. His leaving the island was marked by a painfully significant act. He took with him one of his native friends. Several were desirous of going with him to see Sydney. The man selected was one who had been notorious for his opposition to the mission, and was the person in the Anelecauhat district to whom a portion of the body of Waiwai was sent. The idea of such an one being taken by an Englishman on a voyage with him, as a mark of special favour, is astounding, and will convey a stronger impression than any mere description, as to how low a man may sink, notwithstanding the advantages of highly respectable family connections, and a liberal and Christian education, in the most enlightened country on the face of the earth. Alas! what is man? Without religion, what is man?

"Therefore let no man glory in men." He that glorieth, let him glory in the Lord."

From this time the work made steady and rapid progress. Of this, every month furnished interesting and delightful evidence. Under date February 4th, Mr. Geddie writes: "The natives on several parts of the island are giving up their superstitions, and abandoning their objects of worship. Lately, two celebrated disease-makers have joined us. They declare that they will no more be the servants of the devil, and ruin their souls in doing his work; and, as an evidence of their sincerity, they have sent me their disease-making apparatus. These I received one day while engaged in my school, and opened up and exhibited to the great amusement of all present. The charms were done up in two native bags. On opening the bags, I found an earthern jar in one, and a tin case in the other. I poured out their contents, and then examined them minutely. The contents were black earth, chewings of the leaf of a plant sacred to the natmases, human hair, fragments of a native female dress, made of the pandanus leaf, fragments of sugar cane from which the juice had been sucked, etc., etc. When a disease-maker wishes to make any person sick, he endeavours to procure a lock of the hair, a fragment of the dress, or a little food belonging to the person. Any of these things will answer his purpose. He then chews up a quantity of sacred leaf, and puts the whole into his charming-pot, which he places on the fire, and prays to his natmases to inflict disease on the person or persons whom he wishes to charm. The process is called *Naragess*, and the persons whose profession it is are more feared than any other class on the island; nor is this strange, seeing that they are believed to possess the power of life and death." These professional gentlemen carry things with a high hand among their deluded countrymen. They were wont to ask freely for anything they wished, and woe to the luckless wight who had the hardihood to refuse their demands! They were of course hated as much as they were feared. It is no wonder that this class of men was violently opposed to Christianity, seeing it owed its wealth and influence to a craft which the progress of Christianity must inevitably destroy.

The following interesting record bears cheering testimony to the progress of the good cause:—"The natives whom I sent out yesterday (Sabbath, February 14th), met with much encouragement in their work. They had worship in the morning at Umetch, after which they divided themselves into two companies, one of which went inland into the mountains, and the other went along the shore to the villages beyond. The mountain party succeeded in gathering a large body of people, whom they addressed on the subject of Christianity, and with whom they prayed. The people were delighted with what they heard, and begged that they might be visited every Sabbath. They agreed then and there to go to work next morning to build a house to meet in for worship. This is the first effectual attempt to introduce the Gospel among the inland tribes. They are very wild, and as degraded as can well be imagined." The shore party met with no less encouragement. At one village, which had been visited on former occasions, all the people turned out to hear about the new religion. After the visitors had discoursed to them fully as to the folly of their superstitions and practices, one of them asked if they were willing to give up heathenism, and place themselves under Christian instruction. They replied that they were. They were then asked whether, as an evidence of their sincerity, they would destroy their village natmas. They replied that they were afraid to do that; but that they, the Christian party, might do as they pleased. "The said natmas," remarks Mr. Geddie, "was neither more nor less than a piece of heavy, durable wood, with extended branches that might be mistaken for the horns of a reindeer. It had been worshipped from time immemorial."

Having got the consent of the people, one of the party seized the helpless deity, and, as it was too heavy to carry home entire, he broke it in two pieces, and burnt part of it on the spot; the remainder he brought with him as another trophy to the cause of truth.

On the following Sabbath an incident of a different character occurred. Waihit had gone to Umetch to conduct worship, the Samoan teacher who occupied that station being ill with an attack of fever and ague. As he was on his way to the place of meeting, a man, who had concealed himself near the path, came upon him armed with a club, and in great wrath threatened to kill him. During a storm which had occurred about ten days before, the tide had risen beyond its usual height, and destroyed the man's taro. He imagined that Waihit and some other parties belonging to Anelecauhat had caused the tide to rise; and on this account sought revenge. Waihit tried to reason with the man, telling him that God only could control the winds and waves; but he was too much excited to listen to reason. Waihit then said, "I will not run away from you; you can kill me if you will, I am not afraid to die." By this time several people had come up on their way to the service. They interfered, and so the matter ended. The people entreated Waihit not to forsake them on account of the treatment he had met with; and when the chief of the place heard of the occurrence, he was much grieved, and gave the man a severe reprimand before all the people. On the same day, the inland village mentioned above was again visited. The people had been as good as their word, and had built a rude chapel. It was too small, however, to accommodate the congregation that assembled to hear the Word of God.

The following incident contrasts delightfully with the general character of night visits in past days. It occurred on the Sabbath. Mr. Geddie had been preaching from the parable of the sower. "This evening," he writes, "I heard, about nine o'clock, a knock at my door, and on opening it found a man, named Kiho, apparently in distress. When he came in he burst into tears, and was some time before he could tell me the cause of his trouble. As soon as he was able to speak, he said he could not go to rest, for he thought he was one of the unprofitable hearers whom I had described when explaining the parable of the sower. He said his heart was very dark and very hard. I gave him what direction I thought suitable to his case, and prayed with him, and bade him pray for himself. He requested me to explain to him a passage of Scripture that I had preached from some time before, and which seemed to have arrested his attention, 'Behold, I stand at the door and knock,' etc. He seemed to draw some comfort from this beautiful and soul-reviving passage. This man lives about four miles distant. Directly in his path lies a heathen village, the people of which have shown much opposition to the cause, and have more than once threatened Kiho's life. On this account he comes to this place in his canoe, or else takes a long circuitous route through the bush, to avoid his enemies. He usually comes on Saturday, and returns on Monday. The village in which he lives is heathen; most of his relatives are decided in favour of Christianity, but are afraid openly to avow their sentiments."

Trials of another kind now came upon the mission family. As regards storms from without, there was a lull; but domestic afflictions pressed heavily. Mr. Geddie was seized with an attack of slow fever, somewhat resembling the jungle-fever of India. He was reduced to a state of great weakness, and suffered probably much more than he would otherwise have done, on account of the lack, not only of comforts, but of necessaries. "The most of my nourishment during my sickness," he writes, "was a bit of toasted, musty bread, and a few pieces of hard biscuit, which a poor shipwrecked sailor was kind enough to send me out of his weekly allowance. May God repay him! his kindness was invaluable to me."

It is pleasant to hear of the "poor shipwrecked sailor," who, being made acquainted with Mr. Geddie's necessities, unsolicited, divided with him his own scanty supply of bread. Mr. Geddie never had the satisfaction of seeing and thanking his kind benefactor, as he left the island before he was sufficiently recovered. All that he could learn of him was, that he was a Scotch sailor. During Mr. Geddie's illness, the whole party to which this man belonged, having heard of his distress, sent and offered to supply him out of their own limited means with anything they had which might be of use. They were themselves on allowance. Mr. Geddie declined their generous offer, but felt their kindness very deeply. It does one's heart good to hear of these instances of generosity on the part of British seamen. May they reap a rich reward! "Inasmuch as ye did it unto one of the least of these my brethren, ye did it unto Me."

Relief soon came. The *John Williams*, with supplies, was at hand. Early in May, the writer, in company with the Rev. J. P. Sunderland, visited the island, as a deputation from the Samoan Mission, and had the high satisfaction of seeing what God was doing for the Aneiteumese. And oh, how cheering were the indications that everywhere met us of the mighty and blessed change that was in progress!

Hope deferred had tried our faith; hope realised now filled our hearts with joy, and our lips with praise. Past labour, sufferings, and perils were forgotten, while the results, so happy and full of promise, were before our eyes. We did not need to be *told* that a change had taken place. The evidence was too palpable to be mistaken. The following extracts from our report, published in the *Samoan Reporter*, will give an idea of the state of things as we beheld them:—

"Everything we saw and heard indicated, in a way not to be mistaken, that an amazing change had taken place since our last visit. At that time scarcely any visible impression had been made. Five or six individuals had begun to discover some signs of awakening interest in the truths of Christianity, but the great body of the people were scarcely a single remove from the lowest heathenism. Now, in the neighbourhood of all the principal stations, four in number, there are not a few who have totally abandoned heathenism, and who are steady and consistent attendants on the means of grace and instruction. At the harbour, the Sabbath congregation averages one hundred; the daily schools eighty. About forty can read tolerably, and a considerable number quite fluently. About sixty are members of a select class, the conditions of membership being, external conformity to the requirements of the Word of God.

"A church has been formed, consisting of thirteen members, six male and seven female. They were baptised on the morning of the Sabbath we spent on the island. In the afternoon, they were constituted a Christian church, and the ordinance of the Lord's Supper was administered to them. The occasion was one of thrilling interest.' It was the first time the sacred ordinance had been administered to natives of Western Polynesia, and will be regarded as an era in the future history of the great western division of the Polynesian family. Viewed in this light, the transactions of Sabbath, 18th May, 1852, on the island of Aneiteum, assume an interest and importance of the first magnitude. Let the friends of missions take courage, and let the God of missions be magnified, who hath thus given us a pledge of ultimate and complete success!

"At Umetch, another station on the island, occupied by a Samoan teacher, the Christian party form also a decided majority;'and at Apame, which is next in importance to the place where Mr. Geddie resides, the state of things is not less encouraging than it is there. The number that attend schools and services is about the same; and there are other decisive indications that the work is taking hold of the hearts of many. Articles of wearing apparel are in great demand at all the stations; for, instead of bedaubing themselves with paint, as they were wont, all now wear clothing, as far as their means will allow. Long hair and other indications of heathenism have almost entirely disappeared among the Christian party, and no such thing as a weapon of war is to be seen. The people are most desirous to learn to read; many are learning to write also. Mr. and Mrs. Geddie have about eighteen boys and girls, as boarders, who can write well. Their progress in learning to read is somewhat impeded for want of books. They have, at present, a very scanty supply of these. What they have are valued beyond all price. A case was mentioned to us, where a family had their house and all their little property burned. The loss of the house and property appeared to be thought nothing of; the only regret seemed to be, that the *books* were destroyed.

"The happy change now in progress, according to Mr. Geddie's opinion, has been brought about in a great measure by *native* instrumentality. There are six natives who go out as evangelists, and address their fellow-countrymen on the subject of religion. The chief of these, and the one who has been most extensively useful, is Waihit, a remarkable character. He was a very considerable personage in former days. He had, as was supposed, authority over the sea, and exerted a great influence for evil. So late as the voyage in 1849, he was a debased, cruel, savage, and would not so much as enter the house of God. Now he is clothed, and in his right mind, and employed from day to day in testifying to his countrymen the Gospel of the grace of God. How amazing the change! What hath God wrought!

"Our space will not allow of our attempting anything like a full enumeration of the trials through which the mission has passed. The worthy man and his devoted partner, who, without any succour from man, have borne the burden and heat of the day, have been 'in labours more abundant,' and in perils great and imminent. They have been in perils by their own countrymen, and in perils by the heathen. But out of them all the Master whom they serve has graciously delivered them; and He has given them to see, to a most gratifying extent, His work prospering in their hands. Thus they have, even now, their reward. We cannot enumerate all the beneficial effects of the happy change which has taken place. Some of these the Christian heart contemplates with peculiar satisfaction; such as the very general cessation of the horrid practice of strangling widows, on the death of their husbands. Even among the heathen, the missionary and his adherents frequently succeed in saving parties doomed to death by the cruel usages of superstition. The unnatural and revolting practice is not confined to widows. Not long ago a woman was strangled at her own request, on the death of her son. The youth had no wife to accompany him to the other world, and his mother chose to do so. The probability is, that ere a great while, these remnants of the reign of darkness and superstition will cease throughout the island. The light is fast spreading; and they cannot live in the light."

Such was the state of things at the time to which these extracts refer. The reader acquainted with the history of modern missions will notice in the preceding pages a striking similarity to what took place at Tahiti, and also on some of the Society and Hervey Islands,—Raiatea, Raiotonga, and Aitutaki, for example.

During the period of transition from darkness to light, and so long as the truth takes little or no hold of the minds of men, all goes on with comparative smoothness; but no sooner does the Gospel begin to exert a decided influence, than all the powers of darkness seem aroused to unwonted activity. The devil comes down, as it were, having great wrath, knowing that his time is short; interested parties, heathen priests, and sometimes despotic chiefs—and not seldom men bearing the Christian name—are his ready tools; so that the poor defenceless missionary and his adherents are literally as lambs in the midst of wolves. It appears as if hell were let loose; and the witness for the truth is at his wit's end. But his extremity is God's opportunity; and when he is ready to conclude that all is lost—*then* appears the "salvation of God." What joy then fills his heart! What wonders of wisdom and grace does he see in those very things that appeared most threatening and inexplicable! How is his faith strengthened, and his arm nerved for future conflict! He

ISLAND SCENERY.

was not aware that these very things were a necessary discipline, to prepare him and others for receiving the mercy that was in store for them. But for these, his heart might have been lifted up, and he might have been in danger of arrogating something to himself. Now he is prepared to give all the praise to Him to whom it is due.

It was considered desirable that Mr. Geddie should embrace the opportunity which was now offered of seeking relaxation and invigoration of body and mind, by a short sea voyage; so he determined to go with us in our cruise among the adjacent islands. We sailed on the 13th of May, and got back to Aneiteum on the 13th of June. Mr. Geddie returned much improved, and with recruited health and spirits resumed his arduous labours. Nothing untoward had happened during his absence; Mrs. Geddie's chief troubles had arisen from the intended case of strangling mentioned in the preceding chapter.

Mr. Geddie had not been long home when an event took place, furnishing a painful contrast to scenes recently witnessed on the island. Mr. Geddie thus describes it, under date June 24th:—"A sad event has just occurred. Four young men set out from Anauantchai to come to this place this morning. They had been sent by the chief to beg a teacher for his land, and some of our native catechisms. They had to pass through a place about three miles distant on their way; the chief of that place, and also some of the people, have joined us, but the body of the people are still heathen. The young men were attacked by the heathen, and one of their number barbarously murdered. The young man who was killed belonged to Aneito, but had been some time at Anauantchai, teaching the Christian party there to read. It was not on account of his Christianity that the young man was killed, but to avenge the death of some parties who had fallen in former wars with the Aneito people."

The adjacent village made an unsuccessful effort to get the body of the murdered young man for burial. When they went and applied for it, it was concealed; and afterwards it was brought forth and cooked. It is worthy of remark, that those who endeavoured to preserve the body from this indignity were politically connected with the murderers. Little more then a year before they would have joined with them in avenging their common quarrel, and in the subsequent cannibal feast. Well may Mr. Geddie exclaim, in reference to this case, "What a change the Gospel makes! Among the Christian party all former grievances and animosities appear to be forgotten, and an injury done to one is regarded as an injury done to the whole body.

It is not easy for any except those who have been placed in similar circumstances to conceive what must have been the feelings of the solitary missionary and his estimable wife, when they were surprised by the arrival of Bishop Selwyn, in his schooner, the *Border Maid*, with the Rev. John Inglis and Mrs. Inglis, to labour on the New Hebrides. Mr. Inglis is connected with the Reformed Presbyterian Church of Scotland. He had laboured several years in New Zealand, chiefly among British settlers, by whom he was held in high esteem; and, guided by providential indications, he had now come to Mr. Geddie's aid. Bishop Selwyn kindly and generously brought him and his goods from New Zealand free of expense. Mr. and Mrs. Geddie were delighted to welcome these esteemed friends to be their companions in labour; and all was speedily arranged for their settlement on Aneiteum. It was on the 1st of July, 1852, that Mr. and Mrs. Inglis arrived.

The place at which Mr. Inglis settled is named Aname. It adjoins Ipece, were the first teachers were landed. It was a joyous day on that side of the island, and, indeed, all the island over, among the Christians, when Mr. Inglis took up his abode at Aname. Mr. Geddie accompanied Mr. Inglis to his station, and has this record in reference to the first Sabbath spent at it:—"July 4th, Sabbath.— A lovely day. The assemblage of people so large that the house would not nearly contain them. I preached twice, and introduced Mr. Inglis to his future charge. This was to me a most pleasing service. May God bless the labours of his servant! He enters upon his labours with most pleasing prospects."

Mr. Inglis had brought with him from New Zealand the frame and other materials for a house; and in a very short time, a comfortable home was ready for the reception of himself and his excellent wife. Many hands and willing hearts made light work; and in about a month from their arrival everything was ready for their reception, and they took up their abode at Aname. Seldom have fellow-labourers been more equally yoked than Messrs. Geddie and Inglis. To them and their esteemed partners, the beautiful words of inspiration are strikingly appropriate—"Behold, how good and how pleasant it is for brethren to dwell together in unity!" Lovely and pleasant, indeed, has been their connection; and the God of love and peace has been with them, as He always will be with those who live together in love and peace.

The work now made steady progress. Old things were rapidly passing away, and all things were becoming new. The following extract, bearing date July 14th, 1852, furnishes pleasing testimony to this:—"What a revolution has taken place on the subject of feasting! At the time of our arrival on this island, giving and receiving feasts seemed to engross the attention of the natives more than anything else. Pigs, taro, cocoa-nuts, fish, etc., were all tabooed for this purpose; and the natives lived in misery, that they might be able to make great exhibitions of food at their feasts. The people of this place have just made a collection of food to repay a feast received by them from the people inland. There was no waste of time, no ceremony, no heathenism: when the food was all collected in the chief's yard, and the inland people came to receive it, Nohoat addressed them seriously, and told them not to think of the perishable food they were receiving, but to seek the Word of God, which only could save them from ruin. He declared to them the choice he had made, and exhorted them to follow his example. The chief has come out more decidedly of late than ever before; and it is the opinion of our most judicious men, that he is in earnest about the one thing needful. He sent to me this morning, requesting me to send some of our most enlightened men to talk to the people from the interior, for he says his heart is very dark." Poor Nohoat! His heart was, no doubt, very dark; but what a marvellous change had he undergone: How different the Nohoat we now meet, to the poor grovelling heathen who kept dunning us about the "long-eared pig," all the way round from Ipece to Anelecauhat, when we first visited that place. Verily nothing is too hard for the Lord. Of this, the history of the mission at this time furnished ample evidence. Witness the following:—" Sept. 8th. We have had several accessions of late. Some who were the most determined enemies of the cause have joined us, and wish to be taught the Word of God. Many, whom we least of all expected so to act, have turned their backs on heathenism, and ask for Christian instruction. Our natives wonder, and exclaim, 'This is the Lord's doing!' How strange and pleasing to see those who so lately raged against the cause of God, and those who are friendly to it, now willing to sit at the feet of Jesus, that they may be taught the way to life and happiness!"

On Sabbath, the 19th of September, a very gratifying scene was witnessed at Anelecauhat. Mr. Geddie describes it thus:—"An interesting Sabbath. Our chapel was crowded to excess. Witnessed a very interesting scene. Mr. Inglis came round yesterday, and brought with him an influential chief named Iata, formerly a great warrior and notorious cannibal. He had not been on this side of the island for years before our arrival. He met in the house of God, to-day, a man of a similar stamp to himself, named Nimtiwan. The last time they met was on the field of battle. I wondered how they would act now; and oh! how delighted I was to see these two men come out of the house of God with their arms round each other! I could not help calling the attention of brother Inglis to the scene, and saying, 'See what the Gospel hath wrought!'"

On the 27th of October, a very old man from an inland

village, ten miles distant, came to Mr. Geddie, to seek Christian instruction. The Gospel had reached his village some time before through native agency, and had taken so much hold of his heart that he had cast off his god, a stone idol, and sent it to Mr. Geddie.

Nothing of a very marked character occurred during the remainder of this year. At its close, the little church had increased to twenty-four members; four small books had been printed; a chapel capable of containing 500 people had been opened; and every department of the work was steadily progressing. Nearly one-half of the entire population of the island, including the principal chiefs, had abandoned heathenism and embraced Christianity.

The struggle between Christianity and heathenism was now (January, 1853) drawing to a close, and the state of things was more quiet and settled. The heathen did not cease, however, occasionally to make attempts to revive their sinking cause, and check the progress of the new religion; but the result was uniformly loss to them and gain to Christianity. Indeed, in the most troublous times, this was the case; although, amid the strife and tumult of the conflict, it was not always apparent. The truth of God was steadily and surely making its way towards victory; the savour of the Redeemer's name was being spread abroad.

About the middle of January, the people of Anauunse, who were still heathen, determined to make an attack upon the district adjoining their own, because that district had renounced heathenism and embraced Christianity. A combined effort on the part of the Christians from other districts, headed by the missionaries, was successful in preventing the attack; and the usual result followed, viz., loss of influence on the part of the heathen, and corresponding advantage to the Christian cause. The heathen were overawed, and promised that they would not again molest their Christian neighbours.

The spread of Christianity brought more and more fully

to light the cruel and abominable practices to which the people had been addicted in their heathen state. Under date March 1st, Mr. Geddie writes :—" In taking a census of different villages, I have been much struck with the disproportion between the number of boys and girls, the former being much more numerous ; and also between the number of children and adults, the former being comparatively few. I knew enough about the horrid practices of these islands to suspect the cause. Infanticide has prevailed to a considerable extent. Parents have been accustomed to put their children to death, in order to be relieved from the trouble of bringing them up. The practice has been to take the newborn infant to the bush, and leave it there to die. Many, thus exposed, have been saved by others, and adopted as their own children. We have now two living in our family who were thus exposed in infancy. Male as well as female children were destroyed, but especially the latter."

From such disclosures as the above, it is delightful to turn to the following :—" May 18th. Nokoai died to-day. His end was peace. His life has been very consistent since he made a profession of Christianity. He was our first native teacher on this island ; and during the few months that he acted as teacher he appears to have done much good. A few days ago I had a conversation with him, and asked him about the state of his mind in the prospect of death. His answer was, that he was a great sinner, but that he felt peace in looking to the blood of Jesus ; and, as for death, he was willing to meet it, if that were the will of God."

In the month of June of this year, a case of strangling occurred in the district of Anelecauhat. The people were greatly excited when they heard of it. The guilty parties were sought out and bound, and well lectured on their wickedness. They were released on promising to engage no more in such deeds.

In October, the writer, in company with Mr. Sunderland,

NATIVES OF ANEITEUM CARRYING TIMBER TO BUILD A CHURCH.

again visited the island, and had the happiness to witness the continued progress of the good cause. The following extract from the report of the voyage exhibits some of the cheering results that had been realised. After noticing the arrival of Mr. Inglis, the report proceeds:—"At Anelecauhat, the cause has been steadily progressing since last visit. The Sabbath congregations have been nearly trebled, and a proportionate increase has taken place in the Schools. A new place of worship has been erected, in which a congregation, averaging 350, assemble every Sabbath. Besides the principal congregation, there are seven others connected with the Anelecauhat station; and, in addition to more regular services, a good deal is done every Sabbath, in the way of visiting and conversing with different parties. The number of native assistants is about fifteen; and three Samoan teachers aid the missionaries in their various labours. Mr. Geddie has a select daily class of about forty young men; many of whom, it is hoped, will be found eligible for teachers, when further instructed. Seventeen have been added to the Church since last visit; it now numbers thirty, and further additions are about being made. The number of schools on the island is twenty-five. Some of them are very small; but the aggregate number under instruction is about 1,400, and of these about one-third can read tolerably. Many also can write à little.

"At Aname, the station occupied by Mr. Inglis, the state of things is very similar to what it is at Anelecauhat; somewhat less advanced, as might be expected, from the fact that a much less amount of labour has been expended on it. The work is rather retarded at present, for want of a suitable place of worship. That hindrance, however, is in the way of being removed. An excellent chapel is being erected. It is far advanced, and when completed will be of immense advantage. It is seventy feet by thirty. Its erection is exciting great interest. Even the heathen are coming voluntarily forward, and lending a hand.

"The present Sabbath congregation at the principal station is about 300. There are three other congregations in other parts of the district; and a fourth, which is suspended at present, will shortly be resumed. Mr. Inglis has also a select class of young men, similar to Mr. Geddie's, which numbers about fifty.

"The usual happy effects are following the spread of Christian truth on Aneiteum. War, cannibalism, infanticide, the strangling of widows, heathen dances, feasts, and other Pagan practices, are either passed, or rapidly passing away; and the characteristics of a Christian community are beginning to appear.

"The sandal-wood establishment is obliterated. As much of the property as could be removed without much difficulty was taken away, and the remainder was burned by parties employed by the owner, who has taken up his residence on a neighbouring island. Thus the opposition to the mission from that quarter, once so formidable is at an end. The cause of truth and righteousness has triumphed, as it always ultimately will.

"It was our privilege to be the bearers of an inestimable treasure to the Aneiteum people, the Gospel of Mark. It had been translated by Mr. Geddie, and was taken to Sydney by Mr. Sunderland; and during the stay of the *John Williams* there, we got an edition of 3,000 printed. This is the first complete portion of Scripture that has been printed in any language or dialect of Western Polynesia."

On this occasion two natives of Aneiteum, Waihit from Mr. Geddie's district, and Josefa from Mr. Inglis's district, went with us to be located as Christian teachers on the adjacent island of Fotuna. This was the first decidedly missionary effort put forth by Aneiteum. Mr. and Mrs. Geddie went with us on this voyage. We sailed from Aneiteum on the 25th of October, and returned on the 13th of November. Nothing calling for particular remark occurred during the remainder of this year. The labourers, foreign and native, went steadily and zealously forward with their work, and the pleasure of the Lord prospered in their hands.

The following extract will give the reader an idea of the kind of travelling which missionaries have sometimes to encounter in visiting inland villages. "We then pursued our course up the valley, and, after a walk of four miles, reached Anumetch, in the interior of the island. The road was dismal, such as I never before travelled. Our only path was the bed of a small but rapid stream; we were obliged to jump from stone to stone a great part of the way. In places where the water was too deep, we clambered up the precipitous sides of the banks, and, clinging to roots of trees, and projections or excavations in the rocks, we made our way along. In many places the road was dangerous, and we were obliged to proceed with caution. The mountains rose almost perpendicularly on either side of the narrow stream, to the height of several hundred feet. It seems as if the mountains had been cleft by some great convulsion; and the narrow pass thus formed has become the bed of the stream, and serves also for a path. Anumetch is a pretty level spot in the interior, surrounded by a circular ridge of mountains. It looks just as if it might be the basin of an extinct volcano. Into this secluded and inaccessible spot, some seven or eight miles inland, the light had found its way. A place of worship had been built, and the people were anxious for a teacher to instruct them more fully in the way of the Lord." After an account of visits to several other places, Mr. Geddie concludes: "I feel much encouraged by this visit. How delightful to see the poor natives hungering after the Word of God: What a contrast between the present and the past! The time was, when I durst not visit any of these places; but now my visits are greatly desired."

In March of this year (1854), a second church was formed on the island; and the new chapel at Aname was opened. "A day of much interest," writes Mr. Geddie, referring to the occasion. "We assembled in the new chapel at Aname for the first time, on Sabbath, March 12. At the close of the sermon, Mr. Inglis baptised nine persons, and constituted them a Christian church. In the afternoon we again met, when the ordinance of the Lord's Supper was administered. The whole occasion was one of surpassing interest. There were present between nine hundred and one thousand persons. They came together from different parts of the island. How pleasing, how delightful, to see so many persons, formerly regarding each other with deadly enmity, now meeting as friends and brethren! The events of this day will not, I am sure, be soon forgotten by those who were present."

On the Monday following this interesting Sabbath, the brethren " had a meeting with all the principal chiefs and people, and advised them to do something towards forming a political constitution for the suppression of crime, and the general good of society. This suggestion was well received; and the chiefs will meet, on a future occasion, to enact a few simple laws."

In April, Messrs. Geddie and Inglis made a tour of the island, and met with much to interest and encourage. "We were gratified, and in some instances astonished," Mr. Geddie remarks, "to see the rapid improvement of the natives in some of the more remote districts." Let the reader note the following remarks, as an illustration of heathen life:—"Among the party who accompanied us were some chiefs of high rank, who had never been round the island, small as it is. In the reign of heathenism, life was so insecure that it was not safe for a man to pass beyond the boundaries of his own district. Oh, what a change has the gospel wrought!"

In the month of July, a new place of worship was opened at Anelecauhat. It was built in the short space of three and a-half months, and was capable of accommodating about nine hundred persons. The old chapel, which was built only about two years before, had become too small. On the 9th of July, when this was opened, a congregation of about a thousand persons assembled.

Messrs. Hardie and Sunderland visited the island in October of this year, and found the work in a highly satisfactory state. It had been ascertained, by the brethren labouring on the island, that as many as two thousand and six hundred had embraced Christianity. Thirty schools were in operation throughout the island; churches and congregations were increasing; and everything indicated the most cheering progress. "The Christian party," writes Mr. Hardie, "has gained a very decided ascendency all over the island; and the ancient customs are everywhere on the wane. War, cannibalism, and heathen orgies, may be now reckoned among the things that were. The natmases are everywhere being cast away or neglected. For eighteen months no case of strangling has occurred." On this occasion two other natives were set apart for missionary work, and proceeded in the *John Williams* to Tanna.

An attempt was made at Anauunse, a place famous from of old for its opposition to Christianity, to revive the custom of strangling widows. A heathen chief had died, and the heathen party, still large in the village, determined to strangle his wife. Times were so altered now, however, that the teacher, with the aid of some Christians, to whom he applied for help, had little difficulty in saving the woman. More than two years had now elapsed since a case of strangling had taken place on the island. How many lives, during that period, must have been spared, that, but for Christianity, would have been cruelly cut short!

The long-continued opposition of the people of Anauunse to Christianity, appears to have been owing, to some extent, to the influence of a fearfully wicked man, named Yakanua. This man was one of the most awfully depraved wretches that ever disgraced humanity—a perfect demon. He was a chief, and a sacred man, and had the reputation of being a great disease-maker. The first teachers who were stationed in the district found very few children; and the reason assigned for this was, that Yakanua had killed and eaten great numbers. The grown-up people were also in great fear of him, lest they should become his victims. He was in the habit of surprising those whom he killed in unguarded moments. When this man embraced Christianity, which was towards the close of this year, the poor people were greatly rejoiced, and remarked that *now they would be able to sleep in peace.* One wonders that such a monster was allowed to live. It was, no doubt, owing to his sacred character. Certain destruction would, according to the notions of the deluded people, have overtaken any one who should have ventured to molest him. Hence, he was allowed to roam at large, and do as he pleased. He is still alive; he has not given evidence of a radical change, but the indirect influence of the Gospel has rendered him harmless. Very recently the writer met and shook hands with this man of blood.

At the close of this year (1854), a very interesting death occurred; perhaps the most interesting that has yet taken place on Aneiteum. On the 25th of October, 1854, Mary Ann, a young woman of much promise, was called away from her island home, to join the "great multitude which no man can number." The following account of the life and death of this young woman, written by Mrs. Geddie, in a letter to a friend, will interest the reader:—

"When we commenced our labours among this people. Mary Ann was a young, thoughtless heathen. She was a very interesting-looking girl, and being of high rank—she was the only female of the same rank on the island—I was anxious to have her with me when I commenced my boarding-school. Several times she came, and promised to remain with me; but after continuing a day or two, I would see no more of her for some time. One morning her parents came to our house, bringing, as a present, a large basket of bread-fruit, and asked us if we would take their daughter and take charge of her; urging, as their reason for this application, that they were afraid the foreigners would take her to live with them. We told them we were anxious to get a number of promising girls to live in our family, that we might instruct them, and that we would take her as they desired. As the parents were heathens, they could not appreciate our motives, but they wished her to remain with us, and said she was to be our child, and from that time they called her so. For some months after Mary Ann came to live with us, she continued to be very thoughtless and unsteady, often going away, and staying several days. One evening I called her and Mary, her companion, who also lived with us, into my room, and had a long conversation with them. I told them I was grieved to see them so thoughtless, especially Mary Ann, and added that I had left my own home that I might teach them the Word of God, and that I parted from my own child, who was very dear to me, that I might remain among them. I said that I should never regret leaving my home and friends, and parting with my child, if I should have the happiness of seeing them seeking the Saviour; and that now, as my dear Charlotte had left me, they should try, as much as possible, to fill her place to me. They both cried very much, and said they knew what I told them was true, and that they were very bad and dark-hearted. From this time I could see an evident change in them both. Dear Mary Ann became quite a changed girl, and, we have every reason to believe, a decided Christian. She tried in every way to please me, and to be a daughter to me. We all loved her very much, and never, as far as I remember, had reason to reprove her. As she was a girl of highest rank, she was very much annoyed by the heathen chiefs; when preparations for a feast were going on especially, they insisted upon her assisting in heathen ceremonies, but she never yielded. She and some others of our first converts were often much persecuted by the heathen, and their lives were threatened. About the time Mary Ann became serious, she formed an acquaintance with a young man on the other side of the island. They soon became strongly attached to each other; and, as they were both promising young people, we were pleased to see it. After Mr. Inglis had settled at the other side, he appointed the young man as a teacher to a distant village; and, as we knew of no obstacle to prevent, we all thought it well for him and Mary Ann to be married, that she might assist and cheer him in his labours. After Mary Ann was settled in the land where her husband was teacher, we did not see her very often, as the place was distant, and the road was bad; but she never failed to write to me by every opportunity. Her letters were very affectionate, and written in a most pious strain. In almost every one of them she thanked me for my care and instruction; and always added, 'What should I have been if you had not taken care of me? You are my mother; and, although I love my parents, I love you and Mr. Geddie better than I do them.' Mr. Inglis was very much pleased with our dear Mary Ann as a teacher. Last July she wrote me that she was not well, from the effects of a bad cold. Her husband got medicine from Mr. Inglis, which relieved her, but did not remove the complaint, which proved to be an affection of the membrane lining the windpipe. She suffered much pain, and her strength rapidly failed. In October H.M.S. *Herald* called here; we immediately sent for Mary Ann, and consulted the doctor about her. He approved of what Mr. Geddie and Mr. Inglis had done for her, but gave us little hope of her recovery. From this time she lived at her father's, who lived close beside us. In as gentle a manner as possible, I told her that the doctor thought her very ill, and said it was doubtful if she would recover, and added, that she was in the hands of a kind and heavenly Father, who, if He thought fit to restore her, was able to do so. I was surprised to hear her say, with the greatest calmness, that she did not expect to recover; and that she felt very happy at the thought of going to her Saviour. Her parents, husband, and sisters, who were present, could not restrain their grief, but she remained quite composed. From this time

AN ISLAND CHAPEL.

I visited her daily, and read portions of Scripture to her. Mr. Geddie also visited her frequently, and prayed with her. Her strength gradually declined, and she suffered very much from pain in her throat, and severe cough. She could not swallow anything without great pain, yet she always appeared cheerful and happy. She talked a great deal to her parents, brothers, and sisters, advising and urging them to be zealous and devoted to the cause of Christ. To her two sisters, who are mothers, she gave much good advice about bringing up their children. To her eldest sister, who often disputed with her husband, she talked very seriously, and told her how happily she and William, her own husband, had lived together; and urged her and her husband to follow their example, as they soon, too, might have to part, and give account of themselves to God. One night Mr. Geddie and I were sitting beside her, thinking every minute would be her last. Appearing comparatively easy, Mr. Geddie asked her how she felt now, in the near prospect of death. She said she felt very happy at the thought of being soon with her Saviour, who she knew had died for her sins. She added that, often when in great pain, and, as she thought, just about to depart, she felt unspeakably happy at the prospect of soon being in heaven; and that when she became a little better, she felt disappointed. Soon after, she took her husband's hand in hers, and, looking affectionately at him, she said, 'William, I feel very sorry for you; great is my love for you, and I would like to live for your sake; but my desire to be with Jesus is greater.'

"She lingered a week after this, and suffered less pain than she had formerly done; but she had lost the power of swallowing. On Christmas morning her husband came to me, saying that Mary Ann desired to see me; that she felt different to what she had ever done, and thought she was dying. I hastened to her. She was quite sensible, but scarcely able to speak. Mr. Geddie prayed with her, and soon after she became, as we all thought, insensible, as she took no notice when we spoke to her. But when her husband asked if she was resting on Jesus, she distinctly answered 'Yes.' Her face wore a calm and happy expression; her breathing became fainter; and soon after her spirit took its flight to that happy land where she longed to be.

"Thus my dear Mr.———, have I given you a hasty and imperfect sketch of one who, we have every reason to hope, is now rejoicing in the presence of the Saviour; one of the first fruits of the Gospel on Aneiteum, whom you, and all who have lent their aid in sending the Gospel to this isle of the ocean, have been instrumental in saving from eternal misery, and directing to the Lamb of God that taketh away the sin of the world. I have never met with any native who had the same ideas of modesty and propriety that Mary Ann possessed. Mr. Geddie and I often remarked, after she became decidedly pious, that her views appeared quite above those of a young person brought up in heathenism."

The above sketch presents us with a striking and beautiful exemplification of the powerful and benign influence of the Gospel. How great, how marvellous, the contrast between the "thoughtless heathen," and the meek, loving, patient saint, lying at the threshold of heaven, and longing to depart and be with Christ! What a happy system must that be from which such effects flow! Soon may its holy and blessed influence be felt in every land beneath the sun!

It is pleasing to add that Mary, the friend and companion of Mary Ann, became also a decided Christian. The conversation which Mrs. Geddie had with them appeared to have been blessed to them both. Mary was married to Lathella, the son and successor of Nohoat. She was a character of high promise, but she was not long for this world. She closed her brief career, happily, at the age of twenty-four or twenty-five. She died in May, 1861, of pulmonary consumption, brought on by an attack of measles, which she had early in the year. She has left behind her a fragrant name, which will long be held in affectionate remembrance on her native isle.

So closed the year 1854. And here terminates the more eventful period of the mission's history. From this time forward we meet with little calling for particular notice.

The storms in which the mission had been cradled had spent themselves, and the stream of events flowed smoothly on. Now and again we meet with an outburst of heathen rage, in the shape of an assault on those who sought to lead them from darkness to light. Such outbursts, however, were now no longer to be dreaded, and they became more and more infrequent.

The last case of strangling that occurred was of a peculiarly revolting character—a meet winding-up to so horrible a practice. It took place in March, 1857, at an obscure inland village, a great distance from the mission stations. Between three and four years had passed since a case had occurred; and the missionaries and the Christian party were resting in the conviction that there would be no more strangling on Aneiteum. It was on the occasion of the death of a child; the father and uncle of the child strangled their *own mother!* The whole Christian party were startled and filled with indignation when the strange news reached them. The chiefs determined at once to punish the guilty parties. "They assembled accordingly," Mr. Geddie writes, "from all parts of the island, at the place where the deed was committed; and after tying the criminals hand and foot, spoke to them about the awful wickedness of the deed they had committed. They were heathens, and pleaded the darkness of their hearts, and their ignorance of right and wrong. As a punishment their long hair was cut off, their houses destroyed, and a fine imposed. Mr. Inglis and I had previously taken a promise, that no injury should be done to their persons. They seemed thankful to escape with so lenient a punishment. The heathen of the place, though greatly terrified at such an august meeting in their land of the chiefs of the island, were much and favourably impressed by their visit, and have declared their determination to give up heathenism and embrace Christianity, and nave requested that a teacher may be sent to them without delay. The chiefs and people are decidedly of opinion that strangulation will never more be practised on Aneiteum."

And so it has proved. There has been no more strangling on Aneiteum. The reign of darkness and cruelty, as regards its grosser and more revolting developments, terminated with that dark deed, and henceforth the kingdom of peace and love was to sway its sceptre over Aneiteum. Occasionally, deeds of darkness, committed under the influence of heathen superstition, did occur after this date, but they were few and far between. The following case occurred about the close of April of the year 1857. A young man, of a small inland village, named Annuce, had been sick, and become delirious. His relations believed he was possessed by the devil, and, under the influence of this delusion, his own brothers and others took him and threw him into the river. The poor fellow struggled to ascend the banks of the river, but was pushed back by his deluded murderers into the stream, and was drowned. The chiefs assembled on this, as on the strangling occasion, and punished the perpetrators of the deed in the same way. The insane are put to death on the island of Vate also; perhaps from a similar notion to that entertained by the Aneiteumese.

Another incident, which occurred a considerable time before this, may be mentioned in further illustration of the benign and happy influence of the Gospel. A woman died in the neighbourhood of Anelecauhat soon after giving birth to a child. "This event," Mr. Geddie writes, "gave rise to some conversation on the change which Christianity has made. In the days of heathenism, the tender infant would have been rolled up in the same mat with the dead mother, and thrown into the sea. To Christianity does this child owe its existence. What a boon has the Gospel been to this people!" Yes; how many other children, and how many widows on Aneiteum, owe their lives to this Gospel!

The next deputation that visited the island, Messrs. Harbutt and Drummond, were much gratified with what they witnessed. Their visit was in June, 1857. They reported as follows:—"We spent the Sabbath at Mr. Geddie's station, and it was truly a day of refreshing from the presence of the Lord. The substantial plastered chapel at the station was crowded. Mr. Geddie preached a sermon in the native language to a peculiarly attentive congregation: every one present seemed in earnest to catch the words as they fell from the preacher's lips. After sermon, we assembled with the church around the table of the Lord, to commemorate the dying love of our blessed Redeemer. Around this table were assembled with us all belonging to the *John Williams* that are members of the church, the Rarotongan and Samoan teachers, and no less than a hundred natives of Aneiteum, all of whom, a few years ago, were degraded cannibals. Addresses were delivered in the Aneiteum, Samoan, and English languages; and all present seemed ready to exclaim, ' This is none other but the house of God, and this is the gate of heaven.' It was to us a day of sweet and hallowed enjoyment. In the afternoon a sermon was preached in English to as many as could attend from the *John Williams*, and others, residing on Aneiteum, engaged in the sandal-wood trade; and in the evening we held a prayer meeting at Mr. Geddie's house, which closed the services of a Sabbath ever to be remembered as one of the happiest we have ever spent in this vale of tears.

"On Monday we held a missionary meeting in the chapel. The place was well filled with a deeply attentive congregation. Money has not yet come into circulation on this island; but the people offered willingly of such as they had, to help forward the work of God on the neighbouring islands. They brought large quantities of mats, native dresses, and cinnet, for their teachers placed on Fotuna and Tanna; and also a large present of mats for Mr. and Mrs. Gordon. They also brought for the *John Williams*, a large pig, and a great quantity of taro and bananas. At this meeting some of the native Christians were set apart for missionary work at Fotuna and Tanna; and words of encouragement were spoken to them, and to the congregation assembled. One of the native teachers, about to proceed to Tanna, made also a very excellent speech, which was translated to us by Mrs. Geddie."

The report of the Rev. G. Gill, of Rarotonga, and the Rev. G. Stallworthy, of Samoa, was equally satisfactory with those of former visitors. All went to show that the labours of the esteemed brethren, Geddie and Inglis, and their native teachers, were still being signally owned and blessed of God.

During the year 1859, the mission sustained a serious loss in the death of the chief, Nohoat. He has frequently come before us in the course of our narrative. We have seen what he was at the commencement of the mission, and we have seen something of what he became under the influence of Christianity. Let us hear Mr. Geddie's testimony as to what Nohoat was after he came out on the Lord's side, and avowed himself a disciple of Christ.

"He took the side of Christianity at the very time when the mission was in the midst of its greatest trials. His previous hostility had been so marked, that his sincerity was for some time doubted. But he soon gave very satisfactory evidence of it, by giving up many heathenish customs; parting with one of his wives; abandoning the use of *Kava;* cutting off his long hair, etc. All his influence was now exerted in favour of Christianity. When the heathen were threatening our own lives, and the destruction of the whole Christian party, and when my house was set on fire by the heathen at midnight, I shall never forget his kindness to myself and family. For more than two months after this event he slept in my house every night, for our safety; and said that the heathen must kill him before doing any injury to us. Indeed, had not this man been raised up to befriend the mission, it is questionable if it could have risen above the opposition arrayed against it. After Nohoat embraced Christianity, he became a humble disciple at the feet of Jesus. Though sixty years of age, he attended school very regularly every morning; and his seat in the church was never vacant when he was able to attend. It was not to be expected that a man who had been under the influence of a degrading heathenism till far advanced in life, would become an intelligent, and, in all respects, a consistent Christian. He was naturally proud, passionate, and deceitful; but, with all his infirmities, I believe he was a good man. No man did more for Christianity on this island than Nohoat, and yet none suffered so much as he did from the change effected by it. The class of chiefs to which he belonged were regarded with religious veneration while they lived; and were worshipped after death. But when Christianity divested him of his sacred character, he was no longer dreaded by the people, and having been an unpopular man in the days of heathenism, he lost much of his influence, which he never recovered. When the mission to Tanna was undertaken by teachers from this island, Nohoat rendered them valuable aid. Having spent several years on Tanna in early life, he could speak the language of that island fluently, and his influence there was great. He made frequent visits at our request, and travelled through different parts of the island, telling the Tannese what Christianity had done for Aneiteum; and urging them also to embrace it. Being an eloquent and earnest man, his visits did much good, and served to prepare the way for the entrance of missionaries to that island. He was on a visit to Tanna when he was seized with his last illness, which was brought on by severe cold. He suffered much after his return, and died after an illness of about three weeks. The last interview I had with him was two days before his death. I was going from home on duty, and was called to see him before leaving. I saw that he was a dying man. He told me that there was one thing which gave him great uneasiness, and that was, his suspension from the church some months previously. The offence for which discipline was exercised in his case was not a grave one. It was intended to restore him, as he had given very satisfactory evidence of penitence. After I left, he sent frequently for Mrs. Geddie, and she had some very interesting conversations with him. He confessed the wickedness of his life, but expressed a humble hope of salvation through Jesus Christ. His end was peaceful.

"Nohoat is now no more, and I have lost in him a sincere and valuable friend. He is succeeded by his son, Lathella, who is one of my deacons and teachers; he is an excellent young man, and will, I trust, be a blessing to the island: though young in years he is much respected by the people. He is now by far the most influential man on the island."

So passed away Nohoat, the most remarkable character, except perhaps Waihit, that appears in the early history of the Aneiteum mission. Only a few brief years remained when he was brought out of darkness into light, but how important were those years to the cause of God on his native isle! They embraced the critical period of the mission's history; just the period during which his influence was specially needed. Nor, as we have seen, was his usefulness confined to Aneiteum. The missionary schooner *John Knox* scarcely ever made a voyage to the neighbouring islands without Nohoat; and during some of his visits, especially to the island of Tanna, his simple faith and earnest zeal in the cause of Christ shone out beautifully. On one occasion he set out with a small party to visit a district on Tanna which was on terms of hostility with another district, which had consented to make peace if their enemies would agree to that. Nohoat had influence in the district to which these belonged; still it was a hazardous mission on which he embarked. The parties to be pacified and conciliated were bent on fighting. They heard of Nohoat's intended visit, and took counsel on the subject, the result of which was, that they should try and shoot Nohoat before he reached their village—

feeling, as they did, that if he once got among them, they would be obliged to give up their war. And they actually fired two or three shots at him. Nohoat pressed on to his journey's end, without heeding the shafts of death that were flying around; and succeeded in inducing the people to give up the war. Mr. Geddie afterwards asked him if he were not afraid. "No," said he, "I knew I was going on a good errand, and I believed God would protect me."

There are few things more interesting to contemplate than the zeal and devotedness of first converts from

MISSIONARIES LANDING.

heathenism to Christianity. Never does the religion of the Gospel appear more fresh and beautiful than in those who have passed out of darkness (such as Christian lands know not) into marvellous light. Their faith appears so childlike, and their appreciation of the excellence of Christianity is so vivid, that to encounter danger and suffering on its account seems to be thought nothing of. To put forth efforts for its extension, and, if need be, to endure hardness and hazard in so doing, seems to be regarded as a matter of course. And what is this but the genuine spirit of Christianity developing its native tendency to diffuse and extend itself?

During the course of the following year (1860), another of the early fruits of the Aneiteum mission was, as we trust, gathered into the heavenly garner. Namuri, one of the first who avowed himself a follower of Christ on the island, finished his course in his Master's service on Tanna. Namuri was not a man of much energy of character, nor was he a man of rank, hence he does not figure prominently in the history of the mission. He seems, however, to have been a sincere, good man, and to have done what he could.

About two years before his death, he went as a teacher to Tanna. During the last year of his life he was in a declining state of health; and, a few months before his death, a heathen struck him a severe blow with a stone which probably hastened his death. Mr. Paton, near whom he was stationed, attended him during his illness, and was a witness to the spirit and conduct which he manifested while descending into the dark valley, and grappling with the last enemy. Mr. Paton writes as follows:—" On Tuesday, Namuri said to me, 'I am not afraid to die; I love the things of God, so I do not fear. Long ago I did much bad conduct—I was very wicked; but since Mr. Geddie taught me what was right and wrong, I have hated evil and loved good. I lean on Jesus.' I spoke to him a little, when he answered, 'Thank you, you speak to me just like Mr. Geddie, and Simeona, and Peter, and your word is like theirs, and brings all things to my mind that they told me long ago.' He said many such things to me, showing how his mind was occupied with spiritual things, though it wavered for the last two days before his death. As his life, so far as seen by me, corresponded with his death, I hope he sleeps in Jesus! I buried him beside Vasa, a Samoan teacher, killed on Tanna some years ago, at the other end of the old house, from Mrs. Paton's grave." Thus these witnesses for Christ, from lands far remote, sleep side by side on Tanna's dark and savage shore, awaiting the glorious resurrection morn. What scenes will that blest morn disclose!

> " Faith sees the bright, eternal doors
> Unfold to make her children way;
> They shall be clothed with endless life,
> And shine in everlasting day."

But to return; we have little more in the shape of narrative, to add to our sketch of the Aneiteum mission. An extract from Dr. Turner's report of his visit to the island in October, 1859, will form an appropriate conclusion. Dr. Turner writes:—"Found Mr. and Mrs. Geddie and family well, and the affairs of the mission making progress in the right direction. The walls of a new stone church are rising, beautifully figurative of the steady advance of the cause of Christ on this island; and I was struck also with the fact, that the place on the beach where the natives were digging up the sandstone for their church was about the very spot where Mr. Murray and I had our first meeting with the chief Nohoat, and some of his people, when we first visited this side of the island, fourteen years ago. In the afternoon we attended a meeting of about 400 of the people. I spoke a few words to them, expressive of my great joy in seeing what God by the Gospel had done for them; reminded them of our struggles with the heathenism of former days, and exhorted them to be thankful to God for having sent his servants to lead them from darkness to light.

"On Friday the 8th, I left the ship in company with Mr. Inglis and Mr. Copeland, and visited the first station we had on the island on the north-east side, and where Mr. and Mrs. Inglis have laboured for seven years. After the visit of 1845, war broke out, and the station was abandoned. In 1848, Mr. Nisbet and I recommenced the mission by locating two teachers, and, ever since, it has gone on. Instead of the uncultivated heathen shore, without a house to be seen, there are now at Aname the lovely mission premises, church, class-room, and dwelling-houses, and a cheerful group of young men and women living in the neighbourhood, and under regular instruction. There were only seven young lads there who knew their letters in 1845; now there are a thousand people in the district who can read the New Testament!

"On the Sabbath day, I attended Divine service; about 400 were present, and listened with marked attention while Mr. Inglis and I addressed them. Some of them after the service, shook hands, and said they could hardly suppress their tears while I spoke to them of the heathen times of eleven and fourteen years back. I was also pleased to see the people pretty well clothed.

"There are at this station 130 church members. But one of the most hopeful prospects for future progress which I saw here, was the select class of sixty young men and women, who are under tuition with a view to their being employed as native teachers.

"The entire population of Aneiteum is 3,513. All, I may say, are professedly Christian. Hardly one can now be found who calls himself heathen. The church members number 297, and the candidates for admission to the church 110. The island is encircled by fifty-six school-houses, eleven chapels, and sixty native teachers and assistants. I was glad also to learn that the missionaries of this group have formed an auxiliary to the British and Foreign Bible Society; the sum raised during the last two years amounts to £60."

Let the facts mentioned in the above extract be duly weighed, and the state of things which they, in connection with the preceding narrative, evince, be considered; and let it be remembered what Aneiteum was but a few years ago, and it will be evident that a wonderful work has been accomplished. And when the instrumentality by which these results have been realized is taken into account, our wonder will be further heightened, and our conviction deepened, that God's own hand has done it. What short of Divine power could have effected such a transformation under any circumstances? And, pre-eminently, what else could have accomplished it under the circumstances before us? During the most critical period of the mission's history, when the decisive struggle took place, there was, as we have seen, but a single European labourer. What can we say, therefore, but that " It is the Lord's doing"? " His right hand, and His holy arm hath gotten him the victory." " And He shall bear the glory."

Perhaps it may not be amiss to add a few words as to the apparently disproportionate space which the Aneiteum mission occupies among the sketches. As regards extent of territory and population, there can be no doubt the place it occupies is disproportionate; but, on other grounds, we think it quite entitled to the prominence we have given it. It is not the extent of the battle-field nor the number of the combatants that determines the importance of the contest, but the interests involved and the issue of the struggle. Now, on Aneiteum, a battle has been fought and a victory won, which will materially affect the interests, for time and eternity, of all the thirty islands which compose the group to which it belongs, to the latest generations. Already it has sent forth evangelists to five islands; and doubtless the work will continue to advance. The leaven which has been hid will work till the whole be leavened. The light which shines on it, and which has exerted so blessed an influence, will spread till, instead of one solitary island shining as a light in a dark place, every island of the group shall " be filled with the light of the knowledge of the glory of the Lord, as the waters cover the sea."

We may mention, in conclusion, that the entire New Testament, and various portions of the Old, have been translated into the Aneiteum language, printed by the British and Foreign Bible Society.

CHAPTER VI.

TANNA.

" And let us not be weary in well doing: for in due season we shall reap, if we faint not."—Galatians vi. 9.

" For He is faithful that promised."—Hebrews x. 23.

A DIFFERENT scene now opens to that which has just passed before us. The Tanna mission, though dating considerably earlier than that on Aneiteum, and having for several years had a larger share of our attention, and been regarded with deeper interest and more sanguine hopes, presents, as yet, only a painful contrast to the happy results which have there been realized. A dreary, forbidding page is the history of our Tanna mission so far; but not, perhaps, the less instructive on that account. Assuredly it has many important lessons to teach, which may we, by God's help, not be slow to learn.

Very strikingly do the natural character and features of Tanna contrast with the state of its inhabitants. It is a lovely island, by far the richest and most beautiful of all the islands of the southern division of the New Hebrides. It was discovered by Captain Cook, on the 5th of August, 1774, and was estimated by him to be about thirty miles in length, and from nine to twelve miles in breadth. It is therefore about eighty miles in circumference. The population is probably about ten thousand; the estimate of some is much higher, and they may be correct. The island presents a very interesting appearance. It is mountainous, but the mountains being generally rather low, and round, or table-topped, and covered with dense forests to their summits, it appears soft and beautiful, rather than grand and imposing. "The purple peak, the pointed spire," the frowning battlement, and hoary cliff, which look so grand and picturesque, on many of the islands of Polynesia, are not found on Tanna. Tanna, however, has its own beauties and objects of interest, many and great. The most striking natural object on the island is a volcano, which has been in a state of constant activity from the days of Cook, and no one knows how long before, to the present time.

Any one approaching the island now find Cook's description just as apt as it was when he penned it. "The light seen in the night," he says, "we now find to have been a volcano. A rumbling noise was heard, and it threw up great quantities of smoke and fire." Again he remarks: "On Thursday, the 11th, during the night, the volcano was very troublesome, and threw out great quantities of fire and smoke, with a most tremendous noise, and sometimes we saw great stones thrown into the air." Nothing strikes one as more remarkable than the prodigious stones it emits. Immense blocks are scattered around the neighbourhood of the crater, which at different times have been thrown out. At the distance of miles the ground is hot and cracked; and smoke is seen issuing from fissures in several places. Hot springs abound in the neighbourhood; and vast quantities of sulphur are found. Sulphur is now becoming an article of export. There are several craters, some of which are extinct. Two or three are generally in a state of activity; and occasionally the noise is, as Cook describes it, tremendous, being heard at a distance of forty miles. The mountain is not high, and over an area of perhaps three or four miles it is covered with ashes and scoria.

The island is amazingly fertile. All the usual productions of Eastern Polynesia are found, and others also, such as figs. The yams of Tanna are perhaps the largest of any to be found in Polynesia, or anywhere else. Cook says, "One of our people weighed a yam which exceeded fifty-five pounds."

Port Resolution, in which Cook anchored, is a tolerable

harbour; it is formed by a bay, or creek, about three-quarters of a mile deep, and about half that broad, the head of which is only about four miles from the volcano. It is situated on the north side of the most easterly point of the island, and is about thirty miles distant from Aneiteum.

The following extract from Cook embraces various points of interest connected with the Tannese:—

"These people are rather slender made, and of the middle size. They have agreeable countenances, good features, and are very active and nimble, like the other tropical inhabitants. The females are put to all laborious works, and the men walk unconcerned by their side, when they are loaded with heavy burdens, besides a child at the back. Perhaps the men think that their carrying their arms and defending them are sufficient. We often saw large parties of women carrying various kinds of articles, and a party of men armed with clubs and spears to defend them, though now and then we have seen a man carry a burden at the same time, but not often. The women of Tanna are not very beautiful, yet they are certainly handsome enough for the men who put them to all manner of drudgery. Though both men and women are dark-coloured, they are not black, nor do they bear any resemblance to negroes. They make themselves blacker than they really are, by painting their faces the colour of black-lead. They use a sort of pigment which is red, and a third sort which is brown; all these, especially the first, they lay on with a liberal hand, not only on the face, but on the neck, shoulders, and breasts. The women wear a petticoat made of leaves, and the men nothing but a belt and wrapper. Bracelets, earrings, and armlets are indiscriminately worn by both sexes. The armlets are made of the green stone of Zealand,* and the bracelets of sea shells

---

* New Zealand we suppose is here meant, but the stone referred to must be obtained on the island itself, or on some of the neighbouring islands. It was very highly prized by the Tannese and others in former years, and in many places it is so still. It is the Green Jade.

or cocoa-nuts; and the necklaces, chiefly worn by the women, mostly of sea shells. The valuable earrings are made of tortoise-shell."

The Tannese pay great attention to their hair. They part it into small locks, which they wind round with the rind of a small plant to within about an inch of the ends. Each of these is about the thickness of whipcord; they

GOING OFF TO THE MISSIONARY SHIP.

are bound together, and hang down behind like a parcel of strings. This mode of wearing the hair is found only on Tanna, Anciteum, Fotuna, and Niua. Something very much resembling it appears to have prevailed among some ancient nations. See "Kitto's Daily Bible Illustrations," vol. v., p. 68. The women wear their hair cropped short, as do also boys till they approach manhood.

The Tannese are a very fierce, savage race. Settled peace is a thing hardly known among them. Very recently, when one of their chiefs, who had been residing for some time on Aneiteum, returned home, and reported that there was no more war on that island, his testimony was derided, and his sceptical countrymen asked, "When was ever such a thing heard of as a country living without war?" Other parts of his wonderful report might be true, but *that* could not. What a tale does such a fact as this tell as to the state of the people! They are, moreover, inveterate cannibals, and are addicted to all the vilest abominations that are usually found among the most debased tribes of the human family.

Such were the Tannese in the days of Cook, and such they are at the present day, though we have had Christian teachers among them, with but a brief interval or two, for upwards of twenty years. "Ye have need of patience, brethren." So, indeed, with regard to Tanna, we have need of patience; but the reaping time will come. Sooner or later, "we shall reap, if we faint not." "My word shall not return unto me void." God grant that the dreary "night of toil" may speedily pass away, and be succeeded by a morning whose brightness shall be in proportion to the preceding gloom!

It was on the 18th of November, 1839, that Christian teachers were placed on Tanna; or, perhaps, it would be more correct to say the 19th, as on the 18th the teachers only slept on shore, while the vessel stood off and on, that it might be seen how the people would treat the strangers during the night, and that they might have an opportunity of looking about, and be able to form some idea as to how the natives would be likely to behave when they might be left wholly to their mercy.

The result of their observation was favourable; their property was landed on the 19th, and the first decisive step was taken towards the evangelization of Tanna The teachers, Lalolangi, Salamea, and Mose were all

Samoans. Salamea died on Tanna after two or three years' labour. The other two returned to Samoa after several years' residence on Tanna, and are still alive. The placing of these teachers on Tanna, as is generally known, was the last work that the enterprising Williams was permitted to accomplish. That act done, he might have said with the Apostle, "I am now ready to be offered, and the time of my departure is at hand." His heart, however, was set on rendering further service to the great Master; and he was pressing on to that when the voice was heard that bade him rest from his labours, and go to the kingdom and the crown. Glorious exchange! What a transition! From the clubs and spears of the debased and deluded people whose salvation he sought, to the presence of his Saviour, and the pure and holy society of saints and angels in the world of light!

After an interval of a few months, the teachers were visited by Mr. Heath, from Samoa, and everything was found in as promising a state as could be expected. Mr. Heath reinforced the mission by placing two additional Samoan teachers on the island, Pomare and Vaiofanga. This visit and the addition made to the number of the teachers, exerted a favourable influence, and things began to look decidedly hopeful, when, in the inscrutable providence of God, circumstances occurred which very severely tried the mission, and threatened its utter extinction. All the teachers were taken severely ill. Not one was able to help his brother. Happily, before their illness commenced, some of the natives had attached themselves to them. These were wonderfully kind. When the state in which the natives then were, and their after conduct are considered, it does seem a marvel that they should have acted as they did. After they had been ill about six weeks, Pomare and Salamea died. Poor fellows! what a sad death was theirs, in as far as human succour was concerned! We trust, however, that they were not forsaken by Him in whose work they died. The kindness of their native attendants failed not, as long as they required their aid; and when they were dead, they performed for them the last offices of friendship, which their fellow-labourers were unable to do. After a while those who remained recovered, and were able to resume their work; but, alas! there was no work to do. The natives had pitied them in their illness, but they were wholly indisposed to give any further heed to their instructions, or have anything more to do with the new religion. They attributed the fact of the teachers having been ill, and two of them having died, to the displeasure of *Alema*, their principal God; and thence inferred that their god must be more powerful than the God of the teachers. The consequence was, that for several months the teachers were entirely deserted, and were often in great straits. By some means, however, they managed to struggle along, and when they were visited by the writer, in April, 1851, a slight improvement had taken place in the state of things. When they found themselves deserted, they set to work to plant yams, taro, etc., so that they were no longer wholly dependent on the natives for the means of subsistence. We found, at the above date, that a few had again attached themselves to the teachers, and were giving heed to their instructions. At a meeting which was held with the principal chiefs, in and near Resolution Bay, on board the *Camden*, they expressed themselves very decidedly in favour of the new religion, and declared their wish that the teachers should continue among them, and that missionaries might soon come to instruct them fully. Though it was thought desirable to ask them whether they were prepared to welcome missionaries, and whether they would attend to their instructions, and treat them kindly, it was expected that a considerable time would elapse before European labourers were sent to occupy the island. On reaching Sydney, however, we were agreeably surprised to find two esteemed brethren, Messrs. Turner and Nisbet, waiting an opportunity of getting to Tanna, to which they had been appointed by the Directors of the London

Missionary Society. Messrs. Turner and Nisbet came in the *Camden* to Samoa, where they remained several months preparing for their important mission, and waiting an opportunity of proceeding to their field of labour.

In the month of June, 1842, they sailed in the *Camden*, with their wives, accompanied by Mr. Heath, of the Samoan mission, who had been appointed to give them the benefit of his experience in the difficult and perilous undertaking in which they had embarked. They met with an encouraging reception, and entered upon their work with as fair a prospect of success as, under the circumstances could be expected. With a zeal and heartiness proportioned to the greatness and difficulty of their enterprise, they commenced their labours, and in a very short time, some three or four months, they were able to begin to instruct the Tannese in the great truths they had gone to teach. The commencement, on the whole, was auspicious and promising; but the season of promise was of short duration. Clouds soon began to gather, and the symptoms of an approaching storm was unmistakable. The Tannese have firm faith in the supernatural. They believe in, and, after their manner, worship, "gods many and lords many." Like all other unenlightened nations, they regard their gods only as objects of terror. All disease and death are viewed as the effects of the displeasure of the god or gods in whom they believe, occasioned by something done, either by themselves or others. They have among them a crafty and avaricious priesthood, who make it their aim to exalt and enrich themselves by taking advantage of the notions of the people respecting the origin of disease and death. They pretend to great powers in such matters, and so work upon the credulity and fears of their countrymen as to maintain a great ascendency, and possess themselves of such property as the people have to give. These men soon discovered the incompatibility of the new religion with their pretensions and practice. They saw that their craft was in danger; their enmity was aroused, and their ingenuity set to work to counteract the efforts of the missionaries, and get them either murdered or driven from their shores. Opportunely for them, an epidemic broke out, and proved extensively fatal among the tribes who had not attached themselves to the missionaries and teachers. The district where these resided was wholly exempt from the visitation. This remarkable circumstance was turned to account by the crafty priests. They gave out that the missionaries and the new religion were the cause of the calamity, and urged that the missionaries should be either killed or driven from the island. The parties who had received the missionaries, and among whom they resided, were strongly inclined to protect them, and, in order to this, were ready to wage war, or at least, to stand on the defensive should an attack be made. Their number was wholly inadequate, however; and, in the event of their enemies coming upon them, defeat and the murder of the whole mission party seemed inevitable. The crisis approached.

Two or three significant acts, which had well nigh proved fatal to individuals belonging to the mission, were the precursors of a more general movement. The arm of an enraged native was seized by an old native woman, in whose heart pity still had a place, while uplifted, and in the very act of throwing one of their deadly war-stones at the head of one of the missionaries, who had gone some distance from home to preach. On two other occasions, also, attacks were made on parties connected with the mission. At length war was declared against the little party of strangers and their native adherents. All the preliminaries were arranged, and the hostile party were on the move.

Deeply-anxious days and nights passed: the danger became more and more imminent; the enraged savages, like ravening wolves, thirsting for blood, were drawing nearer and nearer. The mission party were in circumstances which no language can describe. One after another of the natives, who were kindly disposed towards them, was losing courage or proving treacherous, till they were almost left alone. A gun which they possessed was an occasion of trouble and perplexity. The friendly natives were most earnestly importunate to have the gun, in order to defend their own lives and those of the missionaries. How natural that they should, and how strange and unaccountable must the refusal have appeared to them! The noble-minded missionaries were not to be moved. True to the spirit of their sacred cause, to the advancement of whose interest they had devoted their lives, they would by no means give up the destructive weapon, though death, under circumstances the most appalling, stared them in the face. They had but one refuge left—that of betaking themselves to their Divine Protector. Of that refuge they availed themselves, and it did not fail them. Night closed in upon a day of agonizing anxiety: matters had reached a crisis. The following morning would, in all probability, bring the dreaded issue. What was to be done? If they abode where they were, their worst fears would in all likelihood be realized. But what could they do? The only thing that seemed to offer any chance of safety, was to endeavour to escape to some one of the neighbouring islands. But in the way of this there were the most formidable difficulties and dangers. The perils of the sea in a dark, stormy night, in an open boat, the danger of missing land, and being subjected to the horrors of a lingering death at sea, or of landing on some other shore equally inhospitable with the one they were leaving, made it no easy matter to determine on which side lay the greatest hazard. The scale turned in favour of an attempt to escape. Let the reader imagine what must have been the danger apprehended on the other side which led to this decision!

Preparations were speedily made, and in the darkness of the night the party embarked. How shortsighted is man, and how unable to choose his own way! The night was unfavourable for the escape of the party. A strong wind was setting into the bay, and a rough head-sea, against which, with all their struggling, they could make scarcely any way. How sad were their circumstances! The very elements of nature seemed to conspire against them. The result was, that cold, wet, and weary, they turned their faces again towards the inhospitable shore they had left. What a night must that have been: But "joy cometh in the morning." The stormy elements were only seemingly adverse. Deliverance was on the wing: the eye of the unslumbering One was upon them: their cry had reached his ear; their extremity was His opportunity. In the morning a ship appeared off the bay! It was as life from the dead. Communication was speedily had with the captain; an agreement was made; and in a short time the whole party were safe on board the *Highlander*, Captain Lucas, from Hobart Town, and on their way to Samoa. How must their hearts have swelled with gratitude to their adorable Deliverer! and how delightfully illustrative were the whole circumstances of His faithfulness and watchful care over those who confide in Him! After a tedious and rough voyage they reached Upolu in safety, in the month of February, 1843. Thus did the poor Tannese put away from themselves Heaven's richest boon to the family of man; but they knew not what they did. Alas for them! how sad have been the consequences of their misguided conduct!

It was in January, 1843, that the mission was broken up, and the island was not again visited till April, 1845. At that time the writer, in company with Dr. Turner, visited it in the *John Williams*. The following account, written by Dr. Turner, gives a glimpse of what took place upon the expulsion of the missionaries and teachers, and of the state of things at the time of our visit. At that time appearances were such as to awaken hopes which were not to be realized.

"At Aneiteum we heard most cheering accounts of a reaction at Tanna in favour of Christianity, and in a few minutes after we cast anchor in Port Resolution, we saw that it was really so. Our arrival was hailed with delight, not only by those who were formerly friends, but also by many who once were our avowed enemies. The war raised against us by the heathen party, and which occasioned our expulsion continued for a month after we left, and ended in favour of the Christian party. The epidemic for which we were blamed made fearful havoc among the enemy after we left: so much so that the people declared their dead lay scattered about in the villages, so numerous that they could not bury them. They could only regard it as a judgment; and, when every house became a house of mourning, they began to dread the name of Jehovah, and determined to give up the war, and live at peace with the Christian party. That party were deeply grieved at the loss of their missionaries. It was amongst our parting counsels to them that they would remember the Sabbath, and this they have never forgotten. Up to the present time they have assembled regularly on the Lord's Day for prayer and religious conversation. The mission premises were made sacred, and the strictest prohibition given not to steal from the garden. One old man broke through all restraint, and stole some taro; he died the next day after the theft; others trespassed on the forbidden ground, and they too were suddenly cut off. Some others, who mocked at the religious services which the Christian party were accustomed to hold on the Sabbaths, were also seized with disease, and died. These things made a deep impression on the minds of the people. No one after their occurrence dared to jeer at any who assembled for worship on the Sabbath; nor would any one go near the mission-house, not touch an article that grew in the garden, so that breadfruit and other produce were allowed to ripen, and fall, and rot untouched.

"Our visit was hailed by all with unmingled delight.

We had a full meeting of all the district at Port Resolution. The principal chiefs of the more distant tribes were present; these were our bitterest enemies at the time the mission was broken up, and were the chief originators of the war that was raised in order to exterminate the whole mission party.

"All were now united in wishing us to return, entreating us once more to put confidence in them, and at least to leave Samoan teachers with them, if we did not at once feel disposed to take up our abode among them. They readily promised all that we could desire, and, to their great delight, we selected three Rarotongan and four Samoan teachers, and located them at three separate stations. And thus have our fondest hopes respecting Tanna been more than realized, and all our fears scattered to the winds." Such were the sanguine hopes and high expectations we were led to entertain on the occasion to which the above extract from Dr. Turner refers. Appearances were certainly very promising. Appearances, however, are apt to mislead, especially among a savage people. So it was in the present case.

Deeper trials were in store for the Tannese mission than it had before encountered; fierce storms were yet to assail it, ere success should crown our efforts. So far, life had been spared. In the hour of deepest peril, and when hope was all but extinct, deliverance had been extended. Now it is to be otherwise. The deluded savages are to be allowed to go the length of shedding the blood of those who sought to lead them to a participation in the blessings of the Gospel. The report of the Deputation, the Rev. H. Nisbet, and the Rev. W. Gill, who visited the island in September, 1846, tells a mournful tale. The following is the substance of their statement.

For some months after the recommencememt of the mission, the teachers pursued their work with encouraging prospects. This continued till an epidemic broke out. Many died, and the suspicions of the people were again aroused against the teachers. They became greatly enraged, and took counsel together to murder the whole party. They assembled in order to carry their resolution into effect, but were prevented from so doing by the interposition of a friendly and powerful chief named Viavia, who was the staunch friend of the mission through all the vicissitudes of its early history. At this juncture the disease seems to have abated, and the teachers were again allowed to pursue for a season their work without molestation.

A fresh storm, however, soon gathered. Disease again broke out among the people, and an attempt was made on the life of one of the teachers. It was, no doubt, the intention of the savages to murder their victim. They struck him repeatedly with a club, and probably left him supposing him to be dead. He was severely wounded, his under jaw-bone was broken, and other injuries were inflicted upon him, the marks of which he carried with him to to the grave. After his recovery, he and his companions continued at their post till matters again came to extremities.

Another epidemic broke out, and proved extensively fatal, especially among children. Now the rage of the people was no longer to be restrained. The poor defenceless teachers were still the objects of their suspicion—still regarded as the cause of their sufferings. No wonder, therefore, that they proceeded to extremities; indeed, the wonder is that they were so long restrained, and that any of the obnoxious party escaped from their fury. Their first act was to set fire, during the night, to the dwelling-house of the teachers at the principal station, hoping probably to effect the destruction of the inmates as well as the house. They, however, were mercifully preserved. Two days after one of the teachers, Vasa, was waylaid and murdered while returning from the bush, to which he had retired for prayer. It was evening. The savages had probably noticed that at that hour the teachers were accustomed to seek solitude, and hence watched their opportunity in order to wreak their vengeance on the man who sought their salvation. Mistaken men! But "they knew not what they did."

It was now quite manifest that evil was determined against the mission party, and that the natives were only waiting their opportunity to cut them off. Hence they determined, that should an opportunity of leaving the island offer, they would embrace it. Such an opportunity

MURDEROUS ATTACK OF NATIVES.

was providentially afforded the very next day after the murder of Vasa. A vessel anchored in Port Resolution, the captain of which kindly received the teachers and their families on board, and took them to the neighbouring island of Aneiteum. But for this most opportune interposition of a gracious Providence, the great probability is that, with perhaps a single exception, the whole party would have been murdered. At one place the people continued to treat their teacher with kindness throughout all the changes and difficulties that occurred. There was little reason to hope, however, that they would have been able to protect him should he continue among them; hence he left with the others, and the mission was again totally suspended. It would weary the reader were we to notice particularly all the ups and downs which followed. A cursory glance at the leading occurrences is all we shall attempt. When the island was visited by Mr. Nisbet and Mr. W. Gill, in September, 1846, the state of things was found as above described. Nothing could be attempted at that time towards recommencing operations; but two teachers, who had been on Tanna, were left on Aneiteum, with instructions to take advantage of any favourable change that might occur, which might indicate the practicability of resuming their work on that island. These teachers had not very long to wait. In March, 1847, a chief of Resolution Bay sent his son to Aneiteum expressly to try and get teachers; this was regarded as a providential call, and the devoted men returned immediately to the scene of self-denial and danger. The *John Williams* visited the island again in July, 1848. At that time there was not much to encourage hope. A little progress appeared to be making, but no decided indications of success were apparent. A third teacher was left to encourage and aid the two by whom the mission had been recommended.

In September, 1849, the island was again visited. The teachers were all found in good health; they had been enabled to keep their ground, and perhaps had made a little advancement. Appearances certainly were more encouraging than they had been for a long time before, but the time to favour Tanna had not yet come; deep waters of tribulation were still before the already severely tried mission. If ever a mission was cradled in storms, surely that mission is the one which forms the subject of the present sketch.

The following extract from the report of the deputation, consisting of the Rev. J. P. Sunderland and the writer, who visited the island in October, 1853, will explain our meaning.

"Tanna, unhappy Tanna! is still the same repulsive, forbidding field it has so long been; or, rather, it is in a more sad and discouraging state at present than it has been at any time since the expulsion of the servants of Christ from its shores in 1843. It will be recollected that the mission was reinforced last voyage, and that, though the prospects were far from bright, still there appeared no reason to apprehend another total eclipse, such as has come over the island. Nor, in all probability, would it have been so, had not a calamity come upon it from without, which was the manifest occasion of the breaking up of the mission.

"The *abandonment of one of the stations* did, indeed, take place long before the occasion referred to; and, of course, *it* had no connection with that. It was occasioned by the breaking out of an epidemic not a great while after our last visit. The old notion that the disease was in some way connected with the Christian religion was revived; the teachers were in danger, and were obliged to escape for their lives. The infatuated people, generally removed to a distance from them, destroyed or stole their property, killed their pigs, and threatened themselves. The chief, under whose protection they were, stood by them to the last; still, they thought it advisable to retire from the storm. They joined their brethren at Port Resolution, and continued there till the melancholy occurrences took place which terminated their lives and labours, and led to the suspension of the mission.

"An effort was made, shortly after the last visit, towards the erection of a chapel in the bay; but the attempt was frustrated by the opposition of the perverse people. Materials were collected and prepared, and all was ready for commencing the erection of the building, when difficulties arose respecting a site, and the issue was, that the chiefs commanded that the work should not proceed. As opposition on the part of the teachers would have been useless, they quietly submitted.

"From this time, direct missionary work was almost entirely suspended; and about the month of May, last year, the bark *Edward*, Captain Thomas, from California, anchored in Port Resolution, having the *small-pox* on board. No steps were taken to prevent the spread of the disease. The teachers and natives were not aware of the hazard to which they exposed themselves by coming in contact with their visitors, who, from whatever motive, did not apprise them of their danger. The natives were allowed free access to the vessel, and the foreigners were frequent visitors at the houses of the unsuspecting teachers. The vessel remained about three weeks; and it was not until after its departure that the fatal disease appeared on Tanna. In the course of the week after it left one of the teachers was seized. The progress of the disease was rapid, and the patient sank about a week after he was taken ill. Another of the teachers was speedily seized, and he also died. A third was taken ill, and, though the attack seems to have been somewhat milder in his case, it terminated fatally. The two who were first seized were unmarried, but the third had a wife, and she also died. We were unable to learn any particulars respecting her death—whether she died of small-pox, of a broken heart, or how, we could not ascertain.

"Only one of the mission families now remained, Pita a Samoan—one of the two who were left on Aneiteum by Messrs. Nisbet and Gill when the mission was broken up the second time—and his wife and child. They lived in another part of the bay. They had been warned by a foreigner residing on shore of the infectious nature of the disease, and, though they did not abandon their fellow-labourers in their affliction, they were careful to expose themselves as little as possible. Happily they were preserved, and survived the melancholy wreck.

"But the calamity did not end here. About a fortnight after the death of the teachers, the natives commenced stealing the property they had left, and caught the infection. About fifteen died. The infectious character of the disease, however, becoming well-known, the house that the deceased teachers had occupied was burned, with the remaining property. All that the natives and foreigners could do to check the progress of the disease was done, and it does not appear to have spread widely. But other diseases appeared about the same time, and carried off a number; and the infatuated people, as usual, ascribed all to Christianity and its teachers and adherents, and began loudly to demand that the remaining teacher should leave. They said they would not kill him—they knew that *that* was bad, but that he must leave. He was loath to abandon his post, and did not make up his mind to do so till it was quite plain that there was no alternative. The first decisive indication of that was the murder of a woman belonging to the family of Kuanuan, the principal supporter of the teachers. Complaints and threatenings became louder and louder, and matters were brought to a crisis by Kuanuan, who has been the staunch and faithful friend of missionaries and teachers through every vicissitude, coming to the teacher with tears, and telling him that he thought he must go; for, however desirous he and a few others might be for him to remain, they could not protect either him or themselves. The path of duty was now clear; and the faithful teacher, with his wife and child, escaped in a boat kindly lent by a foreign resident, and reached Aneiteum in safety. And that the time had fully come for taking such a step, was made additionally clear by a most mournful occurrence which took place while the teacher was making preparations to leave. Four women belonging to the small party who are friendly to Christianity were murdered by the deluded savages. Thus Tanna is again in the unenviable position of a land that has put away from it the servants of God, and the words of eternal life. Oh, when will the time to favour this wretched people come! How mournful is it to see them in their troubles acting in a manner which can only make their condition worse, instead of turning to Him who smiteth, and who alone can heal!

"One is at a loss for language to characterize the conduct of the parties who introduced the disease among the unsuspecting teachers and natives. Their crime is not of a character to be taken cognizance of by human law; but they have already been tried and condemned at the bar of public opinion, and there is a higher tribunal before which they must ere long appear, and answer for their reckless disregard of the lives of their fellow-creatures.

"From all we have been able to learn, we think there is reason to conclude that the progress of the disease has been checked, and that it has not extended beyond Port Resolution. The Tannese, as is well known, are so unsocial in their disposition, and so barbarous in their habits, that intercourse is confined within very narrow limits. Parties living on opposite sides of Tanna know about as little of each other, and are as effectually separated, as if they lived on opposite sides of the globe. Such being the case, the information we obtained from masters of vessels who have visited the island within a few weeks is most probably correct, that the disease had not spread beyond the neighbourhood where it first appeared. We have introduced *vaccination* to all the islands we have visited.

"Notwithstanding the present state of Tanna, there is every probability that foreign missionaries might settle on it; and the opinion expressed in former reports is more and more confirmed, that nothing further of consequence will be accomplished till it be occupied by men fitted to grapple with the peculiar difficulties of the field."

Thus for the third time were missionary operations entirely suspended. The interval, however, was not of long duration. Messrs. Hardie and Sunderland, who visited the island in October, 1854, remark, in the report of the voyage, "It will be gratifying to our Christian friends to know that a gleam of hope has again burst through the dark cloud that envelopes this hitherto difficult field of labour." The report goes on to narrate how the reoccupation of the island by the Christian teachers was brought about. While the reign of darkness continued unbroken on Tanna, and while such melancholy occurrences were taking place in consequence on the neighbouring island of Aneiteum, the Sun of Righteousness had arisen, with healing under His wings; and precious fruits, as we have already seen, were being reaped by the privileged labourers who were employed in cultivating that field. And to this it was owing, under God, that the Tanna mission was so soon recommenced. A party of people belonging to Aneiteum went to Tanna to visit some of their relations there. They reported the wonderful things' that were in progress on their island, and the result was a wish on the part of the Tannese to visit Aneiteum, and see for themselves. In order to accomplish this object, they built two canoes; and in the month of September, 1854, shortly before the visit of the *John Williams*, they went to Aneiteum. They were greatly astonished, and most favourably impressed. The most wonderful thing to them was, that the whole island was, and had for a length of time been at peace. They remarked that, "they never imagined that a people could live on an island together without fighting." They made a tour of the island, and so had a full opportunity of witnessing the state of things. They were persuaded by their Aneiteum friends to leave their clubs and spears behind them when travelling, as being only useless encumbrances in their land of peace. The result was, that they determined to embrace Christianity, and requested that teachers might be given them, to instruct them in the new religion. On the 3rd of October, about a week after they left Aneiteum to return home, the *John Williams* reached that island; and on the 14th of the same month she visited Tanna, and left two Aneiteum teachers, with their wives, at a place called Iuakaraka, on the south-east side of the island, with the chief who had visited Aneiteum, whose name was Iarisi.

The teachers received a most encouraging welcome from the chief and his people, and thus hope dawned once more on Tanna. Some 300 people were assembled on the beach to gaze upon and welcome the strangers; and influenced by what some of them had seen at Aneiteum, and what others had heard respecting the change on that island, they had laid aside their weapons of war. A wonderful thing for them to do while having dealings with strangers. A new thing under the sun! A Tanna man never ventures far from his own door without his club.

The next visit of the *John Williams* to the island was in June, 1857. On that occasion the deputation, Messrs. Harbutt and Drummond, had the satisfaction of finding the state of things more encouraging than it had been at any former time. The Rev. G. N. Gordon, then newly arrived, was on board the *John Williams*, and was prepared, with his devoted wife, to have taken up his abode among the Tannese, had that been judged advisable by those on whom it devolved to counsel him as to the selection of a sphere of labour. The precise state of the mission at the time referred to will be best learnt from the report of the deputation, which is as follows:—"It will be remembered that the *John Williams*, when she called at Tanna, in 1854, landed two teachers from Aneiteum on the south-east of the island, at a place called Iuakaraka, about twelve miles from Resolution Bay. Prosperity has attended the labours of these teachers at the above station. They live their in safety, and most of the people, if not all, listen to their instructions. Three other Aneiteum teachers were placed some time ago in the bay of Port Resolution. On the morning of our arrival, these teachers met us on board the *John Williams*. Some of them had been sick, but were again well. They stated that the people had been very kind to them, and that they had never suffered from hunger. They had plantations of their own; but some of their taro was rotting, as they needed not to use it, they were so abundantly supplied by the liberality of the people. But we must not omit to state that these teachers are all chiefs of some importance on Aneiteum, that they have connections among the Tannese, and that they would have been supplied with food even if they had not been teachers. They also stated that all the people at the harbour, whether heathen or professedly Christian, respect the Sabbath. They do no work in their plantations, nor fish nor fight on that day. The only kind of work done is the cooking of their food. A superstitious fear is said to be one of the causes of this. They are afraid lest yams planted on that day might not grow, and their fishing excursions not be attended with success. At one station, all the people had at one time abandoned heathenism; but sickness broke out among them, and only twelve remained firm to their first resolution. At another station, formerly the residence of Messrs. Turner and Nisbet, two individuals only profess to be Christian. There were many more some time ago, but an epidemic broke out among the people, and they all returned to heathenism, except the two mentioned. At ten villages, all the inhabitants used to meet for Divine worship at their places for holding public assemblies; but, since the epidemic broke out among them, only two or three attend, and the others talk of killing the teachers. Some time ago, on a Saturday, the people all assembled, and held a consultation, and determined that they would kill the teachers on the Sabbath; but on that day they met as usual, and held their meetings, and nothing was done to them. Captain Edwards, who happened to be at Tanna at that time, kindly offered to take the teachers to Aneiteum; but they chose to remain, and wait coming events. It was pleasing to hear the testimony given by the teachers to the kindness shown them by this gentleman and others engaged in the sandal-wood trade.

"In addition to the three stations hitherto occupied by Aneiteum teachers, other three have been opened; and the Aneiteum brethren hold themselves in readiness to occupy other stations as openings occur.

"The practice of strangling widows on the death of their husbands, prevalent on Aneiteum in the days of heathenism, was introduced into Tanna, from that island some years ago. This diabolical custom is practised in Resolution Bay, and is said to be spreading widely over the island. Some of the inland tribes are now at war; and it was reported that three bodies of those slain in war had been cooked and eaten near the harbour about the time of our visit.

"On Saturday, the 13th, we had a meeting on board the *John Williams* with all the principal chiefs residing in the vicinity of the bay. They all professed a desire to have a missionary to reside among them; but they said they were afraid, lest an inland tribe of disease-makers should declare war against them, if they received one; and then, should they be conquered, they would not be able to protect him. They therefore expressed a wish that Aneiteum teachers only should be left with them for another year, during which time they would try and get the tribe of which they were afraid to consent to their receiving a missionary. Among these chiefs was old Kuanuan, the missionary's unchanging friend. He is now a very old man; he was much delighted to see us. After hearing the decision of the chiefs, we were unanimous in thinking that Mr. Gordon should not take up his abode on Tanna, but proceed to Eramanga, and examine that field of labour.

"In company with the ladies and children, we walked all round the bay, and went inland a little way, and examined one of the villages. We also went to see one of the teacher's houses, which is a very comfortable little cottage, all things considered. Wherever we went the people seemed friendly; and we fondly hope the day is drawing near when the adamantine walls of the prison house in which this unhappy people are confined shall be broken down, and the iron fetters with which they are bound burst asunder, 'and the prisoners brought out from the prison, and them that sit in darkness out of the prison house.'"

The above extract, it will be observed, decidedly indicates progress; and when the island was again visited in July, 1859, the state of things was found to be increasingly promising.

The report of the deputation, which consisted of the Rev. G. Gill, from Rarotonga, and the Rev. G. Stallworthy, from Samoa, supplies ground for encouragement and hope. "We anchored at Port Resolution," these brethren remark, "on July 16th. There are now on Tanna eleven teachers, all of them from Aneiteum; we found them all in good health. The wife of one of them died about six weeks before our visit. That was the first death in the Tanna mission since its recommencement, four ears ago, by Aneiteum teachers; a fact which contrasts encouragingly with the mortality in past years among Samoan and Rarotongan teachers in some islands of the New Hebrides, and indicates the advantage for the prosecution of our work in that group which we shall gain from a truly native agency, consisting of *Western Polynesians*, instead of that really foreign one, composed of *Eastern Polynesians*, on which, in the commencement of our operations in those parts, we necessarily relied. With the exception of a district of about four miles on the coast, the teachers occupy fourteen miles of country, beginning at Port Resolution, and extending southward to Iuakaraka. Most of the people at the latter place attend Christian worship. The number on the shore of Port Resolution who profess Christianity is about twenty or thirty. Among the chiefs of that locality, Nauwar is the most steady and constant adherent of the teachers. Miaki, the principal chief of the neighbourhood, is favourable to them, and his countenance may be calculated upon in the future prosecution of the mission. He attends the services held by the teachers on the Sabbath, but does not appear at the week-day meetings. It is hoped that the confidence of the people on the north side of Port Resolution, who were hostile to the mission from Samoa, is now gained. A teacher has been accepted in a district called Enekahi; and Nauwar has considerable influence with the adjoining tribe of Kasuremene. The people of a district about eight miles to the northward of Port Resolution have requested a teacher, and the brethren on Aneiteum hope soon to supply them with one. Viavia, an old and steadfast friend of missionaries and teachers, died about two months ago; Saiviri, who killed the teacher Vasa, died more recently.

"The people of Iuakaraka and those at Port Resolution are desirous of missionaries. We had heard of this desire at Aneiteum; and on our arrival at Tanna we learned that, the day before we anchored in Port Resolution, the people in the neighbourhood of that place had held a meeting for the purpose of coming to a formal decision on the subject, and the result was in favour of receiving one. It appears to Messrs. Geddie and Inglis very desirable, that, to allay jealousies, the two places should be simultaneously occupied; and their advices from Nova Scotia and Scotland justify the expectation of their being in a position to accomplish that important object at no distant period.

"Mr. Geddie conducted worship on Friday evening, with the teachers and their adherents, in a house in which they are in the habit of assembling. On Sabbath morning he preached in the open air, through the Aneiteum chief, Nohoat, as interpreter, to nearly a hundred natives; and in the afternoon held a special service with the Aneiteum teachers. On returning from the last-named service, he told us that the teachers had informed him that a man was murdered on the preceding day, about three miles inland of the bay, and that on that day his friends had avenged his death by killing another. These deeds of blood seemed to excite no general attention; they do not affect the safety of the teachers. We learnt that the people on the south side of the bay had, within the last three months, killed three of their own people and eaten them—there being at that time great scarcity of food. These things show that Satan still holds sway on Tanna; but his sway is now disputed there, and there are grounds to hope that many of his captives will soon be released from their heavy bondage."

We now approach what we may designate the second principal era in the history of the Tanna mission, namely, the reoccupation of the island by foreign missionaries. It had long been the conviction of all acquainted with the circumstances, that not much in the shape of results, beyond opening the door and smoothing the way a little, was to be expected from the labours of our native agents. Hence, to obtain labourers better fitted to cope with the peculiar difficulties to be encountered, and to get such labourers introduced to the field, had been all along an object of earnest desire. That object was at length realized. Towards the close of 1858, three missionaries, Messrs. Paton and Copeland, from Scotland, and Mr. Matheson, from Nova Scotia, were located on the island. Messrs. Paton and Copeland were stationed at Port Resolution, and Mr. Matheson at Iuakaraka. How full of promise this apparently auspicious movement seemed, and how it cheered the hearts and revived the hopes of those who had so long striven to impart the blessings of the Gospel to the benighted Tannese, will be readily conceived. Surely the long, dreary night of toil must be well-nigh past; surely the storms, which have so long and so fiercely raged, must have well-nigh spent themselves. So we hoped, and so may the event yet prove. Thus far, however, there is little to encourage, except it be that the darkest hour precedes the dawn; except, indeed, it be that man's extremity is God's opportunity. Our last tidings present about as gloomy a picture as we have had to contemplate at any former time, except, perhaps, when our operations have been totally suspended. Dr. Turner, of the Samoan mission, who visited the island in October, 1859, writes as follows:—"Wednesday, 13th October.—Anchored at noon in Port Resolution. Found Mr. Paton well; but since his arrival, twelve months ago, he has been deeply afflicted. In March last he lost his wife and infant son. Mrs. Paton died very suddenly, apparently from the rupture of a blood-vessel, on the 5th of March; and on the 21st of the same month, her infant son followed her to the grave. She was devotedly attached to the cause of Christ, seemed healthy, and bade fair to labour long in the mission. But how short-sighted is man! In addition to this heavy affliction, Mr. Paton has had fourteen attacks of fever and ague during the twelve months he has been on the island. He is pretty well at present, but we fear he will soon break down, if not speedily aided by some other missionaries, to share with him in the toils of this difficult mission. Like other missionaries and teachers who have been there, he is blamed as the cause of disease, and his life has been repeatedly threatened; but hitherto, men have been raised up in each extremity to stand by him, and oppose all attempts on his life. As the tribes are all hostile in the neighbourhood, he has never been able to venture more than a mile or two from his door, on the south and west sides of the bay. He has walked once, however, twelve miles to the south-east, as far as the station lately occupied by Mr. Matheson, where Aneiteum teachers are now labouring with some encouragement.

"Mr. Paton thinks there are at least two dialects on the island, widely differing from each other, and both Papuan. He is about to erect a house on a hill immediately behind the present mission premises, and we took from Aneiteum a large quantity of wood with which to build a chapel close by it. He is fast acquiring the language, and, if spared to get the chapel up, hopes to be able to conduct service there regularly every Lord's day. I only met with some three or four of the people who were there seventeen years ago. Many are dead, and many survive, but they have been carried in war away inland. The district on the east side of the harbour has of late years completely changed hands.

"It is still thought that Tanna is densely populated. Some think there may be 20,000 on the island. It is all guess-work; but, from appearances, I should expect there are at least 15,000.

"We found a Sydney vessel at anchor, collecting sulphur. The captain said he had procured close upon forty tons in three weeks; but, owing to the hostile state of the tribes between the head of the bay and the volcano, it was difficult to procure it. He got some from the natives on the rocks on the west side of the bay, but had to send his boats for most of it round three miles to Sulphur Bay, as it is called, at the entrance of the volcano valley; and where they bought it from the natives for tobacco, pipes, etc. The action of the volcano is much the same as it was when I was there eleven, fourteen, and seventeen years ago, namely an eruption every five, seven, or ten minutes.

"We left Tanna on Thursday, the 14th. We tried to pursuade Mr. Paton to come on board with us for a three weeks' cruise, to invigorate his weakened system; but he declined, fearing lest his absence should cause any reaction, and occasion the loss of a little hold which he thinks he has obtained. He is aided by eleven Aneiteum teachers, and occupies nine different points; but at least three other European missionaries are urgently wanted for this important field. May the Lord of the harvest send them forth!"

Mr. Matheson was compelled, on account of the state of his health, to retire to Aneiteum after a brief residence in Tanna; and Mr. Copeland has been removed to Aneiteum to take charge of the station and institution there. Hence, Mr. Paton was found alone at the above date.

It makes the heart sad to think of the solitary labourer who, in circumstances so deeply trying, remains on the island. What a bitter cup has he been called to drink! What a sorrowful initiation has he had to missionary labour! Fourteen attacks of fever and ague within twelve months; deprived of his fellow-labourers; motives suspected, and his life often in danger; and, most heartrending of all, deprived of his beloved wife and child! How desolate his situation, and how strong his claims on the sympathy and prayers of the friends of missions.

CHAPTER VII.

ERAMANGA.

> " Here sleeps the martyr's weary head,
> Here softly moulders holy dust."—BONAR.

> " Surely the wrath of man shall praise Thee."—*Psalm* lxxvi. 10.

THE island next in importance to Tanna, in the southern group of the New Hebrides, is far-famed Eramanga. The distance between the nearest points of the two islands is, according to Cook, about eighteen miles. Eramanga lies to the north-west of Tanna, and the middle of the island is in latitude 18° 54′ S.; and in longitude 169° 19′ E.

Besides the one never-to-be-forgotten occurrence which has given Eramanga a world-wide notoriety, and invested it with undying interest to the friends of Christian missions, it has at least another distinction among the adjacent islands; it is famed for the production of large quantities of sandal-wood of very superior quality; and on this account it has been resorted to by large numbers of foreigners for many years past. Brief have been the intervals when parties have not been occupied on some parts of the island in search of that article; and for some time past a number have been permanently residing in Dillon's Bay. Although Eramanga has been so much and so long resorted to by foreigners, our information respecting it is but scanty. Cook, its discoverer, who has left such accurate and copious information respecting many other islands, had not an opportunity of learning much respecting Eramanga, and its people. It would seem as if a kind of fatality had marked the intercourse of the Eramangans with foreigners, from the first day of their coming into contact with them. A serious encounter took place between them and Cook, and their subsequent quarrels with foreigners have been very numerous; and many of them, like the first, attended with fatal consequences to themselves. In their quarrel with Cook, as in some other of their quarrels, they appear to have been the aggressors; but in very many cases they have been

SKETCH OF NATIVES AND THEIR HOME.

deeply wronged, and the blood of many a murdered Eramangan cries to heaven for vengeance. Captain Cook's account of the discovery of Eramanga is rather confused, but it appears to have been on the 1st of August, 1769, that he first sighted the island. He was much in want of wood and water at the time, and it was in endeavouring to procure these that the unhappy quarrel to which we have alluded took place. The account of the affair in Cook's narrative is too long to transcribe entire. The following extracts contain the pith of it:—

"Their behaviour was in every respect agreeable, yet we

did not much like their appearance, as they were all armed with bows, arrows, clubs, spears, and darts. On this account we kept a sharp look-out." The result was that the natives, after trying to induce the party to haul the boat on shore, attempted to detain it by force. They seized the oars and wrested them from the hands of the people, and appeared bent on obtaining the boat. Alas! they little knew the character and resources of the parties with whom they were contending. "Our own safety," says the narrative, "was now becoming our only consideration, for signs and threats had not the effect we expected. The captain therefore resolved to make the chief suffer alone, a victim to his own treachery; but at this critical moment his piece did not go off. This increased their insolence, and they began to assault us with stones, darts, and arrows. We were now ordered to fire. The first discharge threw them into confusion; but they were very reluctantly driven off the beach by the second. After this they continued a kind of bush fight, by throwing stones from behind trees, and sometimes a dart or two. Four of them lay, to all appearance, dead on the shore; but two of them afterwards crawled in among the bushes. It was a fortunate circumstance for these assailants that more than half our muskets missed fire, otherwise we should have done much more execution among them. One of our crew was wounded in the check with a dart, which entered nearly two inches; and an arrow struck Mr. Gilbert's breast, but hardly penetrated the skin." Such was the inauspicious commencement of intercourse between the Eramangans and foreigners. When the skirmish was over, Cook and his party returned to their ship, weighed anchor and put to sea. As they were getting the ship under weigh, several of the natives appeared on a low rocky point, displaying the oars they had seized during the quarrel. "We thought," says the narrative, "they were desirous of returning the oars, and that their manner of behaving might be a token of submission; nevertheless, that they might understand the effect of our great guns, we fired a four-pound shot at them, which, though it fell short, terrified them so much, that we saw no more of them, and when they went away they left the two oars standing up against the bushes." So ended Captain Cook's intercourse with the Eramangans. One would hope, though the narrative does not say so, that the four-pound shot from the great gun was *designed* to fall short of the natives.

The following is all Cook says about the Eramangans: "The natives of this island are of a middle size, regular features, and pretty well made. They are of a different race from those of Malicolo, as well in their persons as in their language. Their complexions are naturally dark; yet they paint their faces, some with black, and others with red pigment. Their hair is curly, but somewhat woolly. The women are not very inviting, but rather ugly. They wear a petticoat made of a plant like palm leaves; and the men go in a manner naked, having only a belt and wrapper round their waist. They live in houses covered with thatch, and their plantations are laid out by line and fenced round. We saw no canoes in any part of the island."

The Eramangans, in some respects, differ considerably from their neighbours, the Tannese. They are physically inferior, and, if possible, more deeply sunk and debased.

They are darker in colour, and seem more closely allied to the purely negro races. I have seen parties among them who might have been mistaken for genuine negroes. As regards war, cannibalism, polygamy, and other heathen practices, they do not differ much. Theft, quarrelling, and murder are of frequent occurrence among themselves; and woe to the stranger that by any mishap falls into their hands. Shortly before our second visit to the island, a party, consisting of ten persons from Fotuna, had been compelled by adverse winds to put themselves in their power; and, sad to say, they had all been murdered.

And this is not an exceptional case. No, it is the rule; the exception is when any so circumstanced escape. On one occasion we had the happiness of taking a native of some adjacent island, a poor fellow who by some means had escaped with his life, on board the missionary vessel. We were standing close in with the ship when he sprang from a cliff into the sea, and dashed through the waves towards us, with all the energy and determination which the hope of escape from impending death could inspire. Teachers had been a few months on the island, and from them he had heard of the missionary ship. As soon as he was discerned, we of course stood towards him. We succeeded in picking him up. An unhealed wound in his temples, from the blow of a club, told of the danger he had escaped. Poor Lengolo became quite a favourite on board the *Camden*. His long hair and paint soon disappeared; decent apparel was supplied; and he was speedily among us as one clothed and in his right mind. We could never make out to what island he belonged; most probably he was from one of the more northerly islands of the New Hebrides. We left him on the Isle of Pines, with the teachers whom we had been obliged to remove from Eramanga, where he remained until the breaking-up of the mission on that island. The teachers were all murdered, and Lengolo, being identified with them, shared their fate. Poor fellow! One would fain hope that it was for the welfare of his soul he was saved, when his companions fell a sacrifice to the ferocious Eramangans, and enabled to reach the missionary ship, and thus put in the way of hearing of Him who is able to save to the uttermost. He must have learnt something considerable of Him and of His work before his death; and it may be that through Him he has been washed, and sanctified, and admitted to the society of those who have been redeemed from among men out of every kindred, and tribe, and tongue.

It is but what one would expect that the Eramangans,

should be greatly dreaded by the neighbouring islanders, and that they should be regarded by them as savages of the most invincible ferocity. This we have sometimes found, to our no small inconvenience.

I have spent hours in fruitless efforts to induce a native of Tanna to go with us to Eramanga, to assist us in our attempts to get teachers introduced to the island, though he would not have been required to leave the ship, and would have been taken back to his own land in a few days. Such impressions have the Tannese of the extreme badness of the Eramangans, and especially of their man-eating propensities, that all entreaties and arguments were vain. Were not the subject so painful, it would be amusing to hear how the Tannese regard and speak of the Eramangans. It is not only their ferocity that they speak against, but their shameless *indecency* is perfectly shocking! As if they themselves differed much in these respects! The fact is, the difference is very slight indeed. To them, however, it seems immeasurable.

The following extract, from the report of a visit to the island in October, 1859, by the Rev. G. Turner, of the Samoan mission, embraces several points of interest connected with the manners, customs, religious beliefs, etc., of the Eramangans, which we could not ascertain at an earlier period :—

"Mr. Gordon, if spared to labour on Eramanga, will be able, in a few years, to furnish many details respecting the manners, customs, and traditions of this interesting branch of the Papuan tribes. For the present, the following fragments, partly from him, and partly from a Samoan teacher, who was three years on the island, will not be uninteresting. The population may be set down at 5,000. They are a kindred race to the Tannese. They are scattered, and without any settled, well-ordered villages. They are migratory in given localities, as war and planting may require. Their chiefs are numerous, but not powerful. There are two dialects on the island, differing widely from each other; but the one is only partially known on the north-east end of the island, and among a tribe which numbers but a few people. Children are kindly treated in general; but Mr. Gordon thinks there are some instances of infanticide, and that on the death of a mother her infant child is buried alive with her. There are but few children in a family. Four are considered a large family. One albino has been seen. The population of the island is thought to be less than formerly. The dysentery, which raged in 1842 in other parts of the group, and which led to the breaking up of the Tanna mission, and the massacre of our teachers on Fotuna, raged fearfully on Eramanga. They traced it to some *hatchets* taken on shore from a sandal-wooding vessel, and threw them all away. It is supposed that about a third of the population of the island died at that time. Women carry the children on the side. Circumcision is practised. Connected with marriages there is a formal dowry. Polygamy prevails. A great chief has, perhaps, ten wives. The wife of a deceased husband is taken by the brother of the departed. Bread-fruit, yams, taro, fish, and pork, are the principal kinds of food of the people. The women cover their persons, from the waist to the heels, with leaf girdles. The men prefer nudity, and a thick rope-work of leaves or cloth in front, half a yard long. The women tattoo each other about the mouth, cheeks, and chin, with rude devices of leaves and flowers. The people are fond of such amusements as dancing, racing, and dart and stone throwing. The principle articles of manufacture are clubs, and bows, and arrows. A number of old people are to be seen. The sick are not well cared for. They have some medicines for cases of poisoning, etc. They believe in witchcraft, and other things, as causing disease. There are few hunchbacks. Ulcerous sores are common, as also elephantiasis, and fever and ague. The dead are buried, in some cases, without any covering, and, in others, with a winding-sheet of cocoa-nut leaves. They do not *raise* any mark over the grave; it is known rather by a *depression* in the earth of a few inches, and by two sticks standing up, the one at the head, the other at the feet. Some also are laid in caves, without any earth or covering. They do not eat anything which grows within about a hundred yards of a place where *their own* dead are buried; but strangers from another district will pluck cocoa-nuts, and eat freely of such things as grow there.

"The spirits of the dead are supposed to go *eastward*, but they do not know where. Spirits are also thought to roam the bush. *Nobu* is the name which they give to their great god and creator. They say, that after creating the human race at Eramanga, he went to another land. When they first saw white men, they concluded that they were made by the same great spirit; and to this day call foreigners, whether white or black, by the name of Nobu. They say that, 'once upon a time,' men walked like pigs, and pigs walked erect. The birds and some reptiles had a meeting about it. The lizard said he thought that the pig should go on all-fours, and the men walk erect. The water-wagtail disputed this. It ended in the lizard going up a cocoa-nut tree, falling on the back of the pig, making it stoop and walk on all-fours, as it now does; and ever since pigs go on their four legs and men walk erect. The first of the human race, they say, was a *woman;* then her son; and from them sprang the race of men. They have many tales about the doings of that woman and her son. Rain they supposed to be caused by the sun; and say, that if he is a long time without giving any, some of the stars get angry, and stone him till he causes rain to fall. In another curious fragment we trace the Scripture account of the prophet Jonah. One of their people, they say, fell into the sea, and was immediately swallowed by a *whale*. After a time the projecting pieces of wood which he wore as earrings pricked the inside of the whale, and made it vomit him forth. He was still alive; but as he walked up from the beach he was thin and weak."

The island is of a triangular shape. According to Cook, it is seventy-five miles in circumference. It is not, as a whole, equal to Tanna in fertility and beauty; still, it is a fine island, and in many parts it is not devoid of beauty. It is mountainous, and some of the mountains are so high that they can be seen at a distance of forty miles. A large part of the south-east, or windward side of the island, looks rugged and barren.

Mr. Gordon's estimate of the population, as given in Dr. Turner's report, is probably near the truth. It will no doubt strike the reader, that if this be the case, the number of the people is very small, compared with the size of the island. This is partly accounted for in the above extract; but there are many causes constantly operating among a savage people tending to the decrease of population, such as their interminable wars, polygamy, sensuality, neglect of the sick, the improper treatment of infants, etc. The mortality among infants, in savage states of society, is very great; indeed, it is only the decidedly robust and healthy that stand any tolerable chance of surviving the injudicious treatment and rough usage to which they are subject. On Aneiteum it was the custom, when a child was born, to commence immediately to feed it with fish, taro, and other substantial articles of food; and probably the same custom prevails on Eramanga, and other islands of the group. When the state of the case is fully known and considered, the wonder seems, not that the population in such circumstances is generally small, but rather that it is so large as it is usually found to be. In the case of Eramanga, something considerable is also to be put to the score of their intercourse with foreigners. I am not aware that foreign diseases have to any great extent been introduced among the Eramangans; but in other ways foreign influence has tended to reduce their numbers. It is a matter of great satisfaction to those who, for the last twenty years, have been striving to promote the temporal and spiritual welfare of the Eramangans, that of late years a great change has taken place in the character of those who resort to the island for purposes of trade. This we acknowledge with devout gratitude to God. But it is a fact with which we are too well acquainted, that for many years the treatment of the Eramangans by parties in search of sandal-wood was of a most outrageous character. Seeing, however, that the times have changed, and that a different line of policy has been adopted, we will not

SOUTH SEA FISHERS.

enter into particulars on this painful subject, though it is a matter on which we have had occasion to feel very deeply. Let us hope that the days of cruelty and wrong have passed away, never to return; and that whatever may be the calamities that may yet come upon Eramanga, wrongs inflicted by the white man may be heard of no more!

But it is time for us to return to our main business, which is to narrate the efforts that have been made with a view to put the people in possession of the blessings of the Gospel. To other matters we give only a passing glance.

As all the particulars of the first missionary visit to

Eramanga have long been before the world, we shall pass over that, only remarking, that in the "Memoir of the Rev. John Williams," or in "Ellis's History of the London Missionary Society," a full account of it may be found.

At a meeting of the missionaries of the Samoan mission, held on the arrival of the *Camden* with the stunning intelligence that the first mover in the work of evangelizing Western Polynesia had fallen, it was resolved to take up the work at once, and push it forward to the full extent of our resources. The senior member of our mission, the Rev. T. Heath, was appointed to proceed in the *Camden*, in order to follow up what had been begun by Mr. Williams, and commence operations in other islands or groups as Providence might direct. Mr. Heath stipulated, as a condition of complying with the wish of his brethren, that in case he should be cut off as Mr. Williams had been, the work should not be abandoned, but that another should follow in the great enterprise in which we had embarked. There was no backwardness on the part of his brethren to pledge themselves to this ; and with this understanding he started on his voyage. Mr. Williams had placed teachers on the island of Rotumah, and, as has already been stated, on Tanna also.

Mr. Heath, following in Mr. Williams's track, visited Rotumah, where he found everthing going on prosperously, after which he proceeded to the New Hebrides, where he visited the island of Tanna and the small island of Niua, on which he commenced operations by leaving two teachers. From Niua the missionary party proceeded to Eramanga. It was thought advisable to try another part of the island than Dillon's Bay on the present occasion. The attempt to obtain intercourse with the people, and to induce them to receive teachers, was successful. Christian teachers were located among the Eramangans in May, 1840, a few months after the murder of Williams and Harris. In April of the following year it was the writer's privilege to visit the island. We made the island on the morning of the 5th April. We stood in close to the bay where the teachers had been left, and looked long and anxiously for something that might assure us that they were alive. A few of the natives came out some distance from the shore, but they would not come near the vessel; and their shy, distrustful appearance, awoke painful apprehensions that something was wrong. Failing in our efforts to induce the natives to come near the ship, we lowered a boat and pulled in towards the shore. We were soon gladdened by the sight of a canoe approaching us with Lasalo, one of the teachers. He was accompanied by Nauari, the principal chief, under whose protection he and his fellow-labourer had been placed. The chief and teacher came at once into the boat. This was encouraging, and our hopes were sanguine that, notwithstanding first appearances being unpromising, all was right. We requested that Taniela, the other teacher, should be brought down to us, or that he should be furnished with the means of coming. To this request the natives would not accede. Nothing would serve them, but we must go in with the boat and land. This we did not consider it advisable to do. The entrance to the landing-place was a narrow inlet between two high cliffs. These were covered with crowds of armed savages, who would have had us entirely in their power had we landed; and, with what had so recently occurred; on the island fresh in our recollection, and present appearances being far from inviting, we did not feel inclined to trust them. Hence we kept out a short distance, and continued to urge the people to bring the teacher, or allow him to come to us. All our efforts were vain; the natives would neither bring off the teacher nor allow him to come; and when the chief perceived that there was no hope of our going in with the boat, he sprang into the sea, and made the best of his way toward the shore. Now we were in a dilemma: the teacher at the mercy of the savages on shore, and we about to lose our only hold upon them by the escape of the chief. We pursued him with all speed, and were soon close upon him. Seeing that he was in our power, he came again into the boat. He was in great trepidation, poor fellow! We soon succeeded in getting his confidence somewhat restored, and now he was ready to unite his efforts with ours to get the teacher brought off. Notwithstanding this, it was a long time before we succeeded in our object. At length a canoe appeared, with the teacher in it, and came out some little distance towards us; but still matters were not much improved, as the people in the canoe would not come sufficiently near us, nor allow us to get sufficiently near them for him to get into the boat, without our putting ourselves in the power of the crowds that were collected on the beach. They kept tantalizing us for a long time, advancing and receding just as we did, till the teacher brought matters to a crisis by leaping from the canoe into the sea, and making his way towards the boat. There was no time for hesitancy or reflection, so we dashed forward and succeeded in getting him safe into our hands. The teacher had made an unnatural effort, and that the effort was successful was a marvel. When we got him into the boat he sunk down perfectly exhausted into a state of stupor, from which he did not recover till after we reached the ship.

Having obtained the teacher, our prisoner was of course at liberty. We gave him presents, and did our utmost to induce him to accompany us to the ship, but to this he would by no means consent; so with great reluctance we let him go. Our reluctance to his leaving us as he did arose from the fact that his so doing was the closing of the door—the extinction of hope for Eramanga on that occasion. No choice was left us, however; so we had the pain of seeing the little light which for a season had glimmered on Eramanga's dark and gloomy shores extinguished, and with heavy hearts we returned on board.

The teachers had a doleful tale to tell. That we found them alive was a wonder, almost a miracle. The chiefs, who had engaged to protect them and provide for them, had been unfaithful to their engagement. Their lack of fidelity, however, was compensated in some measure by a party from the island of Niua, who had relations on Eramanga, and one of whom had an Eramangan woman for a wife. This party was on a visit to their relations, who lived near the place where the teachers were landed. They remained till within about five months of our arrival, and up to that time the teachers were tolerably provided for. Long before the party from Niua left, the Eramangans had deserted them: so that when the Niuans were gone, they were left in a state of destitution. And in addition to being thus cast off, they were taken ill; and it really seems that they must have perished, had not God provided for them in a manner almost as remarkable as that in which He sustained the prophet of old by the brook Cherith.

There was *one* man, a native of Eramanga, whose name was Vorevore, who was moved with pity for the friendless, destitute strangers. Day after day, and week after week, this man brought them regular supplies of food; and by his instrumentality their lives were sustained. Vorevore used to steal quietly down to the hut in which the teachers lived, lift up the thatch, and hand them in their daily supply. It was necessary that he should go about his work of mercy unobserved, as he was acting against the orders of the chiefs. It would appear as if they had intended to leave the teachers to perish for want; and great must have been their wonder as to how their lives were sustained. If this was their design, it was mercifully defeated. Vorevore's kindness held out as long as it was needed. For five months he ceased not to make his daily visits. What were the motives under which he acted it is difficult to conjecture. Whatever view we take of the matter, it is certainly very remarkable that a poor untutored savage should have so acted. That he should have pitied the teachers at all, was remarkable for an Eramangan;

but that he should have *so* pitied them, as at the risk of his own life to provide for them for so long a time, seems inexplicable on any other supposition than that he was acting under an influence not of man. " Your Father knoweth that ye have need of these things." Yes ; He who feeds the fowls of the air and clothes the grass of the field had His gracious eye upon those who were His witnesses in that land of darkness, and He touched with pity the heart of the savage, and inspired him with the needful courage and resolution.

Fain would we have seen Vorevore, and made him some recompense for what he had done. We feared, however, to inquire after him, lest we should draw upon him the wrath of his countrymen for having acted contrary to their known wishes. So we could only leave the matter in the hands of Him who has said," Whosoever shall give to drink unto one of these little ones a cup of cold water only in the name of a disciple, verily I say unto you, he shall in no wise lose his reward." " Verily I say unto you, inasmuch as ye have done it unto one of the least of these My brethren, ye have done it unto Me."

Thus ended the first attempt to introduce the Gospel to Eramanga. Mr. Williams did not go to the island with the intention of landing teachers, but only with the design of preparing the way by having intercourse with the people, and doing what might be practicable towards gaining their confidence, with a view to future operations. A long interval now followed, during which all our efforts to regain our hold upon the island were unsuccessful, These efforts were renewed every successive voyage of the missionary ship; but it was not till 1849 that we were able to take any decisive step towards the re-occupation of the island. In September of that year the writer visited the island, in company with the Rev. Charles Hardie. We succeeded in inducing four natives, named Joe, Mana, Nivave, and Nebore, from Dillon's Bay, to go with us to Samoa. They were place in the institution at Malua, where they remained for nearly three years. It was in the month of April, 1852, that the *John Williams* sailed from Samoa on one of her voyages to the Western Islands, with these four youths on board, in order to be taken back to their native land. It was again the privilege of the writer, in conjunction with an esteemed brother, the Rev. J. P. Sunderland, to visit the island. All went on prosperously for some time after the commencement of our voyage, and we were high in hopes of being permitted to return all our Eramangans safely to their native land. This we very much desired to do, fearing that, unless we did, our hope of gaining through them an entrance to the island would be frustrated. It pleased Him who sees not as man seeth to order it otherwise. One of the lads was taken seriously ill during the voyage. All our efforts, anxieties, and prayers availed not. He gradually sank, and when we were within two or three days' sail of Eramanga he died. Deeply did we grieve over the loss of our poor Eramangan. It was ours, however, to be still, and to be devoutly thankful that we sorrowed not for him as those who have no hope. Nivave was a remarkably quiet, gentle man; he had conducted himself with great propriety during his long stay in Samoa. He had been very attentive to the means of grace and instruction, and it was the opinion of those who were with him during his illness, and who witnessed his departure, that there was hope in his death. He had been looking forward with great interest to our reaching Eramanga, which, with all its repulsiveness, was his home. Poor fellow! we trust he found a better home. The consequences we apprehended from his removal, happily, did not follow. We had the full confidence of the three that remained, and their testimony satisfied their countrymen that all was right. Our fears were scattered to the winds and our hopes fully realized, as the following extract from our report of the voyage will show.

"We anchored in Dillon's Bay about noon on Saturday,

the 22nd of May. We were soon visited by numbers of natives, most of whom swam out to the vessel. We saw only one canoe. They came on board without hesitation; the sight of their countrymen, who had been to Samoa, inspired them with full confidence. We were sorry to hear that the tribes all round the bay were in a state of hostility. From all we could learn, everything seemed very dark. In the afternoon a party of us ventured on shore. We landed near the spot where Williams fell, and made our way towards the memorable stream near which he was attacked, and Harris killed. We were all struck with the loveliness of the scenery, while we gazed on it with mournful interest, and longed for the time when it should be the scene of operations which should invest it with other attactions than those of a merely physical character. After our return on board a very touching scene was witnessed. Mana, one of the Eramangans who had been to Samoa, was standing on the deck with his countrymen, to whom he was reading and speaking about Jesus. He was reading about His advent in the flesh, and pointing to his own hands and feet to convey an idea of the crucifixion—and to heaven, to indicate the place where Christ now is. Oh! when shall the name of Jesus be indeed known, and the efficacy of His precious blood felt by the poor degraded sons of Eramanga!

"We succeeded on the morning of Monday in obtaining an interview with Naioan and Kauiaui, the chiefs of the victorious party in the bay. These we found were the rightful owners of the soil, and those who occupied it when the island was last visited were intruders. The result of our conference with the chiefs was, that the way seemed clear for the settlement of teachers. The chiefs were cordially desirous of this, and readily engaged to protect them, provide them with food, etc. The principal chief gave us his nephew, an adopted son, and the other a relative to bring to Samoa for instruction; and, apparently with the design of removing all our anxiety as to the safety of the teachers, Naioan asked us, 'if it was likely they would injure the teachers, when his own son was going with us to Samoa?' The Eramangans who had been to Samoa were satisfied that the chiefs were sincere; and two of them whom we wished to remain with the teachers agreed to do so. In order to satisfy ourselves still further, we thought it well to get the teachers designed for the island to sleep on shore before landing their wives and property. The result of all was a full persuasion that the door was open; and on Tuesday, the 25th, the teachers and their wives and property were landed in circumstances peculiarly interesting and encouraging. We landed them at the mouth of the stream already mentioned, and about 130 Eramangans gave them a cordial welcome. The chiefs begged that a missionary or missionaries might soon be brought to them. This they did of their own accord. We only asked them respecting teachers. Thus Eramanga at length stretches out her hands, if not to God Himself (Him, alas! they know not), to the servants and people of God. Surely they will not be backward to respond!"

It will interest the reader to know that Mana, himself an Eramangan, and who was doubtless the first who ever spoke intelligibly to the Eramangans of the Saviour, has continued steadfast, affording very satisfactory evidence that he has experienced the saving efficacy of that wondrous death, resurrection, and ascension, which he set himself so promptly and earnestly to explain to his countrymen when the opportunity was afforded. We shall meet with him again and again before we close our narrative. Under God, it was owing solely to the aid rendered us by him, and the other two who had been to Samoa, that we succeeded in accomplishing our long-cherished purpose of placing teachers on Eramanga. We could not have communicated with the chiefs without their assistance, nor could we have felt sufficient confidence in them to trust the teachers in their hands. The teachers, whose names were Vaa and Akatangi, were from Rarotonga. They were both married, and were accompanied by their wives.

Only such as have been in circumstances similar to those in which we were placed, will be able to understand the feelings we experienced at beholding our long-cherished, long-deferred hopes realised. On our first arrival, only three days before the landing of the teachers, the prospects seemed as dark as midnight; and, to add to the gloominess of our prospects, a tremendous swell set into the bay after we came to anchor, and we were in imminent danger of being dashed on shore, and falling into the hands of the Eramangans. The sea rose to such a height during the afternoon, that when a boat was lowered, and we went in towards the shore to endeavour to get intercourse with the chiefs, the boat, when in the trough of the sea, could not be seen from the deck of the ship, though at no great distance. And towards evening, and during the early part of the night, the swell increased, and the sea rose much higher. A night of dreadful anxiety was that on board the *John Williams*, and thankful indeed were we when the sea moderated. "Then were we glad because we were quiet." Dillon's Bay is not a harbour, but an open bay: hence our danger. A lovely Sabbath dawned upon us, and was a delightful contrast to what we had just experienced. As to succeeding in our object on that occasion, hope was all but extinct, and we keenly realised the truth of the Divine testimony, "Hope deferred maketh the heart sick." Hence our satisfaction was all the greater when success crowned our efforts. We were prepared in an unusual degree to appreciate the great mercy that was vouchsafed to us, and feelings of grateful joy, such as are not often surpassed in this vale of tears, swelled our hearts, when, in circumstances of so much promise, the heralds of the cross had obtained a footing on Eramanga. Our esteemed brother, Mr. Geddie, who was watching our movements from the deck of the *John Williams* when we landed the teachers, shed tears of joy as he witnessed the cheering reception given to us by the Eramangans.

It is a matter of much satisfaction and gratitude to God, that though, as was to be expected, the teachers have had great difficulties to contend with, and no small amount of trial and suffering to endure, yet we have been enabled to keep our hold of the island up to the present time. The writer again visited the island, in company with Mr. Sunderland, in 1854. The following extracts from the report of our voyage will convey a correct idea of the state of things at the time referred to :—

"We anchored in Dillon's Bay on the morning of Thursday, the 27th. We were glad to find that, though the teachers had been reduced to great straits on account of the scarcity of food, and had suffered from attacks of illness, the prospects were encouraging. Two vessels were at anchor in the bay, and a third came in during the day. The captains were forward to bear testimony to the beneficial effects which have resulted from the residence of the teachers on the island. They told us that every part of the island may now be travelled over by foreigners with perfect safety, except one, Cook's Bay. They spoke very strongly of the harmlessness and docility of the natives about the harbour, their honesty, attention to the Sabbath, etc.

"The natives have behaved kindly to the teachers. They assisted them to put up a dwelling-house and a place of worship. Both are of a very humble character, but not to be despised on Eramanga. We visited both with deep interest. When the natives saw us enter the chapel, a number assembled, and expected service. It would be difficult to describe the mingled emotions we experienced while engaging with them in an act of worship to the true God on Eramanga.

"Services and schools were commenced shortly after the teachers were left on the island. The principal con-

THE "JOHN WILLIAMS." MISSIONARY SHIP.

ductor of these, for some considerable time, must have been Mana. This young man has fully realized so far the high hopes expressed respecting him in our last report. He was greatly delighted to see his Samoan friends again, and we scarcely less so to see him. May he be steadfast unto death!

"The population in and about the bay is not large. To this it is probably owing that the number who have hitherto attended the services and schools is so small. Another reason is, that the time has not yet come for different tribes to assemble in one place. The attendance hitherto has been only about thirty. It is 'the day of small things,' at present, on Eramanga. How cheering that it is day at all, and that there are indications of onward progress!

"One deeply interesting fact came to our knowledge during our visit. Kauiaui, who expressed so strong a desire for a teacher or missionary last voyage, is the murderer of Mr. Williams. He is chief of Bunkar, the part of Dillon's Bay where the murder took place. We had a conversation with him on the subject. He looked sorry and ashamed, but said he did not know Mr. Williams was a missionary. When asked why he killed him, he replied that it was on account of outrages committed by foreigners some time before. Who can wonder at what he did, when it is remembered that, in the affray referred to between the foreigners and Eramangans, *his own son was murdered?* He is still very desirous to have a missionary. We arranged for one of the teachers left last voyage to remove to his part of the bay; and with this arrangement he is satisfied for the present. We succeeded in getting the *club* with which it is said Mr. Williams was killed, and a pocket-handkerchief with Mr. Harris's initials on it, which Kauiaui's wife gave to the teachers.

"Applications for teachers have been made from two different quarters, at a distance from Dillon's Bay. One of these was from Bunkhil, a very eligible place as regards population, the disposition of the people, obtaining food, etc. The chief had seen the teachers, and very earnestly urged them to try and get a teacher for him when the *John Williams* arrived. The place is not very far distant from Dillon's Bay, only about six or seven miles, but is difficult of access from the sea; and, at the time of our visit, the weather was so rough that it was altogether unapproachable. We left a teacher to be taken to it by his more experienced brethren, as soon as that might be practicable. The new teacher was appointed to this place at his own earnest request. He had heard of the opening, and conceived a strong wish to be the teacher of Bunkhil; and, as he was a very suitable man, we were glad to concur in his wish.

"The other application was from a place at a greater distance, of which we knew nothing, so we did not think of attempting to occupy it; but there was another very eligible opening that we thought it well to embrace. This was Navin, or Elizabeth's Bay, about six miles to leeward of Dillon's Bay. To this place belongs Joe, a native of Eramanga, who had been about four years in Samoa, and had now returned. He is a promising and hopeful lad. He was very desirous to have a teacher settled in his native place, and was confident there would be no danger in placing one there.

"We went round to this bay on Friday, the 28th, and dropped anchor. We found everything as it had been represented by Joe and others, and introduced a teacher under very encouraging circumstances. The population in and about Elizabeth's Bay appears greater than at Dillon's Bay. A foreigner, who had resided there for a considerable time told us he had seen as many as 500 or 600 men assembled on great occasions.

"A small spelling book had been prepared by the teachers in the Eramangan language, and printed by Mr. Geddie. This, doubtless, will be of great service.

"On the whole, the state of things is very encouraging, and there is every probability that the missionaries might be advantageously located on the island ten or twelve months hence; perhaps, even now, that is, if one or more of them were men of missionary experience. It is one of those fields on which very little progress is likely to be made till foreign labourers be at work upon it. The sandal-wood trade, not to mention other things, occasions difficulties with which our teachers are unable to grapple.

"There is one important thing connected with Eramanga which ought to be known. It is much more healthy, we have reason to believe, than Aneiteum and other islands in the neighbourhood.

"May an effective force be speedily obtained to occupy this field of imperishable interest!"

When the island was again visited, by Messrs. Hardie and Sunderland, in October, 1854, still more decided indications of progress were found. "Since the last voyage," they remark, "the number attending religious services has been more than doubled. Sixty-seven, young and old, have renounced heathenism, and attend instruction regularly." Respecting Mana we have the following testimony: "The interesting young man, Mana, referred to in former reports, continues steadfast, and is a very valuable assistant to the teachers. He constantly takes part in conducting the school and religious services. Poor fellow! He was quite overcome with joy on seeing his old friends on his native shores." The deputation further mention, that another of the three who had been to Samoa continued steadfast in his attachment to the teachers. The third, who was never promising, had relapsed, we suppose, into heathenism. This, of course, is no matter of surprise. It is a far greater wonder that any of them stood fast than that one should fall away. Besides, he may yet be reclaimed. He was quite a lad when in Samoa, and so is still but a young man.

We come now to a new epoch in the history of the Eramangan mission. It is an event, the importance of which it would not be easy to over-estimate, when a missionary takes up his residence among a heathen people. Such an event involves consequences, both as regards the present and the future, which only the Infinite Mind can grasp. The location of first missionaries is always a matter of the deepest interest, and the most grateful satisfaction to those embarked in missionary enterprise. And, in the case of Eramanga, this feeling was experienced in an unusual degree.

It was in the month of June, 1857, that the Rev. G. N. Gordon, from Nova Scotia, and Mrs. Gordon, took up their abode on Eramanga. Messrs. Harbutt and Drummond, of the Samoan mission, who were on board the *John Williams* as a deputation, reported as follows respecting the state of affairs on the island, and the introduction of the missionary:—

"We had heard at Aneiteum that the tribes in Dillon's Bay were at war; and we found on our arrival that peace had not been restored. The young man named Mana, mentioned in other reports, who was for some time at Malua, and who has been of so much service in commending the Gospel to his countrymen, and aiding the teachers in their work, we found at Aneiteum. He had fled thither in order that he might be able to keep himself out of the war. We were delighted to find him willing and very desirous to return with us in the *John Williams* to Eramanga. As soon as we arrived he went ashore, and shortly afterwards we were visited by several Eramangan youths who had been to Samoa. They were clothed, and looked very respectable. They were delighted to see us.

"On Monday we went ashore, accompanied by the ladies and children. We trod with very peculiar feelings the spot where Williams and Harris fell martyrs to their devotedness to the missionary enterprise; and our feelings may be more easily imagined than described when we shook hands with Kauiaui, the murderer of Williams. He is a savage-looking fellow. He is no longer a man of any importance in Dillon's Bay, having been conquered in in the late war.

"We tried to get an interview with the chief Naioan, but could not. Mana crossed the mountains several times with messages from us to him; but, although he promised to come and see us, he never came. He expressed, however, to us, through Mana, his strong desire for a missionary.

"After serious deliberation with the New Hebrides missionaries, we are unanimously of opinion that the time to favour Eramanga had arrived, and that it was Mr. Gordon's duty to enter and take possession of the land. Accordingly, on the 16th and 17th of June, his goods were landed, and also those of the Rarotongan teachers, Taevao and Tuka, whom we had agreed to leave to assist Mr. Gordon, as there was not a single native teacher left on the island. All of them had been obliged to leave on account of sickness. It is hoped, by the blessing of God on the means used by the missionaries to preserve health, and to restore it, if lost, that those co-workers with him will be enabled to remain on the island. It was intended that one of them should be settled at Bunkhil, which Mana said was in a much more prosperous state than Dillon's Bay. At the latter place we saw very few people; but it was hoped the war would soon be over, and the people would return to the settlement. On the 17th, Mr. and Mrs. Gordon, with the two Rarotongan teachers and their wives, parted with their friends on board the *John Williams*, and took up their abode at Eramanga. We accepted Mrs. Gordon's kind invitation to take tea with her that evening in her new home. It is a very humble one, but we were not the less happy on that account. After tea we had a prayer meeting, and after commending our esteemed friends to the care of Him who slumbers not, nor sleeps, we parted with them, and proceeded to the vessel. We shall not soon forget the happy look of Mana when it was remarked to him at parting that he had now got his missionary.

"At Dillon's Bay we parted with Mr. Geddie. Our esteemed and enterprising friend kindly agreed to remain with Mr. Gordon a short time, to assist him to put together the frame of a house, which had been prepared for him at Aneiteum before his arrival.

"On the evening of the 17th, at six o'clock, we left Eramanga, indulging the hope that the darkness of that terrible night, in which her degraded sons have wandered so long, and sunk so low in the scale of civilisation, would ere long be scattered by the rays of the Sun of Righteousness, and their dark abodes lighted up by the dayspring from on high."

The next visit of the *John Williams* was in July, 1858; Mr. Gordon was found earnestly and zealously employed in his self-denying labours. Mrs. Gordon had suffered much from ill-health, and this, in the circumstances in which she was placed, must have been trying indeed. We heard no complaints, however. All seems to have been borne with the patience and fortitude which the Gospel inspires. The deputation—Mr. Stallworthy, of the Samoan mission, and Mr. Gill, of the Rarotongan mission—write as follows in their report of the voyage:—

"On the morning of the 20th of July we entered Dillon's Bay. We were glad to find Mr. Gordon, the missionary stationed there, doing well. Mrs. Gordon had been very unwell at times; she was better, but still far from a good state of health. An Aneiteum teacher was aiding the work on the island, also two Rarotongan teachers, namely, Meariki, who had been there many years, and Taevao, who was left there last year: the former had lost his wife, and the wife of the latter was unwell; Elia, a Samoan teacher, who had been several years on Eramanga, was sickly; and Tuka, another Rarotongan teacher, who was left on the island last year, had, in consequence of ill-health, gone to the Loyalty Islands. Mana continues steadfast and useful; and others who have visited Samoa, though not manifesting the Christian decision by which he is distinguished, nevertheless exert an influence in favour of the mission.

"The missionary complained of the smallness of the population in his immediate neighbourhood. A stream, or rather a small estuary, divides the narrow valley in which he lives; and, in his opinion, the side opposite to that on which his dwelling is situated would afford the best location for the mission premises, both as regards the nature of the soil, and also the gathering of schools and congregations. He is now erecting a school-house there, near where Williams and Harris fell.

"Mr. Gordon commenced his labours at Dillon's Bay last year. Native teachers from Rarotonga and Samoa, with the native Eramangans who had visited Samoa, had prepared the way for him. The people of the place were engaged in war at the time of his landing; but on the first Sabbath he had a congregation of twelve natives; some time afterward fifty attended; in November, eighty; after that the attendance declined. The chief, Naioan, has attended worship occasionally. He is the only chief who has done so; but when Mr. Gordon has visited other chiefs, they have manifested a less discouraging bearing towards the truths made known to them than that chief has generally done. Mr. Gordon now itinerates on the Sabbath in the neighbourhood of Dillon's Bay, and the people he thus falls in with, together with those of his little home congregation, number about a hundred individuals. Mr. Gordon has school on week-days. A few have learned to read; some of them were taught by the native teachers with such imperfect means as they possessed, and others commenced since Mr. Gordon's arrival. He has prepared and printed one or two small books. Mr. Gordon has made the circuit of the island, and was generally very well received. Stations have been occupied in various parts by the teachers and congregations gathered; but owing to the illness and consequent emoval of the teachers, they have dispersed. Could agents be found, there are few places where they would not be readily received."

The last visit of the *John Williams* to Eramanga was in October, 1859. With reference to the state of the mission at that time, Dr. Turner, the deputation from the Samoan Mission, writes :—

"Anchored in Dillon's Bay on Saturday, October 15th. Mr. Gordon was soon on board, and, accompanied by him, some of us went ashore, and up the hill to his residence, about a thousand feet above the level of the sea, and there we found Mrs. Gordon well. Owing to the unhealthy swamps on the low grounds, Mr. Gordon has built his cottage on the high land. Close by the house he has erected a small chapel, and has a fine bell at the one end which echoes from hill to hill, and calls the tribes to their little Zion.

"We had the pleasure of spending a Sabbath at Eramanga, and met with about 150 of the people in their little chapel. All were quiet and orderly. It thrilled our inmost soul to hear them, as led by Mrs. Gordon, strike up the tune of 'New Lydia,' and also the translation and tune of 'There is a happy land.' Mr. Macfarlane and I addressed them through Mr. Gordon. They were startled and deeply interested, as I told them of former times, when we tried so hard to get intercourse with them, and to show them that we were different from other white men who had visited their shores. When I read out the names of seven who swam off to us in 1845, and to whom we showed kindness, and took on shore in the boat, it appeared, from the sensation created, that one of them was present. He came after the service, shook hands, said some two or three more of them were alive; that our visit that day greatly surprised them; and that they marked our vessel as the one that showed them kindness, and did not take sandal-wood. They thought us quite different from all the white men with whom they had previously come in contact.

"Mr. Gordon was glad to see so many at the service, and considered our visit providential and opportune. There had been a reaction. Reports were raised that the Aneiteum people were all dying, and that it was occasioned by the new religion. The chiefs forbade the people attending the Sabbath services, and the consequence was that the chapel, the Sabbath before our visit, was quite deserted. Only some five people ventured to attend ; we hope that the good effect will not soon pass away. But Mr. Gordon finds it up-hill work.

"The population is not only widely scattered, but constantly occupied with intertribal wars. He thinks the entire population of the island may be set down at 5,000. There is one dialect which is known all over the island ; and in this Mr. Gordon has printed some four-page elementary pieces, catechisms, hymns, etc. The Eramangan teacher, Mana, is stationed on the other side of the island, and has collected a number around him. There is also an Aneiteum teacher assisting Mr. Gordon at Dillon's Bay ; and he has six young men under instruction, who he hopes may yet make useful helpers. But he sadly wants another missionary for Portenia Bay, on the opposite side of the island."

Another paragraph or two from the report from which the above extracts are taken, relative to the tragic events which have invested Eramanga with so deep an interest, will not be unacceptable to the reader. Relative to these events Dr. Turner writes :—

"On the Saturday I saw and shook hands with Kauiaui, who killed Mr. Williams, and on Monday met with him again. I also saw one of his men, Ovialo, who killed Mr. Harris. These two men feel ashamed and shy when the *John Williams* comes. Neither of them was at the service on Sabbath. Probably, they have had a fear also, which they found it difficult to shake off. I hope, however, that Kauiaui has now perfect confidence in our friendly intentions. On the Monday, he and Ovialo walked about with us, showed us the place where Mr. Harris was first struck, the place in the stream a few yards from where he fell, and the course along the road and down the beach where Mr. Williams ran into the sea. Here, too, Ovialo helped us to pick up some stones to take with us as mementoes to surviving friends of the sad event. Mr. Gordon has erected a little printing-office and teacher's residence close to the spot where the first blow was struck at Mr. Harris. I have planted a date palm seed there, in a line towards the stream with the spot were Mr. Harris was struck, and in a line towards the sea with the place where Mr. Williams fell.

"But the most striking and permanent memento of that sad day is a great flat block of coral on the road up the hill, about a gunshot from the spot where Mr. Williams fell. There the natives took the body and laid it down, and cut three marks in the stone to preserve the remembrance of its size. The one mark indicates the length of the head and trunk, and the other the lower extremities, thus:—

| Head and Trunk, | Extremities, |
| 37 inches. | 25 inches. |

A native lay down on the spot, and lying on his right side, with his knees somewhat bent, said that was how he was measured.

"When the *Camden* hove in sight, on the morning of the 20th of November, 1839, the Eramangans thought it was a sandal-wooding party returned, who had but recently killed a number of their people, and plundered their plantations. They were the more confirmed in this impression from the fact that the boat pulled into the very place where that party had landed before, and erected some huts. That morning they had already prepared heaps of yams and taro, for a feast which was to take place close by, up the river. They felt galled by the thought of their being stolen by the white men, and determined to try and prevent their landing; or, if they did land, to attack them if they attempted to go up the river to the place where the yams and the taro were. They sent the women and the children out of the way, and hid themselves in the bush, guarding especially the road leading up along the western bank of the stream. When Mr. Harris made to go up there, and had reached the spot where I have planted the palm tree, the shell blew, Kauiaua rushed out with his party, and commenced the attack. Five out of seven who were foremost in the massacre are dead. The people

SCENE OF THE MASSACRE OF WILLIAMS AND HARRIS, DILLON'S BAY.

were not united in the affair—some were for it, and some were against it; hence the remark of Captain Morgan, 'They made signs for us to go away.' But the principal thing in that sad day, which melted their hearts with pity, they say, was 'the man in the boat, who stood and wrung his hands and wept;' and that, I suppose, was good Captain Morgan.

"After surveying these scenes, so full of affecting recollections, we went off to the vessel, and took Kauaiui with us. We got him into the cabin, and as this is the first time he has ventured to go below, it proves that he has *now* entire confidence in us. We exchanged presents also. We gave him a trifle, and he and the people brought off to the ship forty yams, twenty heads of taro and three bunches of bananas—the first present which the missionary vessel has ever had from Eramanga, and the murderer of John Williams. On showing Kauiaui all over the ship, we stood before Mr. Williams's portrait in the saloon, and told him *that* was the missionary he killed. He gazed with intense interest, said he thought he could recognise the full face and the stout body, and was earnest in leading up to it some others who were with him, and in explaining what it meant. Kauiaui is still a heathen, comparatively. Let us hope that he may soon take a stand on the side of Christ! Mr. Gordon says that Ovialo is a more hopeful character, and seems to be deeply grieved as he thinks of his having had a hand in killing a 'man of God.'"

We are able to furnish but one glimpse more of Eramanga. It is supplied by a letter from Mr. Gordon, dated December 7th, 1859. The letter was addressed to the Rev. G. Stallworthy, who had finished his work, and gone to his reward two months before it was written. We give a short extract, the character of which is the reverse of pleasing; but it is our duty to report faithfully as to the real state of things. It is curious and interesting, moreover, as throwing light on some of the notions and practices of the Eramangans. Mr. Gordon writes as follows:—" The *John Williams* had not left us a week, [referring to the above visit,] when the flames of war were carrying the work of destruction on the south side of Dillon's Bay. The results are the total ruin of some villages and large plantations; some natives wounded and killed; and prospective sickness, from want of food. Marked good resulted from the last visit of the *John Williams*, which the great enemy stirred up himself to oppose. Idolatry has still a strong hold of the natives, even of those who come to worship on a Sabbath. especially a species of idolatry connected with the worship of the moon, the image of which they exhibit at their idolatrous feasts, which are regulated by the moon, and are great abominations. They do not pray to these images, but cleave to them as their protecting gods; and when any of them are stolen, the unhappy owner weeps bitterly, exclaiming with Micah, ' Ye have taken away my gods, and what have I more ?' They believe that these images were never made by man. If a man were to make one now, it would be thrown away. They are in the form of the new moon and the full moon—the latter being like a ring to go on the arm." Mr. Gordon says, in a foot-note, referring to his remark that the Eramangans do not pray to these images he mentions:—"As far as I know they do not, but keep them as household gods." The probability is, that more intimate acquaintance with the language and habits of the natives will convince Mr. Gordon that the natives do pray to these images. There can scarcely be a cleaving to, and trusting in any object such as he describes, without the practice of worshipping it in some shape or other. Prayer is the natural expression of trust and dependence. The reader will remember that practices similar to those described by Mr. Gordon were found on Aneiteum, with reference to the moon.

CHAPTER VIII.

NIUA.

"Whosoever shall lose his life for my sake and the Gospel's, the same shall save it."—Mark viii. 35.

WE have now done with the principal islands of the southern group of the New Hebrides; our record would be incomplete, however, were we not to say a few words about the island of Niua.

This island is small, and comparatively unimportant: still it deserves a brief notice. It is about fifteen miles from Tanna. It is a low, uninviting-looking island, and probably not more than ten miles in circumference. The number of the population is not known; it may be about 400 or 500. Teachers were placed on Niua as early as 1840. During the second voyage of the *Camden*, Mr. Heath landed two teachers under very promising circumstances. The teachers continued for several years to pursue their labours, and others went subsequently to their aid. Little or no impression was made, and up to the present time the island is in much the same state in which it was twenty years ago. During a great part of that time, owing to various causes which we must not stop to particularize, it has been without teachers. Of late years the mission has been resumed; and although one mournful event has occurred since the reoccupation of the island, still the prospects now are more encouraging than they have ever been. On Niua, as on the larger islands in its neighbourhood, Christian blood has been shed by the hand of violence. The teachers by whom the island was reoccupied. Navallah and Nemeian, were from Aneiteum. They were well received, and for some months pursued their work with encouraging prospects, and so in all probability they would have continued to do but for circumstances unknown to the missionaries by whom they were sent, and most likely to themselves. Some thirty years ago, when the darkness of heathenism was as yet unbroken, a party of Niua people set out to visit their friends on Aneiteum. They were overtaken by rough weather, and were unable to reach that part of Aneiteum where their friends lived; hence they were obliged to land on a part of the island where they were unknown; and, according to a barbarous custom which prevailed on the New Hebrides, and in many other parts of Polynesia, they were, with the exception of two who concealed themselves among the rocks, killed, and their bodies cooked. The two who had escaped watched their opportunity, and climbed to a neighbouring height, from which they espied a canoe on the beach. They took their bearings, and when it was night, they stole quietly out of their hiding-place, took possession of the canoe, set up a cocoa-nut branch for a sail, and got safely back to their own land. They told their sad tale to their countrymen, and from that day the Niua people determined to be revenged on the first Aneiteumese from the guilty district that might come within their reach; and to perpetuate the remembrance of the tragic deed, and insure its punishment, they set up sticks, which, as they rotted, were replaced by others, and so the spirit of revenge was kept alive year by year. Of course it would be asked from time to time, What mean ye by these sticks? And as often as the question was asked would come the recital of the old tale of blood, with all its horrors. Unhappily, Nemeian, one of the teachers, was from the very spot where the Niua people were massacred. This was found out by some of the old people, and the sad result was, that Nemeian was waylaid and murdered. The deed was done by two Tanna men who were on Niua at the time, the people of Niua not liking to be themselves the murderers of their teacher.

It was on a Sabbath. The teachers had gone from home to preach, and were returning when they were attacked. Nemeian was struck on the head with a club, and fell dead. Navallah was also struck, but his wound was not mortal. The people were satisfied, the ominous sticks were plucked up and thrown away, and the remaining teacher was entreated to remain among them. This he consented to do, and he still occupies his post. Another Aneiteum teacher, named Nalmai, has taken the place of Nemeian; and the prospects of the mission are encouraging. One of the murderers of Nemeian did not long survive his victim, being shot in a battle at Tanna.

In former years we used to consider our teachers more safe on Niua than on any other island of the southern group of the New Hebrides. More than once they have found it a safe asylum when compelled to flee for their lives from Tanna, but now it also has been stained with Christian blood. It is the *sixth* island of the New Hebrides on which the blood of the servants of God has been shed. And now there remains not one of all the islands of the group, on which missionary operations have been commenced, on which one or more of the labourers have not fallen sacrifices to their zeal in their Master's work. This is especially remarkable in connection with what occurred on the threshold of our entering the field. As many as twelve individuals, including Williams and Harris, have been killed. One of these, indeed, was not, properly speaking, a teacher, but he was truly a martyr, inasmuch as, on account of his adherence to Christianity, he was murdered by his heathen countrymen on the island of Aneiteum. We feel tempted to linger a moment over the memory of the martyrs of the New Hebrides, almost all of whom we personally knew, and to some of whom we sustained relations which death has interrupted, but cannot dissolve. Very touching are our recollections of them. But we need not mourn for them, although one is tempted to feel *as if* theirs had been a hard lot—*as if* there their lives had been thrown away. With the exception of the illustrious man who led the way, they lived and died unknown to fame; in circumstances the most revolting that can well be conceived, their lives were cut short, in some cases before they had well entered upon their labours, and in all before they had seen any fruits of their suffering and toil; yet they lived not in vain; they died not in vain. As surely as the cause in which they fell shall live; as surely as the islands on which their blood was spilt shall be filled with the knowledge of the glory of the Lord, so surely shall their names be cherished, and their memory fragrant, and their influence felt to the latest generations. "The righteous shall be in everlasting remembrance."

Yes! theirs is a lot rather to be envied than pitied. "It is a faithful saying: For if we be dead with Him, we shall also live with Him; if we suffer, we shall also reign with Him." "Blessed are the dead that die in the Lord."

Many and solemn are the lessons suggested by the eventful tale of these missions. We must not, however, dwell upon these. All may be summed up in a few words. Means and instruments, however well qualified and adapted to the end, are nothing—GOD IS ALL. "Cease ye from man." "Trust ye in the Lord for ever; for the Lord Jehovah is the rock of ages." The work in which we are engaged shall be accomplished—must be accomplished; for the mouth of the Lord hath spoken it, but "not by might, nor by power, but by my Spirit, saith the Lord of hosts." Amen, so let it be.

CHAPTER IX.

VATE, OR SANDWICH ISLAND.

"For behold the darkness shall cover the earth, and gross darkness the people; but the Lord shall arise upon thee, and His glory shall be seen upon thee."—
Isaiah lx. 2.

THE island which next claims our notice is the finest of any that has yet engaged our attention. The native name of this island is Vate, or Fate; but Cook, its discoverer, gave it the name of Sandwich Island, in honour of the Earl of Sandwich, who was, at the time of its discovery, first lord of the Admiralty. Cook did not examine the island minutely. He appears, however, like subsequent visitors, to have been delighted with its appearance. He remarks, "The surface whereof appeared very delightful, being agreeably diversified with woods and lawns." The island has indeed a charming appearance. Captain Erskine, who visited it in H.M.'s ship *Havannah*, in 1849, writes as follows :—"The weather being somewhat cleared before sunset, we were enabled to see a little more of the features of the island. The usual belt of vegetation extended on all sides for a few hundred feet above the level of the sea, a white sandy beach running along the shores. Above the first range, especially on the mainland which forms the south side of the harbour, the surrounding hills are of varied and most picturesque forms, being in general bare of trees, but covered with apparently rich pasture, in some places brown, as if burnt for purposes of cultivation. The rainbow-tints caused by the setting sun gave a peculiar beauty to the landscape, and many of the officers considered that none of the islands we had yet visited offered so beautiful

ISLAND OF UPOLU.

a scene as that which lay before us." This is high praise, considering that the gentlemen whose opinion Captain Erskine records had visited the finest islands of Eastern Polynesia, the beauty of some of which has been generally considered to be unrivalled in any part of the world.

Vate, according to Cook, is fifty-four miles to the north of Eramanga, and seventy-five miles in circumference. We have seen but one side of the island. On that there is a large tract of low land, extending in most parts many miles towards the interior, which is occupied by lofty mountain ranges, and hills of various shapes and sizes. The principal mountains are of considerable height, though not, we think, equal to those of Eramanga.

Another thing which gives the island a great superiority over all the islands of the New Hebrides to the south, is its magnificent bays and harbours. In the other islands, if we except the harbour of Aneiteum, there is nothing to compare with them, and we doubt if there is a single island throughout the whole of Eastern Polynesia so well furnished with harbours as is the island of Vate. The finest harbour on the island, so far as our knowledge goes, is that which is now known as "Havannah Harbour." This name was given to it by Captain Erskine when he visited it in the voyage already referred to. The harbour is formed by the mainland of Vate on the south and east sides and on the west and north by two islands. Between the two islands, Captain Erskine states, "there is a passage which would greatly shorten the distance in leaving the port, and spare the ship the heavy squalls from the high land which she is likely to encounter in running down the channel to Hat Island. (An island near the entrance resembling a hat, hence its name.) The passage being apparently shoal, I did not attempt it, but I have since had reason to believe that there are not less than six fathoms water in the centre." The entrance to the harbour is wide, and free from obstruction. The breadth of the bay may average from two to three miles, and its depth cannot be

14

less than seven or eight miles; and by going close in towards the shore, anchorage may be found from a short distance within the heads to very near the bottom of the bay. Such is a glimpse of this beautiful island and its magnificent harbour; but what of its inhabitants? Alas! alas! here we have a contrast most painful and humiliating:—

> "In vain with lavish kindness
> The gifts of God are strewn;
> The heathen, in his blindness,
> Bows down to wood and stone."

Of no part of the world, perhaps, may we say with greater truth:—

> "Every prospect pleases,
> And only man is vile."

And, oh! how vile, how debased, how cruel and heartless is man on this fair and lovely isle of the sea! The heart sickens as we turn to contemplate the revolting picture. Not that the Vatese are much—if at all, more savage than their neighbours, for some of these, as we have already seen, can hardly be outdone; but the contrast between the people and the country is more striking than is the case with the neighbouring islanders, and I may add, also, with the appearance of the people themselves. My own impression of the Vatese, and that of Dr. Turner, in company with whom I first saw them in 1845, was favourable. We thought them decidedly superior to their southern neighbours, though even then some things came to our knowledge that showed that their superiority did not extend much beyond their personal appearance, and some other external matters. And subsequent disclosures showed them to be among the most cruel and relentless savages with whom it has been our lot to come into contact. As regards the crowning abomination found among the neighbouring tribes, they seem to be pre-eminent. They are most inveterate and abominable cannibals. Not only are enemies, slain in war, devoured, but it is said that parties will go to villages at a distance and plunder the graves, carrying off bodies that have been buried two, three, or more days, for the disgustingly unnatural purpose of cooking them. Their wars are very frequent, and when either party desires peace they have a custom which, so far as we know, is peculiar to themselves. The party making the proposal must kill one of their own people and present the body as an offering to the enemy. If it is accepted, which is not always the case, peace is proclaimed; if not, the war goes on. When a woman is offered, or a man not well suited for cannibal purposes, rejection is often the consequence. On one occasion it was our privilege to save a poor fellow who had been marked out by his tribe for the above horrid purpose. The circumstance occurred some time after the introduction of the gospel to the island. We had finished our business, and were just about to take our leave of the teachers, in whose house we were at the time, when a tall, wild, excited-looking man was introduced to us as wishing to go to Samoa. He was from another part of the island, where teachers had formerly been stationed. He had learned from the teachers about the missionary ship, and thinking if he could reach it he would be safe, he had fled from his tribe, and now made his earnest application to us. Poor fellow! we little dreamt how much cause he had for his earnestness. We had already arranged to take two natives with us; we had a very large company on board, and the present applicant was not a likely-looking man to be of use to our cause; hence we felt no disposition to entertain the case. While the subject was being discussed, however, our friend, instead of waiting to hear our decision, slipped quietly off to the boat, where, to our surprise, we found him when about to start. When the true state of the case was explained to us, we could offer no further objection, so he went with us to Samoa, where he remained several years. On his return to his own land, in a subsequent voyage of the *John Williams*, he found safety with the teachers, and among the Christian party.

INFANTICIDE.

Another of the most revolting practices to which heathen nations are addicted, prevails extensively among the Vatese. Very few families, it is said, rear all their children. Here we have the most melancholy proof that a woman *may* forget her suckling child, and cease to have compassion on the son of her womb. Few women rear more than two or three children on Vate. And what is the motive that thus overmatches the strongest and tenderest instincts of the human heart? It is avowedly no other than to avoid the trouble and fatigue of rearing the little ones, and to be free from the hindrance which that would occasion to the accustomed engagements of the mother. Sometimes the father interposes, and a doomed one is spared; and sometimes one is saved by some other party volunteering to adopt it. Such are these "innocent children of nature,", as some would have us believe they are, "without natural affection, implacable, unmerciful," more sunk and debased than the beasts that perish. Like all the neighbouring islanders, the Vatese are polygamists; and the females are oppressed and degraded in consequence, being viewed and treated more as servants or slaves than wives: and this no doubt has much to do with the weakening and extinguishing in them of those affections which ordinarily are stronger than death.

The following extract from Captain Erskine's work will interest the reader:—" These people, although differing a good deal among themselves, had, except the black colour of their skins, few points of resemblance to the Tannese. They were of larger stature and more regular features, some having straight or almost aquiline noses, good foreheads, and beards of a moderate size. As their manners were more composed, so their dress was much more decent, consisting of a broad belt of matting, seven or eight inches wide, very neatly worked in a diamond pattern of red, white, and black colours with a species of maro presented in front. Many of them had their skins tattooed, or rather covered with raised figures, the arms and chest being the part generally operated upon; the cartilage of the nose was frequently pierced, and filled with a circular piece of stone, and the lobes of the ears always so; large ornaments of white shell being hung from them, so as often to extend the orifice to a great size. Round their arms, and in some cases round their ankles, they wore handsome bracelets made of small rings ground out of shells, exactly resembling chain armour, and so neatly strung together in black and white rows or figures, that the inside resembled a course woven cloth. Garters of a green leaf were often tied tight round the leg, under the knee; and in one or two instances the crisp hair, which was in general of a moderate length, was gathered up into a large top-knot, coloured yellow by lime, and a neat plume of cocks' feathers attached to the scratching-pin inserted in it. They seemed to have no wish for tobacco, saying it was 'tapu,' but were clamorous for pieces of red cotton or handkerchiefs; white strips of calico were sufficient to buy yams, which they brought in considerable quantities, or even their bows and spears. The latter were of beautiful design, the heads being either covered with barbs resembling the finest Gothic work, or composed of several prongs, which they told us were poisoned, and kept wrapped up in banana leaves, inserted into sockets prettily ornamented with red and white plaited cord, and decorated with a bunch of cocks' feathers. Two spears were sold to us as particularly valuable, the one being headed by a fragment of human bone about a foot long, and the other by a piece of wood shaped into an exact copy of the former. Their ordinary canoes were constructed with outriggers, and although of coarser model and workmanship, were similar to those in Samoa. We afterwards, however, saw hauled up on the beach a much larger canoe, on the body of which (apparently single) was built a kind of box to sit in, resembling a gondola, without the enclosed top."

We can vouch for the accuracy of the above description, and also for the following account of the native houses' and other interesting matters, which we take the liberty of extracting from Captain Erskine's work:—"The houses, which stood in no regular order, were of tolerable dimensions, of an oblong form, with slightly curved roofs, closed at the sides, but entirely open at one end. The first one we looked into we took for a temple, as from all the rafters were suspended quantities of bones, which we supposed to be offerings to the spirits; and we were strengthened in our opinion by the opposition made to our entering it. We soon found, however, that we were mistaken in our conjecture, and that the desire of giving us the best reception was the only cause for objecting to our entering any of the houses, for another turn of the path brought us to an open spot where stood the large common house of the village, into which we were ushered with evident pride. The building, which we found to be one hundred feet in length, by twenty-eight wide, differed from the ordinary habitations in having the whole of one side open; but to our surprise, the show of bones which we had remarked in the first house, and which we were told betokened the residence of a chief, was here exhibited in a tenfold degree, the interior of the roof being entirely concealed by the bundles which were suspended from the rafters. Here hung strings of the vertebræ of pigs, there the joints of their tales; while dozens of merry-thoughts of fowls, and every conceivable bone of birds and fishes, mingled with lobster shells and sharks' fins. Whether human bones formed any part of the collection, I cannot say, but none came under my observation; and from the people being aware through the missionary teachers of our horror of the practice of cannibalism, I am induced to think, had such been there, we should not have been invited to inspect them. As to the object or origin of this curious custom, we could get no information; but were told that the passion for collecting these bones is so great, that a traffic in them is carried on, not only among the tribes, but with the neighbouring islands."

CAPABILITIES OF THE SOIL, PRODUCTIONS, ETC. 201

The custom alluded to is most singular. So far as the writer has seen or read, it is found among no other tribe or people. On entering such a house as that described by Captain Erskine, one feels as if one were going into a great charnel-house. The bones are covered with dust, and blackened with smoke, and present a most dismal appearance. What can be the use or object of so strange a custom seems utterly inexplicable.

Captain Erskine's notice of the females is very correct:—
"The women are generally tall and thin, their hair cropped close to the head, and the skin occasionally marked with figures, as was remarked on the men's bodies. Their dress did not differ much from that of the males, consisting of a somewhat broader waistbelt, and a square mat in front resembling an enlarged maro. To this must be added the singular appendage of a tail, made of grass or matting, the ends being of a loose fringe of a foot and a half long, and the whole suspended from the waistbelt, and reaching nearly to the calf of the leg."

Respecting the capabilities of the soil, productions, etc., Captain Erskine remarks:—"The land of Vate, of which a minute portion is cultivated, must be exceedingly fertile, and capable of supporting a very large population. In none of the islands did we see a greater supply of both vegetables and pigs, although the people seemed disinclined to part with the latter; they are in fact, sandal-wood being now scarce, the only article of trade with Europeans, and are probably kept to fulfil some contract with a favourite trader, who purchases them here, as at Tanna, to exchange for sandal-wood with the Eramangans."

The Vatese believe in a future state of existence. They have no idols, but they invoke the spirits of the dead, and worship two gods, whom they call Mauitikitiki and Tamakaiā, and to whom they trace the origin of all things. Their hades, which they say is somewhere in the west, the call Lakinatoto. Like their southern neighbours, they believe that disease and death are caused by men.

So when any one is taken seriously ill they make it their business to find out who has caused the attack, and, having succeeded, they present offerings of such things as they think will be acceptable to the supposed author of the malady, with a view to its removal. Of course the disease originators are seldom far to seek, their object being to profit by the folly and credulity of those on whom they practise their impositions. The probability is that a fuller acquaintance with the people will show that the impostors in question are a kind of priests, who impose upon the superstitious fears of their benighted contrymen.

Connected with the beautiful harbour of which we have spoken, there is a sad tale which we must not wholly pass over. From its relation to subsequent outrages committed by the Vatese upon foreign visitors, it ought, in justice to them, to be brought out. The attention of the writer was called to the proceedings referred to in a somewhat singular manner, shortly after their occurrence, which was about the close of 1842. A person who had been an officer on board one of the vessels of the guilty expedition to which we refer, visited the island where he was stationed, and addressed to him a written statement of the matter. The writer of the said account professed to have been connected with these proceedings wholly against his will, and he considered it to be his duty to take the first opportunity of bringing them to light. Subsequent inquiries proved the correctness of his statement. The writer feels it an unwelcome task to dwell on the painful subject, but our notice of Vate would be incomplete were we to omit it.

The expedition consisted of three vessels; the object was to obtain sandal-wood. They went to Tonga, on their way to the New Hebrides, where they obtained sixty men, natives of Tonga, to aid them in accomplishing the objects of their voyage. They made an unsuccessful attempt to increase the number of their company at Lakemba, an island of the Figi group. On reaching the New Hebrides they called at Tanna, and then went to Eramanga, where they commenced cutting sandal-wood. Quarrels soon arose between the Tongans and the Eramangans, which led to their leaving that island. The particulars of their proceedings there do not seem to have been satisfactorily ascertained, so we are unacquainted with their character; but at Vate their conduct was such as one knows not how to characterize. They anchored in the large harbour where they acted the part of regular freebooters, helping themselves to whatever they desired of the property of the natives (hogs and yams were particularly specified); and not only did they rob and plunder, but they also laid waste and destroyed a great deal of property.* And well would it have been had the mischief ended here. Greater evils followed. They fought with the natives, and, according to the account given by a Tongan chief who was present, twenty-six of the Vatese were killed, while none of the attacking party were injured. No wonder; *they* were armed with muskets, while the Vatese had only their native weapons. After this, the natives endeavoured to secure themselves by the construction of a fort. This was besieged, stormed, and taken by their savage visitors, and a number more killed. Those who escaped retreated to an island, where they hid in a cave; they were followed in their retreat by the Tongans, who, after firing into the cave apparently without effect, pulled down some houses in the neighbourhood, and piled up the materials at the mouth of the cave, to which they set fire, suffocating all the poor creatures who had fled to it for refuge. And, notwithstanding these atrocious proceedings, the commanders of the vessels still continued their sandal-wood cutting, that being to them apparently a matter of far greater moment than the lives of their fellow-creatures. For three days after the affair of the cave the party continued their operations, and then departed, having gained their object. But at what a fearful cost was that accom-

* As many as 200 hogs are said to have been carried off, and yams without number.

plished! Fearful to all concerned, but especially to the unhappy men who directed the expedition. These men, indeed, were not made amenable to human law. By the strong hand of power they bore everything before them, gained their object, and departed in triumph. But "the triumphing of the wicked is short." There was an eye that marked their deeds; there was an arm stretched out to avenge the wrongs of the poor Vatese, which they could neither escape nor elude. Their sin found them out. All of them were, within a very few years, summoned before the tribunal of Him who executeth justice and judgment for all that are oppressed; and their memory will go down to posterity loaded with indelible infamy. "The memory of the wicked shall rot." Would that the consequences of their wickedness had died with themselves and those who were the immediate sufferers. Among these consequences are probably to be reckoned the sad events which took place on Vate a few years afterwards, in reference to which Captain Erskine writes as follows:—"Whether an apprehension of such consequences as the above following the white men's visits actuated adjacent tribes, or whether, as the traders would have us believe, their love of treachery and thirst of blood alone prompted them, may be a matter of dispute, but the Vateans were not long in the strangers' debt; the crews of two English vessels, with the exception of a single Englishman, and some natives of New Zealand and the Society Islands, having been massacred a few years afterwards at Olotapu and Vila, two anchorages or ports to the S.E. of where we were lying." Into the particulars of these tales of blood we will not enter, but hasten to what is a vastly more grateful task, namely, to narrate the efforts that have been made to bring the Vatese under the influence of those blessed truths which promote "peace on earth, glory to God in the highest, and good-will to men." We may just remark, in dismissing these matters, that there is no reason to doubt that the Vatese were influenced by the example set them by the white men. It is, indeed, highly probable that, but for that, the massacres perpetrated by them would not have occurred. When they are so treated, what can be

A VIEW IN RAROTONGA, ONE OF THE HERVEY GROUP.

expected but that whenever opportunity offers, they will retaliate? But let the natives be properly treated, and let there be the exercise of due discretion in dealing with them, and it is believed that the instances in which they will be guilty of outrages on foreign visitors will be found to be few and far between.

The introduction of Christian teachers to Vate was attended with circumstances of a very remarkable character. Towards the close of 1845, the *John Williams* was at anchor in Dillon's Bay, Eramanga. Dr. Turner and the writer were on board as a deputation from the Samoan mission. We had tried, without success, our utmost efforts to regain our hold upon Eramanga; we had just learned of the massacre of our teachers at Fotuna, and had seen that door closed against us; we had reserved four teachers, hoping to find an open door at Eramanga. Under the influence of disappointed expectation and hopes deferred, we were feeling sad, and were in doubt as to what course we should adopt, when a light from a most unexpected quarter was shed upon our path. Indications of the Master's will, such as we could not fail to recognise, were mercifully vouchsafed to us. At anchor alongside of us was a small vessel engaged in the sandalwood trade. Such a quarter was about the last to which we should have thought of looking in those days for any aid in our work. The captain of the vessel came on board the *John Williams*, and gave us the following information. He had just been to Vate, there he had found the remnant of a large party of Tongans and Samoans who many years before had lost their way at sea, and had made that island. Only a few individuals remained, but among these was one man named Sualo, who had married the daughter of the chief of the district where they lived, and had acquired great influence. They had heard of the introduction of Christianity to Samoa and Tonga, and of the happy effects which had followed. They were greatly desirous to be made acquainted with the new religion, and they had earnestly begged the captain to do what he could to get teachers sent to them. And to make our path still more plain, the captain had a New Zealander on board his vessel, whom he offered to pass over to us, who had been living on Vate with the Samoans and Tongans, and who was therefore able to lead us to the very spot to which it was necessary to go, in order to communicate with them. The lad was willing to go with us; hence our way seemed quite clear. With grateful hearts we prepared to proceed to Vate, and early on the morning of the 30th of April we weighed anchor and set sail from Eramanga. We stood direct for Vate, and about three o'clock in the afternoon of the same day we made the island. Night overtook us before we reached the part of which we were in search. On the morning of the following day we were conducted by our guide to a bay of immense extent, in which we anchored. In the neighbourhood of this bay resided our Samoan and Tongan friends, in search of whom we dispatched the New Zealand lad, accompanied by two of our own people, Samoans, who were on board with us. After some considerable difficulty they succeeded in bringing to us Sualo, to whom Captain L—— had directed us as the man most likely to be of service to us. Sualo, as already intimated, had for a wife a daughter of the principal chief of the district in which he resided. This was one source of the influence which he had acquired, but another and more considerable one was, that he was a fearless, daring fellow, and had acquired great celebrity for deeds of valour. The terror of his name had spread far and wide; and his aid was earnestly sought by the natives in the wars they were constantly waging. Fortunate was the party considered which succeeded in securing Sualo's services. Liberal rewards were given him by those whom he assisted, so that he was a man of wealth as well as a hero, which added of course to his consequence. He had adopted the habits and dress of the Vatese, and when he made his appearance, tomahawk in hand, he looked as finished a savage as any of those among whom he dwelt. Thus he was an odd character from whom to emanate a request for Christian teachers; and there seemed little congruity in placing these in any way in connection with him. He avowed his conviction, however, that his past mode of life had been altogether wrong, and assured us of his determination to act differently for the future. He was ready to embrace Christianity, and to aid in every way in his power the teachers left on the island. Past experience had taught us that a good deal of dependence might be placed on a formal agreement entered into in such circumstances, even with a savage. The chief, his father-in-law, whose name was Pomare, and many of the people, were also desirous to have teachers, so that the way seemed clear to commence operations. This we did at two points—namely, Pango, a place near where we were at anchor, and Erakor, the place where Sualo and his friends lived. We placed the four teachers, Mose, Sipi, Taavili, and Setefano, whom we had designed for Eramanga, two and two at these places. The teachers were all Samoans; the chiefs and people gave them an encouraging reception, and we left the island much pleased with the result of our visit, and thankful to Him who had so far prospered our way. After about sixteen months the island was again visited. The visitors on that occasion were the Rev. W. Gill, from Rarotonga, and the Rev. H. Nisbet, from Samoa. Their visit was made in September, 1846. Their report was encouraging as the following extract will show:—"The direction of the wind," they remark, "obliged us to make Vate first, which we did on Monday, the 14th. Upon this island teachers had been placed for the first time on the last voyage of the vessel thither. We were naturally very anxious to know how it had fared with the pioneers, and what God had been pleased to do by them. Our anxieties were soon relieved by intercourse with our teachers; they were four in number, and had been located in two districts. The report from each of these wore a highly encouraging aspect. The teachers had all been treated with uniform kindness by the people. The two villages where they are located, with many people of several other settlements, profess to have abandoned heathenism and embraced Christianity. Religious services are regularly held at several places on the Sabbath, at which an encouraging number attend. Attempts have also been made to establish schools for the young and adult population; but, as was to be expected, very little progress has yet been made in this department of labour." The remainder of the report was in harmony with the above extract. The state of things was highly encouraging. Objects of idolatrous worship had been burned or otherwise destroyed by many. The revolting practice of burying alive infants and old people had to some extent been abandoned, as had also cannibalism. Two new stations had also been commenced in the large bay, Havannah Harbour, and a third at another part of the island, so that the number of stations was now five, and of labourers nine. So far all was encouraging, and it seemed as if the time to favour Vate by the general diffusion of the Gospel was at hand. Alas! alas! such was far from being the case. A long dreary period yet remained during which darkness should continue to cover the land, and gross darkness the people. During the interval of the first and second visits, the massacre of part of the crew of a vessel called the *Cape Packet* and the destruction of the vessel, had taken place. So far as the brethren Gill and Nisbet could learn, the natives acted a very subordinate part in the affair, the originators and chief actors having been New Zealanders, Sandwich Islanders, and natives of Borabora, an island of the of Tahitian group.

During the interval of the second and third visits untoward events occurred, which brought out more fully the character of the natives, and the difficulties to be encountered in the evangelization of the island. Another sad affray took place between the natives and foreigners, in which the natives seem to have been the sole aggressors. An account of that and other important matters are embraced the following report of the deputation, Messrs. Turner and Nisbet:—

"On reaching Vate we were grieved to learn that three of the five stations there had been abandoned, and that our devoted evangelists had been exposed to many perils. At one of the stations the teacher died of ague, in May last year. It was the wish of his wife that she should go and reside with the teachers at another station; but the chief, wishing to have her and her little property, would not allow it! Poor woman! this was more than her mind could bear. Preferring death to degradation, she rushed into the sea one day, and was drowned before the other teachers had time to unite in an effort to remove her from that station.

"At another place, where two teachers had been stationed, we found both dead, and the station abandoned in consequence. About the same time that one of them died the other was taken ill. He was visited by his fellow-teachers from another station. They left him on Saturday, under the care of a servant boy, while they returned to their families and Sabbath duties. On the Sabbath afternoon a party of natives went to the house of the sick man, He was suspicious, got up, and went towards the door, and, on attempting to keep them back by asking them what they came for, one of them struck him on the chest with a block of wood which they use as a pillow. He fell, died, and was buried that night. During his illness he was occasionally delirious. The natives say that according to a custom among them, that was the reason they killed him. This is a modifying circumstance; but we have reason to fear they were as much influenced by a desire to get his canoe, chest, and other property.

"But the abandonment of another of the stations on the south-west side of the island, namely, Olotapu, is associated with events more calamitous still. Mose and Sepania, teachers from Samoa, were stationed here. On Friday afternoon, towards the end of April, 1847, a boat reached a bay close by where the teachers were. Two white men were in it, and starving for want of food. The natives resolved on killing them, desirous of getting their bodies, their clothes, and their boat. Mose was the means of saving one of them, a man named John Jones. The other, a stout man, was taken by a person saying he would save him; but he was killed and cooked next morning. This was a boat belonging to the *British Sovereign*, a sandal-wooding barque, which had gone ashore some nights before on the east side of the island, and had become a wreck. The captain and the rest of the crew having escaped from the wreck, arrived at the same place on the following Sabbath, on their way to the large harbour on the south-west side of the island. When the natives saw them they determined to kill them. Some treated them with cocoa-nuts and sugar-cane, while others went off to muster the district for their massacre. Our teachers saw the people arming and running off; they said they were going to fight with a neighbouring tribe; but the plot came out, and then our teacher and the man Jones were all anxiety to be off to the spot to save life. The chief stood up and would not allow them; and it was only a conviction that it would be their death to go that kept them back. The tribes at hand were assembled, all was arranged, and the natives, in company with the foreigners, got up to advance along the road. They walked single file, a native between every white man, and a few on either side. The chief took the lead, and gave the signal, when every one turned round and struck his man. A few Tanna men escaped to the sea, but were pursued and killed, with the exception of one, who fled to the bush. This man and a little boy, together with Jones, were all who escaped the massacre. They are now off in a vessel. Ten bodies of the unhappy sufferers were cooked on the spot; the teachers mention adjacent villages among whom other ten were distributed; they were not sure what became of the rest, nor the exact number massacred. In most cases the white men are the aggressors. In this most cold-blooded massacre, however, we cannot learn any object on the part of the natives but a desire to obtain human flesh and the clothes of these unfortunate men.

"A few days after, another boat touched at the same place, which we suppose was the long-boat either of the *Elizabeth* or the *British Sovereign*, in search of survivors. All on shore were in arms again, bent upon killing the four or five white men who were in this boat; and when they went off towards it, the men fired upon them. The chiefs were enraged at the firing, and determined to be avenged on the teachers and Jones, who was still a refugee with them. A woman hearing of the plot, ran and informed the teachers. Jones and they had scarcely reached the bush, fleeing for their lives, when the party arrived at their house to kill them. They were pursued to another station whither they fled; but, after remonstrance, and in consideration of getting all the property of the teachers, there was no further bloodshed. Before leaving the island, Jones left a document with the teacher Mose, through whose exertions, under God, he was saved, expressing his deep gratitude for the kindness he had experienced.

" But there is a bright side to the picture. The teachers on this island have many opportunities of telling the people of the way of salvation. They have visited other parts of the island, have been well received, and have had requests for teachers. They report a greater unity of dialect than obtains at Tanna, and a great population. They have also been the means of saving the lives of infants, which heathen custom was wont to bury alive. One child was actually buried, and dug up again by its parents, and is now alive. Three aged women would have been buried alive, but for the remonstrance of the teachers. This custom is awfully prevalent here. It is even considered a disgrace to the family of an aged chief, if he is not buried alive. And when the poor old heathen feels sick and infirm, he will tell those around him to bury him. The grave is at once dug, and the old man's dying groans are drowned amid the weeping and wailing of his family and friends. Persons too, at whatever age, if in sickness they are delirious, are buried alive forthwith. A young man in the prime of life was thus buried lately. He burst up the grave, and escaped. He was seized, and buried again. A second time he struggled to the surface; and then they led him to the bush, bound him to a tree, and left him to die. Verily, the dark places of the earth are full of the habitations of cruelty!

"After arranging for the continued occupation of the two old stations, we proceeded to the west side of the island, and made further inroads on the kingdom of darkness at the large harbour there. Here we have occupied two new stations under most favourable circumstances."

The next visit was by Mr. Hardie and the writer, in September, 1849. At that time the mission was found to be in a very discouraging state. The teachers and their families, in addition to other hardships many and great, had all suffered from disease. Three of themselves, with three of the children, had died; and the survivors were in such a bad state of health as to render it necessary to remove them from the island. Sad deeds of cruelty and blood had come to the knowledge of the teachers, and their own lives had been preserved in ways little less than miraculous, as the following extracts from our report of the voyage will show:—

"We made this island on Wednesday, the 19th; and here we had to listen to a mournful tale. Since the last voyage, all the teachers and their families had been very ill. Three of the teachers and three of their children had died, and most of the survivors were still in bad health; in consequence of which one of the stations was abandoned.

"The state of things among the natives generally was far from encouraging. For two or three months after the last visit, considerable numbers attended the services on the Sabbath, at the several stations. Successive epidemics then took place; first disease of the eyes, then of the chest, fever, etc.; and by these many were carried off. For these and other evils the teachers were blamed; and the consequence was a general abandonment of them and their message. From that time the Sabbath was not observed at any of the stations. Seldom any, except a few individuals belonging to the families of the chiefs with whom the teachers lived, attended the services on that day. The people could not bear the restraints of religion. No schools could be held, the parents being angry when their children went to school, as they rather wished them to go to work. No desire was manifested by any for the Word of God. Wars were very frequent, harassing, and distressing. The people were displeased with the teachers for not engaging in them, and angry with them for forbidding them. All the misfortunes connected with them were attributed to them and their religion. Diseases were still very frequent, and often fatal to many; and whether they happened among the people or the pigs, their causes and consequences were ascribed to the teachers. On account of these things, and urged on by their covetous desires, the people at the different stations threatened to kill them. Their plantations and houses at some of the stations were destroyed, and they themselves had to take refuge at the houses of the chiefs.

"About five months previous to our arrival, an attempt was made to murder the teachers who were stationed at the large harbour, by the people of another district, named Mele. Desirous to obtain the pigs and other property of the teachers, thirty armed men set off in a large canoe, with the design of killing them. They reached the teachers' house at midnight, and roused them up, pretending that they had come on a friendly visit, and asked them to go and help them to pull the canoe out of the water; designing when they got them outside the house, to dispatch them. This, however, was not agreeable to the teachers' notions of propriety, and they did not go. That night, these murderous fellows slept at the teachers' house, and next morning the teachers prepared food for them, and treated them kindly. The whole of this day the savages watched for an opportunity to fall upon the teachers unawares. A number of them pretended to go to a neighbouring village to barter, and returned in the evening after sunset. Some of them went up to the teachers' house, and said they had brought cocoa-nuts for them, and requested them to go down to the canoe and fetch them. Meanwhile, others of their number were lying in ambush, ready to rush upon them in the event of their going. In this, also, they were disappointed; the teachers would not go. At length they all went into the teachers' house, taking their hatchets with them. The hour of prayer came, and these savage men, each with his hatchet in his hand, sat down with the family to worship. One of them, with his hatchet over his shoulder, placed himself opposite the teacher who was to conduct the worship. The teacher, observing it, took the hatchet from him, and laid it down beside him, saying it was not proper so to sit during worship; but the man took his hatchet up again, saying there was no harm. The teachers now became alarmed, especially as they heard the savages speaking to each other in a dialect they did not well understand. The teacher who was to conduct worship said to the others, "Keep your eyes open, and look about you; these men must have some bad intention." The worship then proceeded, and the savages raised themselves, and lifted their hatchets; but their hands trembled and their hearts failed them. One of them whispered not to strike, as the teachers were looking. The teachers then tried to go on with the prayer, and again these men made a move and raised their hatchets; but again their hands trembled and their hearts failed. At this moment the prayer was abruptly concluded, and the teachers united in peremptorily ordering the savages out of the house. They wished to remain; but the teachers got up and insisted on their going immediately. They then all rushed out of the door, and shut it after them, made for their canoe, and were seen no more. They fled thus precipitately, no doubt, from fear lest, alarm being given, the people of the village should suddenly fall upon them. Their desire evidently was to dispatch the teachers as they were kneeling at prayer; but the Lord mercifully saved them from the hands of these murderous men. These people returned to their own land, disappointed and astonished, without accomplishing their object. The people of Fila, another district, hearing of their failure, derided them, and said *they* would go and see whether they could not accomplish what the others had failed to do. Accordingly, sixty armed men set off in three canoes for the village where the teachers were; but a strong wind arose, with a heavy sea, and their canoes were dashed to pieces on a point of land, when they were about two-thirds on their way. Thus they were obliged to return, like the others, without accomplishing their murderous purpose. The result of these failures on the minds of the natives was a strong impression that the religion of the teachers must be true, and that their God must be powerful. The teachers referred their deliverance to the true cause when they said, 'God alone saved us.'

"While our vessel lay at anchor at Pango, a report reached us that the people of that place were meditating an attack upon us with a view to take the vessel. Possibly this was a mere rumour. We thought it advisable, however, to get under weigh, and thus avoid risking a collision.

"The death of so many of the teachers, and the very bad health, with a few exceptions, of the survivors, obliged us to abandon for the present all the stations on the island but one—that of Erakor. Before leaving, we saw all the chiefs with whom the teachers had been, and some others with whom they were on friendly terms, and explained to them why we were obliged to take the teachers away. We gave them presents, and promised to do our best to get teachers for them next voyage. We were glad, on leaving the station at the great harbour, to find the chief with whom the teacher had been, and his brother, very desirous to come with us to Samoa, and very thankfully received them on board.

"We had only one fresh teacher to leave at this island, and we decided on placing him at Erakor, with the only remaining teacher on the island. When he was taken on shore the chiefs and people received him most cordially. The chief at this station, Pomare, is very kind to the

RAIATEA.—HOUSE OF THE LATE REV. J. VIVIAN.

teachers. He says, so long as he and his family are safe, the teachers shall be so too; and he has considerable influence among the people. He says he will attend to what the teachers tell him, that he will not do anything to cause war, and will fight only in the event of an attack. Parties there who plotted to kill the teachers, are now ashamed of their conduct, and throw the blame one upon another. Something like kindness towards the teachers begins to show itself among the people, and there is hope that greater attention will soon be paid to instruction, and that things generally will take a favourable turn."

Thus the mission was left in a very low state on the occasion to which the above extracts refer. We were just able to retain our hold upon the island—but just able to keep the door from being quite closed.

The next visit, by Mr. Sunderland and the writer, was in May, 1852. The state and prospects of the mission at that time were found to be more encouraging than had been expected. A favourable reaction had taken place after the visit of 1849, as the following extract from the report of the voyage will show:—

"In the afternoon of the following day we anchored in a bay near Erakor, the missionary station. We had the satisfaction to find the two teachers alive and well. Since the visit in 1849, they had been enabled steadily to prosecute their labours, and we were rejoiced to find these had not been in vain. While war, cannibalism, murder, and other heathen abominations have encompassed the Christian district, unbroken peace has reigned there; the grosser practices of heathenism have been abandoned; and a very encouraging measure of attention has been given to public services. The average attendance on Sabbath mornings has been about 100; in the afternoon, somewhat less. There have occasionally been much larger congregations, sometimes exceeding 200. They have kept up a monthly missionary prayer meeting, which has been attended, on an average, by about fifty. The Sabbath is very generally observed in the neighbourhood of the principal station, and outstations also, by those professedly Christians; some observe family worship, and a few are accustomed to retire for secret prayer. The chapel was erected in 1849. It is built after the manner of Samoan houses, and enclosed with reeds. It holds about one hundred and fifty. The teachers have visited, more or less regularly, two or three outstations. The chief of these are Pango and Olotapu, places in which teachers resided in former years, and at which some impression has been made. At Pango, as many as 200 profess to have received Christianity; and a congregation averaging 100 attend when the teachers visit it, which is very frequently. There has been very little war at either of these places since last visit. Slight disturbances have occurred which have led to the loss of four or five lives. It is not yet safe for foreigners to put themselves in the power of the natives, though a great change has taken place in their views and feelings towards them. This change is partly to be attributed to the visits of H.M.'s ships of war, the *Fly*, Captain Oliver, and the *Havannah*, Captain Erskine. Both these gentlemen acted in such a manner as to produce a very favourable impression. Two boats' crews, who went ashore at Olotapu to trade, in June, 1850, were in great danger of their lives, perhaps unknown to themselves. They were saved by a Christian chief named Talipoa. Infanticide and other revolting heathen practices still continue among the heathen party. Occasionally, the teachers and the chief, Pomare, succeeded in saving parties whom the cruel superstitions of the country had doomed to destruction. In September, 1850, a woman and her daughter were thus saved from being buried alive. Having finished our business at Erakor, we sailed for another part of the island, where we intended to recommence operations, namely, Havannah Harbour. We were obliged to suspend operations in this bay last voyage, and it was now our intention (D.V.) to renew them. Tongalulu, the chief of Sema, a place in the bay, and a young man, his brother, had been in Samoa since last visit, and were now returning to their native land, having witnessed the effects of the Gospel in Samoa. They were anxious to have their own country brought under the same happy influence. The fact of our having the chief on board, made our arrival quite an event. He had been absent so long beyond the time expected, that the people had concluded he must be dead, and had mourned for him as dead. Thus his appearance among them was as one risen from the dead. Their joy knew no bounds. They shouted, laughed, talked; and those more immediately connected with him greeted his arrival with a general burst of weeping. We took the chief, his brother, and their property, with the teacher who had been selected to reside with him, in our boats to Sema. Large numbers assembled to welcome the return of the chief, and expressed their regard for him and their gratitude to us by bringing us a present of mats, yams, and a pig. They attach great value to their pigs; so that to give one of these is the strongest expression of satisfaction. After our return to the vessel, we were visited by Fatutoka and Marikona, two chiefs who, with Tongalulu, have authority over the whole bay. They brought a present of yams and a pig; and one brought his son, and the other his nephew, requesting us to take them to Samoa, that they might return at a future time accompanied by teachers. They begged most earnestly that they might have teachers the next time the vessel visits the island. They said, if they could not have more, by all means let them have one between them. Ten or twelve teachers might at once be located most advantageously on this lovely island; and foreign missionaries might also settle on some part of it."

When the next visit (which was by the same parties) was made, in October, 1853, things were still found progressing favourably. "Here," says the report, "we met intelligence, on the whole encouraging. Some things of an untoward character had occurred; for that we were prepared, but the decided preponderance was on the encouraging side. The teachers at Erakor have met with comparatively little interruption in their work during the interval since last visit. About two months after the vessel left, an epidemic broke out. About fifteen died. Some parties took up an idea that it was to be attributed to the visit of the *John Williams*, and were angry with the teachers on that account. The disaffection rose so high, that they talked of killing the teachers, and were on the watch for an opportunity of injuring them. An attack, which does not appear to have been of a very determined character, was made upon them one day when they were found by some of the hostile party alone in the bush. They thought it prudent to withdraw for a season, till the storm might pass over. They accordingly removed to Sema, where they remained about a fortnight. During their absence the disease raged much more violently than it had formerly done. About thirty were carried off. Happily, the people were now led to take a different view. They became more and more alarmed, but their alarm took the right direction. They traced the calamity under which they were suffering to Him 'who alone is to be feared,' and, at least externally, turned towards Him, welcomed back the teachers, and gave the most attentive heed to their instructions. Services and schools were now crowded, as formerly, and so they have continued to the present time. The disaffection extended to only about half of the community.

"As we spent the Sabbath at the island, we had a favourable opportunity of seeing for ourselves, and greatly were we cheered with what we did see. The little place of worship was filled to overflowing. The congregation must have numbered full 250; and the order, quiet, and heartiness which characterized the service were very striking. We could not but remark a great external change since last visit. The poor people are thirsting for instruction, and the only drawback to our satisfaction in observing the cheering indications of that which it was our privilege to witness was, that we had not a missionary to leave among them, and so little prospect of soon obtaining one. Their desire for a missionary is very great, and the opening is a most eligible one—such an one as first missionaries have seldom had in any part of Polynesia. Here is a congregation of 250 already collected, who would receive a missionary with open arms, and at once give themselves up to his instruction and guidance. And the locality is highly favourable as a centre whence to operate on the surrounding country.

"The service was closed by the chief Pomare, who is one of six native assistants. He is a very interesting and sensible man. He has been the staunch and unwavering friend of the teachers and of Christianity from the beginning, and affords good evidence of having felt the power of the truth on his heart. Family and secret prayer are generally practised; heathen customs are to a great extent abandoned; and the community is externally Christian in a degree that is highly gratifying.

"At Olotapu, Fila, Meli, and especially Pango, the state of things is altogether different; and on this account it is all the more remarkable that a place in the centre of these should be in such a state as is Erakor. At Pango, one of the most horrible outrages was perpetrated, in March last, of which we have ever heard. It was preceded by a deed which was a fitting preparation. The people had built a chapel, and were giving considerable attention to Christianity, when, on account of sickness, they became disaffected, and did not wish to have services conducted any more in their land. The teachers and their native assistants at Erakor persisted in visiting them; and to put, as they thought, an effectual stop to their so doing, they burned the chapel and returned to heathenism. Thus they were prepared for the dreadful deed of darkness to which we refer. A party consisting of twenty-nine persons, six of whom were women, came from Moso, a village of Sema. They went for purposes of trade. The Pango people, without any apparent inducement, except the gratification of their cannibal propensities, and their desire for property, fell upon the hapless party of strangers, and murdered twenty-two of them. Seven escaped; got hold of a canoe, and fled. The ferocious murderers got their victims into their power by reporting that a ship was in sight. They were thrown off their guard, ran out without their weapons of defence, and thus were helpless. Part of the bodies were distributed among the neighbouring heathen villages, and the remainder appropriated by the murderers. Only one was buried.

"This horrible act of treachery and cruelty has not yet been avenged ; but Sema, it is said, is preparing to avenge it. It is possible that, as Christianity has taken some hold there, the people may quietly bear it ; and, if so, it will be well; as to do otherwise will only be to insure an indefinite amount of further mischief.

"On Monday, the 31st, we sailed from Erakor, and on the following day, November 1st, we anchored under the lee of one of the heads of the large bay, Havannah Harbour.

"From among the many eligible openings in and about the bay, we selected one which appeared to us to have the strongest recommendations. This was Lolopa, an island which forms the north-west side of the harbour, which is said to be much more healthy than the main land, and which is most conveniently situated for commanding the whole bay. To this island the two chiefs belong who made so interesting and urgent an appeal for teachers last voyage. The young men, their relatives, whom we took to Samoa, had returned in safety, on account of which they were greatly rejoiced, and their desire for teachers was confirmed and increased. We placed the teachers (two), with their wives, at Tromalla, a large village where Fatutoka, the chief of the island, lives, and which is a most inviting place for a missionary station. When we took the teachers on shore, the joy of the people seemed to know no bounds. Men, women, and children crowded around us. Some of the principal chiefs laid hold of our hands, and led us through the village, while the crowd manifested their joy in a way most unmistakable. We never saw teachers, on their first landing, meet with such an enthusiastic reception. The field is certainly a most inviting one. May it yield an abundant harvest!

"We had so few disposable teachers, and Sema is so unhealthy, that we thought it advisable to leave it unoccupied for the present. It will not be lost sight of, however. We have a considerable hold upon it, and a commencement has been made at two or three other points in the bay. All these, and especially Sema, the Lolopa teachers will keep in view and visit; so that we hope advances will continue to be made. The Christian party at Sema numbers from 150 to 200. While the teacher was there, which was till the month of June last, congregations varying from 100 to 200 usually assembled on Sabbaths and Wednesdays, and about fifty children daily assembled for instruction. The chief Tongalulu and his brother have rather disappointed our hopes, so that the progress that has been made is the more surprising. While the teacher was at Sema, a reconciliation was effected between two parties who had long been hostile. They met, the teachers addressed them, and they agreed to bury their quarrel; and, in token of their sincerity, shook hands, and publicly pledged themselves to mutual friendship."

Alas! how fickle and deceitful is man, and how little reliance is to be placed on appearance among a heathen people! The above extract indicates a very promising state of things. High in hope and with thankful hearts we bade adieu to Vate on the occasion to which the extract refers. Surely the time to favour Vate, even the set time, had come. And so indeed it might have proved, had it been in our power to take advantage of the circumstances which then promised so fairly, by placing missionaries on the island. As it was the opportunity was lost, and a dismal series of calamities followed in rapid succession, the result of which was the all but total extinction of the mission. A sad report indeed was that which the next visitors of the island had to make. These were Messrs. Hardie and Sunderland. Their visit was in October, 1854. They were horrified to find that the teachers and their wives, who had been so recently left in such promising circumstances, had all been murdered and devoured by the wretched people who had welcomed them with every demonstration of cordiality and joy. A more striking and painful illustration of the extreme fickleness of man can scarcely be conceived. Only nineteen days intervened between the landing of the teachers and their murder. One of the teachers had a son, a little boy, who also shared the fate of the parents. Thus the whole party, five in number, were cut off. The deputation were unable to obtain any information as to what led to the murder of the teachers. Superstitious fears that they might cause disease and death may have had some influence; and the property they possessed was no doubt an alluring bait. We have no means of arriving at certainty, and conjecture is useless. If, however, the fear of disease and death had anything to do with the matter, the things feared were by no means averted by the deed of which the people were guilty. On the contrary, that which they feared speedily came upon them, and that in a way so remarkable as to look very like a judgment. Very soon after the murder of the teachers, an epidemic broke out and raged with fatal effect. As many as 150 were reported to have died on the small island where they were stationed. The disease spread to the main land, and on that many also died. Other calamities followed which we must not particularly detail. Two other teachers died, and when the deputation arrived, only one, with the widow of another, remained to tell the sad tidings. These it was necessary to remove; and Sualo also, who had been of so much service to the mission in past years, could not be induced to remain longer. Thus the foreign labourers were all removed, and the natives who professed themselves Christians were left as sheep without a shepherd—as lambs in the midst of wolves. The brethren of the deputation were deeply pained at leaving the island in such a state of abandonment, but there was no alternative.

It was not until July, 1858, that we were able to reoccupy

the island. It had been visited in June, 1857, and the report of the visitors, Messrs. Harbutt and Drummond, was encouraging, greatly more so than could have been expected, considering the circumstances in which it had been left by the preceding deputation. Had every trace of Christianity been obliterated, it would have been no matter of surprise. Instead of that, however, a considerable number were found calling themselves Christians, keeping up the forms of Christian worship, and longing for teachers to instruct them more fully. The Sabbath was being observed, and the people appeared to be striving to walk according to their little light. And when the next visit was made in 1858, the door was found open and the way prepared for the recommencement of the mission. Of that interesting event the following report gives the particulars. The deputation were the Rev. G. Stallworthy, of the Samoan mission, and the Rev. G. Gill, of Rarotonga. Their report is as follows:—

"Leaving Eramanga on the 21st of July, we reached Vate very early on the following morning; and soon after getting opposite the large bay in which Erakor is situated, some natives came off to the vessel, and among them was Pomare, the chief of Erakor, and father of one of the lads on board. We found that peace prevailed on shore. The men who are mentioned in the report of last year's voyage as men who 'speak Sunday,' are persons who conduct worship and schools. The whole village professes Christianity. Thus some fruit of the labours and sufferings of teachers from Eastern Polynesia still remains. We found that the people were desirous of being again supplied with teachers. We had applied to our brethren on Aneiteum for teachers for them, as we thought natives of that island might not suffer so much from the climate as those of our groups, but they had none to spare at that time; and they thought that our teachers would be more acceptable to the people than any from Aneiteum, and also that our vessel, from its size, was best adapted to visit

GENERAL VIEW OF ANEITEUM.

Vate, where the people have large canoes, and any tribes disposed to be hostile might overpower a small vessel. On the previous evening we had called around us the Rarotongan teachers on board, and asked them if they had any desire to be stationed on Vate. Several of them replied that that was the land of their choice. After getting the news from the shore, we again consulted with them; and it was agreed that three of them should be landed, namely, Teamaru, Teautoa, and Toma. We committed them by prayer to God; their supplies were lowered into the boats, and we accompanied them on shore, with their wives and children.

"After leaving an open bay, we passed an island, and pulled a mile and-a-half up a beautiful lagoon, to Erakor, which is on the right hand side, and beyond which village it extends at least a mile and-a-half. We were at once conducted to the chapel, a wattled and plastered building, with a pulpit and seats, which has been built by the natives in the place of one erected by the former teachers, which had been blown down.

"A short time after we landed, the hollow trunks of two decayed trees, standing near the chapel, were beaten as a substitute for 'the church-going bell,' and 130 persons, including a large number of children, assembled for worship. We requested the teachers to conduct the service in the usual way. One of them, named Petela, entered the pulpit, and read out a hymn from a small manuscript book which he held in his hand, and a person in the centre of the chapel started the singing, when men, women, and children joined the song, the language and tune of which was alike unknown to us, except that we recognized in it that Name which is above every name; which it was music indeed to find cherished and adored in so dark a land as Vate, by a handful of people surrounded by cruel heathen, and with about the smallest possible aid from the churches of the Saviour. Petela then requested Pomare to pray, gave out another hymn, made a short address, and concluded with prayer. We then gave a short exhortation to the people, Petela acting as interpreter; we admonished the people to attend to the instructions of the teachers now left among them, and to supply them with food, and aid them in building a house, in order that their health might be preserved in the new and trying climate to which they were willing to expose themselves for their benefit. Whilst the congregation was dispersing, we addressed a few words to the new teachers, advising them to take care of their health, to get a good house as speedily as possible, but not to overwork themselves in building it; and not to be too hasty in changing modes of worship, and other things to which the people had become accustomed, but which they might think objectionable. We were then conducted to the place which had been occupied by the former teachers' house, on which it was proposed to erect one for the new teachers. It was the highest ground in the neighbourhood, and appeared to us to be the best site which could be selected. Each of the teachers presented us with a mat, and others made a present of yams to the ship. The two young men of the place whom we brought from Samoa were enthusiastically welcomed by their friends, and two others were entrusted to our care for the next year. We cannot but feel a trembling anxiety for the health of the devoted men and their families, who have willingly offered themselves to occupy this interesting post; and we earnestly entreat that their lives may be precious in the eyes of the Lord, and that His work may be established in Vate through their instrumentality. At Vate we took leave of the New Hebrides group, and sailed for the Loyalty Islands; not, however, without grief of heart, that the numerous islands of the former group, stretching far away in a continuous line to the northward, the inhabitants of many of which are reported to be accessible, and desirous of Christian teachers, should year after year be passed by, because the churches of Christ fail to furnish agents to go up and possess them in the name of the Lord."

The above extract gives a deeply interesting glimpse of the "little spot enclosed by grace" out of the surrounding darkness. Delightful indeed must it have been to hear the praises of Jesus sung by Vatean lips in such circumstances. Speedily may the day dawn when His dear Name shall be as ointment poured forth throughout the entire length and breadth of this beautiful island! Towards this consummation an additional step was taken when the island was again visited in October, 1860; and with the account of that step, and the information furnished by the report of that visit, our notice of Vate must close. Dr. Turner, who visited the island on that occasion, reported as follows:—

"Tuesday, October 18th.—Anchored in Erakor Bay, on the south-west side of Vate. The Rarotongan teachers, Teamaru and Toma, with a number of the people, came off immediately. The two families were well, but we were sorry to learn that Teautoa had died since last voyage, and his wife also. Fever and ague seemed to be the principal complaint of the former, but the latter died in childbed. The whole of the settlement of Erakor is nominally Christian. The population is about 250. All are kind to the teachers, and supply them with food without stint and without price. Eight natives of the place are employed by the teachers as helpers in the work; and these with six others, they think, might be admitted to church-fellowship were a church constituted. There has been no war between Erakor and the neighbouring tribes for a long time, but still the way for the teachers preaching in other settlements is hedged up. The people forbid their going there to *preach*, owing to the superstitious belief that unusual sickness and death follow wherever the new religion is received. Still, the teachers have done a good deal during the last twelve months. They have acquired some fluency in the difficult language, and have superintended the building of a new chapel, twice the size of the old one.

"As the teachers had suffered from fever and ague, they expressed a desire that we should try and occupy this place by Aneiteum teachers, who are more likely to stand the climate. I said that this was our wish also, and that we had now brought two teachers and their wives from that island, for the purpose of making a commencement. They were pleased with the arrangement, agreed to remain for another year, and we proceeded to give them their supplies. After this, Captain Williams and I went on shore with the new teachers and others we had to land at this place—ten individuals, namely, the Aneiteum teachers, Thevthev and Vathea, their wives, and one child; the two Vate natives who were taken last year on a visit to Samoa and Rarotonga; the two we picked up at Eramanga; and the child of one of the Rarotongan teachers.

"After pulling for half an hour up the beautiful lagoon we reached the landing-place, and there a crowd of natives waited our arrival, who gave us a warm and hospitable welcome. A table was spread for the captain and myself in the house of the teacher; and in another house provision was made for the boats' crews and the newly-arrived teachers. After conversation with the teachers, the chief Pomare, and some of the people, about the new teachers, it was arranged that for the present they take up their abode with the Rarotongan teachers. We then had the native drum beat, to call all to service. The new chapel looks clean, light, and commodious. It is 45 feet by 35 feet, wattled and plastered, thatched with grass, pulpit built with coral stones, and some rough forms throughout as seats. About 150 assembled in ten minutes. One of the teachers gave out a hymn and prayed. I gave an address in Samoan, through a Vate man as interpreter, and he, in conclusion, conducted singing and prayed. All were remarkably attentive and orderly. Soon after the service the captain and I were led to two separate heaps of yams, taro, sugarcane, and cocoa-nuts, covered with a mat or two, the one was a present to him, the other to me. By and by, two lads who had been to Samoa came each with a pig as a present to me; and presently an old lady came along with a cooked fowl and some hot yams in a basket, as a present to the captain and myself. This old lady, who was dressed in a straw bonnet and a Turkey red cotton gown, turned out to be the wife of the chief. Meanwhile, Mr. Griffin, the second officer, was busy on the beach buying pigs and yams for the ship. We were pleased to see the great change at this place in their demands while bartering. Formerly, it was all trinkets and tobacco; now it is calico and shirts. 'Calico, calico, calico!' was the constant cry. Having filled the two boats, and promising to send in again in the morning some more Manchester goods, with which to buy the yams and pigs they had still to sell, we said good-bye, and got out to the ship before dark.

"Wednesday, October 19th.—After another day's friendly intercourse with the people of Erakor, we weighed anchor in the afternoon, and sailed for Maré, of the Loyalty Islands. While at Eramanga, we heard that a Captain Fletcher and a boat's crew from a sandal-wooding vessel were lately attacked by the natives about Hat Island, at the entrance to Sema (or Havannah Harbour). We made inquiry about it while at Erakor, but could not obtain any account of the affair on which we could rely. It is a fact, however, that the natives attacked the said party, and mangled some of them with their tomahawks."

Thus we take our leave of Vate, in circumstances fitted to inspire gratitude and encourage hope. True we have little to show for so protracted and costly a struggle. Still there is much in the past history and present state of the mission that is full of promise. He who so clearly directed our way when the Macedonian cry reached us in Dillon's Bay, has not left us without indications of His gracious approval all along, and these indications are becoming more and more definite. What is wanted now, is missionaries to step in and take advantage of the present favourable opening. Had we four, or even two men of the right stamp, high hopes might be entertained; but, so long as the island is left to native labourers, much advance cannot be expected. "Pray ye therefore the Lord of the harvest, that He will send forth labourers into His harvest." A more promising field on which to prepare a native agency, to push forward the work of evangelization in the islands beyond, can scarcely be conceived than Vate. Would that we had the means of at once fully and effectively occupying it! May the time when our desires shall be realised speedily come!

CHAPTER X.

NEW CALEDONIA AND THE ISLE OF PINES.

NEW CALEDONIA.

" The isles shall wait for His law."—Isaiah xlii. 4.

OLLOWING in our missionary track, we now pass to another group of islands, namely, that of New Caledonia. Under this designation we include the Loyalty group, consisting of Lifu, Maré, and Uea, and a small island named Toka. Besides these, there are several other islets, none of which are inhabited. According to Captain Erskine, the Loyalty Islands are separated from New Caledonia by a channel forty-five miles wide. "They are," he remarks, "unlike the New Hebrides, being low, flat, coral islands, the north-western extremity of the group being apparently still submerged, and forming a prolonged line of dangerous reefs. The Loyalty Islands have scarcely as yet found a place on our charts; and their western sides, and the position of their different points had never been ascertained until our hurried visit in the *Havannah*." We shall return to these islands in subsequent chapters. Our present business is with *the* island of the group, New Caledonia.

Captain Erskine speaks of New Caledonia as follows:— "The important island of New Caledonia, which, from its position and the excellence of its harbours, may be considered as commanding the communication of Australia with India, China, Panama, and California, was discovered by Captain Cook.

"New Caledonia is about two hundred miles long and twenty-five broad; a central rocky ridge of considerable elevation extending along its whole length, and a barrier coral reef surrounding, with the exception of a very few miles, the entire coast, both on its northern and southern sides. This reef, which is distant from the shore from two to twelve miles, with many openings allowing the largest ships to enter, forms a continuous channel round the island, in almost every part of which anchorage may be found in from four to twenty-five fathoms. A continuation of the reef almost connects the south-east end of New Caledonia with the Isle of Pines, and stretches out fully one hundred and fifty miles from the north-west point, occasionally dotted with islands, some of which are inhabited.

"The New Caledonians, who have no name for their whole island, are a fine and intelligent-looking race, resembling in physical characteristics the Figians, although in religion and language they differ entirely."

The island of New Caledonia is the last link of a chain of islands and groups which extends over a space of nearly five thousand miles. Though the last in this mighty chain, it is by no means the least important. On the contrary, it is on some accounts decidedly the most important. If we except New Zealand, which is out of the range of the chain in question, New Caledonia is without a rival among the isles of the Pacific. Its extent, its harbour, Port St. Vincent—which is said to have no superior anywhere—its climate, its streams and forests, and, above all, its proximity to Australia,—these place it at the head of the great island family to which it belongs.

It was on the 14th of September, 1774, after Captain Cook had finished his survey of the New Hebrides, and was on his way to revisit New Zealand, that he fell in with New Caledonia. After some considerable difficulty, arising from the many dangerous shoals which abound on the coast, he found safe anchorage. He anchored on the 15th of September, at a place now well known—Balade. Here he remained a week, diligently improving the

DISCOVERY OF THE ISLAND.

opportunities he enjoyed of gaining an acquaintance with the country and its inhabitants. The natives, as they appeared to him and acted towards him, present a striking contrast to the views given of them by subsequent visitors. No traces of that invincible treachery and ferocity, of which we have heard so much of late years, were discovered by Cook; and the probability is that the altered conduct of the natives is to be charged chiefly to the account of their visitors. Were the behaviour of these fully known, it would be no matter of surprise that the natives act as they do. It would rather seem a wonder that they do not kill every white man that places himself in their power.

The following extracts from Cook give an account of his first intercourse with the natives, and embrace various interesting particulars.

"We had hardly got to anchor, before we were surrounded by a great number of natives, in sixteen or eighteen canoes, the most of whom were without any sort of weapons. At first they were shy of coming near the ship; but in a short time we prevailed on the people in one boat to get close enough to receive some presents; these were lowered down to them by a rope, to which in return they tied two fish, which stunk intolerably, as did those they gave us in the morning. These mutual exchanges bringing on a kind of confidence, two ventured on board the ship, and presently after she was filled with them, and we had the company of several at dinner in the cabin. Our pea-soup, salt beef, and pork, they had no curiosity to taste, but they ate of some yams, which we happened to have yet left, calling them 'vobbee;' this name is not unlike 'vofee,' as they are called at most of the islands, except Malicolo. Nevertheless, we found these people spoke a language new to us. Like all the nations we had lately seen, the men were almost naked, having hardly any covering but such a wrapper as is used at Malicolo. They were curious in examining every part of the ship, which they viewed with uncommon attention.

They had not the least knowledge of goats, hogs, dogs, or cats, and not even a name for one of them. They seemed fond of large spike-nails and pieces of red cloth, or indeed of any colour; but red was their favourite.

"After dinner, I went on shore with two armed boats, having with us one of the natives, who had attached himself to me. We landed on a sandy beach, before a vast number of people, who had got together with no other intent than to see us, for many of them had not a stick in their hands. Consequently we were received with great courtesy, and with the surprise natural for a people to express at seeing men and things so new to them as we must be. I made presents to all those my friend pointed out, who were either old men or such as seemed of some note; but he took not the least notice of some women, who stood behind the crowd, holding my hand when I was going to give them some beads and medals.

"While we were with them, having inquired by signs for fresh water, some pointed to the east and others to the west. My friend undertook to conduct us to it, and embarked with us for that purpose. We rowed about two miles up the coast, to the east, where the shore was mostly covered with mangrove trees; and entered amongst them by a narrow creek or river, which brought us to a little straggling village above all the mangroves; there we landed, and were shown fresh water. The ground near this village was finely cultivated, being laid out in plantations of sugarcanes, plantains, yams, and other roots; and watered by little rills, conducted by art from the main stream, whose source was in the hills. Here were some cocoa-nut trees, which did not seem burdened with fruit. We heard the crowing of cocks, but saw none. Some roots were baking on a fire, in an earthen jar, which would have held six or eight gallons; nor did we doubt of its being their own manufacture."

After mentioning various other matters, which we must omit, Cook gives the following account of another excursion on shore, which throws light on many important things connected with the country and the people:—

"Early in the morning of the 7th, the watering-party, and a guard under the command of an officer, were sent ashore; and soon after a party of us went to take a view of the country. As soon as we landed, we made known our design to the natives, and two of them undertaking to be our guides, conducted us up the hills by a tolerably good path. In our route we met several people, most of whom turned back with us; so that at last our train was numerous. Some we met who wanted us to return, but we paid no regard to their signs, nor did they seem uneasy as we proceeded. At length we reached the summit of one of the hills, from which we saw the sea in two places, between some advanced hills on the opposite or S.W. side of the land. This was a useful discovery, as it enabled us to judge of the width of the land, which in this part did not exceed ten leagues. Between those advanced hills and the ridge we were upon, there was a large valley, through which ran a serpentine river. On the banks of this were several plantations and some villages, whose inhabitants we had met on the road, and found more on the top of the hill gazing at the ship, as might be supposed. The plain or flat land, which lies along the shore we were upon, appeared from the hills to a great advantage. The winding streams which ran through it, the plantations, the little straggling villages, the variety of the woods, and the shoals on the coast, so variegating the scene that the whole might afford a picture for romance. Indeed, if it were not for those fertile spots on the plains, and some few on the sides of the mountains, the whole country might be called a dreary waste. The mountains and other high places are, for the most part, incapable of cultivation, consisting chiefly of rocks, many of which are full of mundicks; the little soil which is upon them is scorched and burnt up with the sun; it is, nevertheless, coated with coarse grass and other plants, and here and there trees and shrubs. The country in general bore a strong resemblance to some parts of New Holland, under the same parallel of latitude; several of its natural productions seem to be the same, and the woods being without underwood, as in that country. The reefs on the coast, and several other peculiarities, were obvious to every one that had seen both countries. We observed all the north-east coast to be covered with shoals and breakers, extending to the northward beyond the island of Balabea, till they were lost in the horizon."

The writer has not seen the parts of the island to which these extracts refer, and so is unable to make any addition to them. The following description, also from Cook, will interest the reader:—

"I shall conclude our transactions at this place with some account of the country and its inhabitants. They are strong, robust, active, well-made people; courteous and friendly, and not in the least addicted to pilfering, which is more than can be said of any other nation in this sea. They are nearly of the same colour as the natives of Tanna, but have better features, more agreeable countenances, and are a much stouter race—a few being seen who measured six feet four inches. I observed some who had thick lips, flat noses, full cheeks, and in some degree the features and look of a negro." Many other interesting particulars are added, which we must pass over. Of their houses he gives the following description:—"Their houses, or at least most of them, are circular, something like a bee-hive, and full as close and warm (they look very much like a hay-rick); the entrance is by a small door, or long square hole, just big enough to admit a man bent double; the side walls are about four feet and a half high, but the roof is lofty and peaked to a point at the top, above which is a post or stick of wood, and generally ornamented either with carving or shells, or both. The framing is of small spars, reeds, &c., and both sides and roof are thick and close covered with thatch,

THE NATIVES AND THEIR HOUSES. 241

made of coarse, long grass. In the inside of the house
are set up posts, to which cross spars are fastened, and
platforms made for the convenience of laying anything on.
Some houses have two floors one above the other. The
floor is laid with dry grass, and there are mats spread for

A NATIVE HOUSE.

the principal people to sleep or sit on. In most of them
are found two fire-places, and commonly a fire burning;
and as there was no vent for the smoke but by the door,
the whole house was both smoky and hot, insomuch that
we, who are not used to such an atmosphere, could hardly

endure it a moment. In some respects their habitations are neat; for, besides the ornaments at the top, I saw some with carved door-posts. Upon the whole, their houses are better calculated for a cold than a hot climate; and, as they have no partitions in them, they have little privacy. They have no great variety of household utensils; the earthen jars before mentioned being the only article worth notice. Each family has at least one of them, in which they bake their roots, and perhaps their fish, &c.

"I have before mentioned that the country bears great resemblance to New South Wales, or New Holland, and that some of its natural productions are the same. In particular, we found here the tree which is covered with soft, white, ragged bark, easily peeled off, and is, as I am told, the same that in the East Indies is used for caulking ships. The wood is very hard; the leaves are long and narrow, of a pale green, and a fine aromatic; so that it may properly be said to belong to that continent. Nevertheless, here are several plants, &c., common to the eastern and northern islands, and even a species of the passion flower, which, I am told, has never been known to grow wild anywhere but in America. Our botanist did not complain for want of employment at this place, every day bringing something new in botany or other branches of natural history. Land birds, indeed, are not numerous, but several are new. One of these is a kind of crow—at least so we called it, though it is not half so big, and its feathers are tinged with blue. They also have some very beautiful turtle-doves, and other small birds, such as I never saw before."

Before coming to our main subject, we may give a little additional information respecting the manners, customs, etc., of the natives. It seems clear, from the account given by Cook of those with whom he had intercourse, and also from the accounts of our teachers who were on New Caledonia, that not only do the natives of that island differ from those of the New Hebrides and other Polynesian races, but that there is considerable variety among themselves. The earthenware jars of which Cook speaks are not found on the smaller islands, nor on the east end of the larger one, nor on any other island or group of the Pacific, except the Figis and Espiritu Santo. This is a curious fact, and would seem to connect a part of New Caledonia with the Figians and the people of Espiritu Santo. The wrapper also, mentioned by Cook, is not found on the smaller islands, nor on any part of the large island which I have seen. I know of no place where it is worn, except the New Hebrides. The Indians on the Isthmus of Darien, it is said, use it, but in a somewhat different way. Another important thing is, that the language which is spoken on the more westerly part is widely different from that found on the east end and on the smaller islands. Thus it seems probable that there are at least two different races on the group; not at all an unlikely thing, considering the extent of the main island. The natives with whom we have had intercourse—comprising those of Lifu, Maré, the Isle of Pines, and the east end of the large island—are a fine race of people. They are, as already intimated, a different race from their neighbours on the New Hebrides; nor have they any affinity, so far as my knowledge extends, to any of the tribes to the east, the difference between them and these being as marked as the difference in the appearance, formation, and physical character of the islands and groups which they respectively occupy. They are rather above the average height, strong, and well proportioned, and their countenances are generally good and agreeable. They seem to have no affinity whatever to the Malay race and about as little to other tribes of Western Polynesia.

On the island of Uea two distinct races are found, the one allied to the Eastern Polynesian tribes, the others to those of the west.

In colour, the natives of the New Caledonian group resemble more the Western than the Eastern Polynesians, but differ considerably from both. They are a sort of dark drab or grey; they do not tattoo, nor do they generally paint their bodies, but many daub themselves over with white sand; and, by some artificial process, they change the natural colour of their hair, which is black, to different shades of brown, and in some cases to white. It very much resembles coarse wool. And when, as is sometimes the case, they paint their faces jet black, and have their bodies stuck over with white sand, and their hair white, they look very singular.

Both sexes wear ornaments; these consist of earrings and necklaces made of tortoise-shell, also armlets made of shells, which they wear above the wrists, etc.

There is one remarkable difference between the natives of these islands and their neighbours, which deserves particular notice. Throughout the New Hebrides and many other islands and groups of the Pacific, the chiefs are very numerous, and possess very little authority. Here the case is different, at least as regards the smaller islands of the group, On the Isle of Pines there is, or was, only one chief, whose authority was absolute. On Lifu there are two, and the same number on Maré; and these, with a few counsellers, rule their respective islands.

Nowhere perhaps is woman more degraded and debased than on the New Caledonian group. Polygamy, with its attendant evils, prevails to a great extent. Woman is not the companion of man, but his slave and drudge, whom he values chiefly, because she ministers to his ease and gratification. What a humiliating view does this give us of man, when left to act under the unrestrained promptings of his own heart! Where, alas! is the boasted nobleness and generosity of his nature? These are assuredly no general characteristics of man as he is found in heathen lands. In order to the development of these, other influences must be brought to bear upon him than he is subject to there. God's remedy must be applied; the Gospel must be made known, and take effect.

The natives of this group are not less addicted to the revolting practice of cannibalism than their neighbours. War is less frequent upon them than upon the islands where a more democratic form of government prevails; but when it does occur, it is of a much more serious character, involving not two or more small districts, but a whole island or islands. This is one disadvantage that arises from so large an extent of territory being subject to one chief.

The houses are very superior to those of the neighbouring islanders, and *they* are the same all over the group. Some of them are not inferior to the general run of native houses in Eastern Polynesia, and they are palaces compared with the wretched huts of the New Hebrides.

Their canoes also are quite in keeping with their houses; they are very superior for a people in their state—they are double. Two large single canoes, thirty, forty, or even more feet long, are fixed together by means of transverse spars; over these, planks are laid and made fast; these form a deck, on which a house is erected which affords shelter. In the house is a hearth, on which they kindle a fire for cooking, or any other purpose for which they want it. They use a large sail made of matting; and with a good breeze and a moderate sea, their vessels sail well. They are awkward and unmanageable, however, in rough weather; and there is no small danger in venturing any considerable distance in them. The Tongans (Friendly Islanders) have similar canoes. Their large and comparatively commodious vessels are a temptation to them to attempt much longer voyages than their neighbours, who have only single canoes; and the consequence is, that a much greater number of them get lost at sea, or carried away to strange lands, than the less adventurous tribes of other groups. We have found Friendly Islanders in every part of Western Polynesia to which we have yet gone; and it remains to be ascertained to how many other islands they have found their way, highly important results have arisen from this, as we shall see hereafter.

Their canoes will carry thirty, forty, fifty, or more persons. When it is remembered that they are made without any iron fastenings, and that till within a few years the natives had no iron tools, one cannot think meanly of their ingenuity and perseverance.

They do not, like the Aneiteumese, throw their dead into the sea, but deposit them in the earth. Cook describes one of their graves, which some of his people saw, as follows:—"In one of them, they were informed, lay the remains of a chief who was slain in battle: and his grave, which bore some resemblance to a mole-hill, was decorated with spears, darts, paddles, etc., all stuck upright in the ground about it." Like all heathen nations, they mourn as those that have no hope. They daub themselves with mud, in token of mourning, and give violent and extravagant expression to their grief— which, however, soon subsides. They make offerings and render a sort of homage to their deceased ancestors. On all great occasions offerings, with prayers and thanksgivings, are presented to these. There is a class of persons who officiate on these occasions. The offerings consist entirely of vegetable food. It is cooked in the neighbourhood of the grave, and part of it, according to the Chinese custom, is presented to the occupant of the "narrow house," accompanied with prayers and thanksgivings. The food thus presented is left to decompose.

Their worship is not confined to human spirits; they believe in the existence of spirits superior to these. The people of the Isle of Pines have four principal deities, and the same probably are believed in and worshipped on the other islands. Our information on these points, however, is very limited.

As regards the population of the island we are not in circumstances to speak positively. Cook says, speaking of the parts he visited, "although the inhabitants upon the whole may not be numerous, the island is not thinly peopled on the sea-coast, and on the plains and valleys that are capable of cultivation."

Our efforts to bring New Caledonia under missionary culture had their commencement in an arrangement entered into between Mr. Williams, on behalf of the London Missionary Society, and the United Secession Church in Scotland (now the United Presbyterian Church), about the year 1834. The agents of the London Missionary Society were to open the door, and to prepare the way by means of native agency; and the United Secession Church was to send missionaries to take up and carry on the work. A sum of money was also contributed by that body of Christians towards defraying the expenses of the preparatory work. It was the intention of Mr. Williams to visit the group, with a view to commence operations upon it, when he set out on his last missionary voyage. That, however, was not to be. He was permitted to plan—it was reserved for others to carry into execution. It was during the second voyege of the *Camden* among the islands of Western Polynesia that a footing was gained on the group. On the 17th of April, 1840, about five months after the death of Mr. Williams, the vessel called, having on board the Rev. Thomas Heath, and a number of teachers. An unsuccessful effort was made on that occasion to introduce teachers to the island. The party visited Port St. Vincent, and did their utmost to obtain a footing there, but no opening could be found.

The next attempt, the circumstances connected with which we proceed to notice, was attended with a different result. It was in the month of April, 1841, that we succeeded in placing Christian teachers on New Caledonia. We had visited the Isle of Pines, on which teachers had been placed twelve months before, and had induced a young man, a native of New Caledonia, whom we found there, to accompany us. We took also one of the teachers from the Isle of Pines with us to assist in our important and difficult work. Matuku, the chief of the Isle of Pines, was very much opposed, from motives of jealousy, no doubt, to our taking teachers to New Caledonia. He threw every obstacle he could in our way, and did everything in his power to dissuade us. We were not to be deterred or diverted from our purpose; so, having got our guide and the teacher on board, we sailed for New Caledonia on the 14th April, 1841. Towards evening of the same day we were abreast of the part of the island to which our guide belonged, and where lived parties who had been to the Isle of Pines, and had learned something about Christianity and the missionary ship from the teachers; the teachers had told them about the time the vessel was likely to arrive, so they were on the look out. As we drew near the shore, large numbers were seen collecting on the beach.

Between us and them was a formidable barrier—a reef, over which the sea broke heavily, and the night was at hand. A boat was lowered, and we pulled in close to the reef, but there was no opening, and, if there had been, it would not have been a prudent step, for us to go in; so we could only lie-to in our boat, and endeavour by signs to convince the natives of our friendly intentions. After some considerable hesitancy they waded out one after another towards the reef. But how was that to be crossed? All were brought to a stand, and it seemed very doubtful whether any would venture. At length, we were cheered by seeing one and another making their way through the foaming breakers towards the boat; and in a short time we were surrounded by a large number of noisy and greatly-excited visitors, all eager to get into the boat. They recognised the teacher and their own countryman from the Isle of Pines, so we had their confidence at once. We had no small difficulty in keeping them from capsizing or swamping the boat. Happily, among those who swam out to us was the very man of whom we were in search— the son of the chief of the district off which we were, who

MISSION PRINTING OFFICE, LEULUMOENGA.

had been to the Isle of Pines, and had had intercourse with the teachers. We got him into the boat, and after a great deal of coaxing, and giving little presents, we succeeded in getting the number in the boat reduced to three or four, and returned to the ship.

On the following morning we again went in with the boat, and found Nathotha, the chief, the father of the young man mentioned above. He accompanied us on board; our object was explained to him; he expressed his willingness to receive the teachers, and engaged to protect them, furnish them with provisions, and aid them in every way in his power. All being arranged, the teachers and their property were landed, and thus the fondly-cherished desire of our hearts was accomplished. A large and rather tumultuous crowd were assembled on the beach when they landed. All seemed much pleased, and the reception of the teachers was all we could expect under the circumstances. It was on the 15th April, 1841, that the important object was effected. The remarkable manner in which the way had been prepared, the facility with which the object was accomplished, and the reception given to the teachers by the chief and the people, were all of the most gratifying character; and sanguine were the hopes to which they gave birth with reference to the future history of New Caledonia.

In the month of August, 1843, the missionary vessel again visited the island. Mataio, one of the teachers whom we placed on the island, had lived only a few months; Taniela, the remaining one, had been joined by another from the Isle of Pines, and matters on the whole had gone on encouragingly. The mission was reinforced by the addition of a very efficient teacher from Rarotonga; and Messrs. Buzacott and Slatyer, who visited the island on that occasion, left it in a promising state.

After this visit the *Camden* returned to England, and upwards of two years passed before her successor, the *John Williams*, came to our assistance. It is a hazardous thing for an infant mission to be left for any considerable time unvisited. Who can tell but that a visit during the interval referred to might have averted the calamities that came upon our missions in the Isle of Pines and New Caledonia?

The *John Williams* reached Samoa in February, 1845, and on the first of April following, she sailed on her first missionary voyage; the Rev. G. Turner and the writer proceeding in her as a deputation from the Samoan mission. We made the island of New Caledonia on the 12th of May. From what we had heard at the other islands we had hoped to find everything going on prosperously. Bitter disappointment awaited us, as will presently appear. One of the teachers had finished his course, and the remaining two had passed through great trials, and been exposed to the most imminent peril. Matuku, who had murdered his own teachers, had been striving with untiring perseverance to accomplish the destruction of those on the neighbouring islands also. The chiefs of Maré and Lifu had given him a positive refusal, declaring that they would never kill their teachers. That *they* could do, as they had no political dependence on the Isle of Pines, but it was otherwise with New Caledonia. A considerable part of that island had been subjugated by the Isle of Pines, and was under the despotic sway of its barbarous chief. Immediately after the murder of his own teachers, he gave the weapon (a hatchet) with which the foul deed was done to Nathotha, the chief of the district on New Caledonia where the teachers were located, telling him how it had been employed, and charging him to take it and kill all the Samoans and Rarotongans on New Caledonia. Happily, Nathotha disregarded the injunction, though by so doing he exposed himself to the anger of one whose wrath was indeed "as the roaring of a lion." When Matuku heard that his orders had not been executed, he was greatly enraged, and sent a message to the New Caledonians to the following purport :—" Why are not the teachers killed ? If you do not kill them, I will come and kill and eat you." Still the teachers were not killed, and the old man, apparently determined to effect his purpose, went across himself, but was prevented by some cause from attempting it. A second time he visited New Caledonia, but was still kept from the execution of his purpose. His object appeared to be to get the New Caledonians to kill the teachers. This they firmly refused to do, telling him he might do as he pleased, but they would not kill their teachers. He seemed to shrink from coming to an open rupture with them, by attempting to force them to do as he wished. Hence his hesitating and irresolute conduct.

The most determined effort to effect the destruction of the teachers was made a few weeks before our visit, by a party sent no doubt by the same enemy. It consisted of sons of his, and others; they seemed to have crossed to New Caledonia for the express purpose of destroying these innocent men. On the day which they had fixed for the perpetration of the barbarous deed, a party of nine or ten went to the house of the teachers. Noa, one of them, was at the door. A man named Uaise, a nephew of Matuku, who appeared to be the leader of the party, abruptly accosted him, with the design, no doubt, of provoking a quarrel, and preparing the way for the accomplishment of their object. "When," said he, pointing to some graves near the house, "when will these men live again ? You say they will live again; when will they live again ?" "It is true," replied Noa, "they will live again; when the Son of God comes at the end of the world they will live again, and all who ever lived will live again, and be judged; the righteous will live for ever in heaven in the presence of God, but the wicked will be cast into everlasting fire." "You are liars," replied Uaise, "they will not live again; how can they live again ? Their bodies are gone to corruption; their bones are separated from each other; how can they live again?" Taunga, the other teacher, who was in the house, heard the conversation, and came out, and invited the party in. They complied with the invitation, and Taunga addressed them, reiterating and enlarging upon the statements of Noa respecting the resurrection, the judgment, etc. The natives also reiterated the charge of falsehood. While Taunga was still talking with them, four men, three of whom were sons of Matuku, came running into the house armed with hatchets. One of these took his station in front of Noa, and close to him; and another stationed himself behind Taunga. The address was of course at an end. One of the ruffians seized Noa's right arm with his left hand, and raised his hatchet above his head to strike the fatal blow. The other, who was by Taunga, also raised his hatchet over the head of the intended victim. The teachers bowed their heads, lifted up their hearts to God, and calmly resigned themselves to His will. All was ready. It appeared as if the deed were done; hope was extinct. It seemed as if nothing short of a miracle could avail. Buma, a son of Matuku, who stood over Taunga, nodded to Uaise, on whom the issue appeared to depend whether they should strike. By some sign which was understood, he replied, "No!" The scale was turned; the arm of the murderer was arrested by an unseen hand; and the party dispersed, leaving the teachers with feelings somewhat resembling those of a primitive servant of God, and in circumstances in which they might almost have adopted his language, "Now I know that God hath sent His angel, and hath delivered me out of the hand of Herod."

The teachers had many other narrow escapes, which we cannot particularize. They had been "in deaths oft." Attempts had been made on the lives of one or both of them six or seven times, and two of these were by parties belonging to New Caledonia, though the chief there and the people generally were their friends.

There is scarcely anything which, under God, contributes so much to safety as calm self-possession. One striking illustration of this had occurred. A party came upon the teachers one day with bad intentions. Instead of attempting flight or resistance, Taunga said to them, "Come, kill us; you may stop our mouths in death, but you cannot hinder the Word of God; that will continue to live and grow." They were struck with amazement, and said one to another, "See, that man is not afraid; it is because their God is powerful; let them alone."

One of the teachers, Noa, wished to return to Samoa. Taunga, notwithstanding the perilous circumstances in which they were placed, was willing to remain. We could not, however, think of leaving him alone, so we were compelled to let go our hold upon the island. Had we had another disposable teacher on board we might have made an attempt at some other part of the island. This, however, was not the case; and, with great reluctance, we made up our minds to a temporary abandonment of the island. Very temporary, as we had hoped. Sad, however, is it to think that now, after the lapse of fifteen years, the island is in much the same state as it was when we left it. Changes indeed have come over it, great changes; but they have not been of a character to benefit the natives. New Caledonia still is a dreary province of Satan's dark domain. The delay in reoccupying the island has been to us a matter of deep regret, but it has been unavoidable. We have never lost sight of it. Among the smaller islands of the group our efforts have been continued, and the reoccupation of it is only a question of time and practicability.

THE ISLE OF PINES.

The brief tale we have to tell relative to the Isle of Pines may as well be appended to our notice of New Caledonia.

The Isle of Pines is a small island, about twenty-five or thirty miles distant from the south-east end of New Caledonia. It is low, having but one small hill in the centre, from which the land slopes gradually down to the sea. Much of the land near the coast, and several islets in the neighbourhood, are covered with pines; and from this circumstance Cook gave it the name it now bears—the native name is Konie. We saw it only on one side, and so were unable to form an estimate of its extent. It has an excellent harbour, and on this and other accounts is very important, as being so near the large island.

The island was visited by the Rev. Thomas Heath, in the missionary brig *Camden*, and Christian teachers were placed on it in April, 1840. A second visit was made by the writer in April, 1841.

We made the island on Saturday, the 10th of April, but did not get to anchor till next day. We found the mission in a very encouraging state. The teachers had been kindly treated. When they had been about two months on the island the people had abandoned heathenism as a body, and professed to receive Christianity: and we found them earnestly desirous to have a missionary or missionaries to reside among them. From all we saw and heard, we thought we might safely venture to land. Arrangements were accordingly made, and a party consisting of four, two of whom were ladies, proceeded on shore. The ladies, were, doubtless, the first foreigners of their sex that ever set foot on the Isle of Pines. The chief, Matuku, with a number of the people, met us at the landing-place, and seemed greatly pleased with our visit. He led us inland about a mile, or a mile and a half, to a village, in the centre of which was a large house, into which we were conducted. All the way between the landing-place and the village our train continued to increase, and when we reached the house we were surrounded by several hundreds. The house into which we were conducted had been a sacred place, in which the natives had been accustomed to worship their imaginary deities. It was now appropriated to a more worthy object, the worship of the living and true God. It was a large house, capable of containing four or five hundred people. An immemorial custom was set aside on the occasion of our visit. Females had been forbidden to enter the house. It was a sacred place, which must not be polluted by their presence. Our attention was arrested by observing them skulking and crouching about outside; the subject was talked of, and permission was given them to come in. There was some difficulty, however, in getting them to do so; they appeared as if they could not believe that it was really meant that they should.

Shortly after we went into the house an occurrence took place which revealed the character of Matuku in anything but an attractive light, and which showed the absolute subjection of the poor people to his tyrannical sway. He was very desirous to make a favourable impression upon us—to appear a man of great consequence; and, in order to this to have all due respect and deference paid to him by his people in our presence, every individual in passing him was required to do so in a crouching position. Some did not bow sufficiently low to please the despotic savage, and, to our surprise and alarm, he rushed upon the offenders and began to beat them most unmercifully with his club. One of his sons flew to his assistance, and commenced using his club freely also. The teachers were speedily between them and their victims: the one ran to the father, the other to the son, and succeeded in getting them pacified. While all this was going on we, especially the ladies, did not feel very easy. We were completely in the power of the savages, and the scene we witnessed was not such as to make us feel very secure. We were safe, however. The chief seemed to apprehend that we should feel alarmed, and when all was over begged the teachers to assure us that we were in no danger. This was rather an odd introduction to what followed. When order was restored, we had a short service. One of the teachers interpreted, and I gave an address from the words, "Unto you is the word of this salvation sent." After the service, the chief, with a numerous train, escorted us to the boat; and we were glad to find ourselves again safe on board the *Camden*.

At the earnest request of Matuku, some of us were induced to repeat our visit on the following day. Matuku wished to make us a present, and he was very desirous that we should go on shore and have it presented to us in due form. His anxiety was to make a favourable impression, with the view of obtaining missionaries. The present was a very formal and tedious affair. A large part of the day was occupied in getting it together and presenting it to us. It consisted of sugar-canes, bananas, yams, etc. Several hundred people were collected, and they did their utmost to please us and show their respect.

Great care is necessary in dealing with a savage people; mistakes and misunderstandings are so apt to arise, and it is often a difficult matter to get them rectified. We had an illustration of this on the present occasion. After making our present to the chief, we had some conversation with him relative to his wish to obtain missionaries, during which I asked, among other things, "Whether he would protect missionaries and their property in the event of their coming?" At this he became greatly excited. He inferred, from my proposing such a question, that the teachers had spoken unfavourably of him, and was very angry with them. He started to his feet, and replied in a very excited manner, that "If a ship had come to his land and been repaired, and gone without being injured; if a canoe from Tonga, the Friendly Islands, had been cast upon his shores, and those belonging to it spared; and if the teachers were all safe, was it likely that they would kill missionaries or deprive them of their property?"

"A soft answer turneth away wrath." A few quiet words, assuring the old man that his suspicions respecting the teachers were altogether groundless, directing him to the fact that we were giving him the best evidence we could that we had confidence in him, by placing ourselves entirely in his power, a thing we had not done at any other island we had visited, and that we wished a promise from him to write to Christians in England for their satisfaction, set all to rights; and the whole passed off in a manner mutually gratifying to the natives and to us. The desire for missionaries was very great, and the prospects on the whole were highly encouraging, and awakened sanguine hopes with reference to the future; and had we

THE MISSION SETTLEMENT AT BORABORA.

then, or even twelve or eighteen months later, been in circumstances to have placed foreign missionaries on the island, these hopes might have been fully realised. Such, however, was not the case. The favourable opportunity passed unimproved, and the consequences have been of the most deplorable character.

It is remarkable that the untoward events which led to the ruin of the mission took their rise from our present visit. So mysteriously are things of the most contrary character linked together in the present world! Very little was known of the island prior to our visit. The attractions it possessed for commercial adventure had not been brought to light. During our visit it was unhappily discovered that there was sandal-wood on the island, and when we reached Sydney one of our crew made this known. There was no lack of adventurers to go in search of the newly-discovered treasure. Vessels, I know not how many, were fitted out; the services of the party who gave the information were secured; and the quiet island, which had hitherto been so little known, became at once a scene of bustle and excitement. It was brought into an entirely new position, and a new set of influences of the most unfavourable character were brought to bear upon it. The pride, haughtiness, and covetousness of the old chief, always great, were immeasurably increased by the treatment he met with from the foreigners, and the large amount of foreign property that flowed in upon him. His attention, and that of his people were entirely diverted from religion to matters far more congenial to the human heart. His mind was gradually alienated from the teachers, and the melancholy issue was that they were murdered by parties commissioned by him, and the mission was broken up. Three teachers—two of them Samoans and one a Rarotongan—and Lengolo, the poor man whom we took off Eramanga, were killed by the merciless savages. And at the same time the *star*, from Tahiti, owned and commanded by Captain Ebril, was taken, and all hands murdered. How altered the state of things since our visit!

An extensive sandal-wood establishment has existed on the island for several years past, the tendency of which is not to make it more accessible to Christian missionaries; and, to crown all, Popish missionaries have obtained a footing on it; so that its prospects are dark indeed.

The events narrated above took place in 1844; and the

cruel Matuku, the main author of them, was arrested by the hand of death about the close of 1845, or the beginning of 1846. His son, who succeeded him, was similar in character to himself.

There are few things more important in the management of missions than that missionaries and teachers should stand entirely aloof from all interference in trading transactions between the natives and foreigners. They should not act as interpreters, or get mixed up in any way with such matters. Yet to avoid this is not always easy; the man who became guide and assistant to the sandal-wood adventurers had lived several years in Samoa, and was acquainted with the language of that group. Thus he was able to converse with our teachers, and it was reported that he imposed upon them by telling them that we had said they were to assist in procuring sandal-wood. At all events there is reason to believe that they did get drawn into the snare; and to this was owing to some extent, perhaps wholly, the sad termination of their lives, and the breaking-up of the mission.

CHAPTER XI.

MARÉ, OR NENGONE.

"This also cometh forth from the Lord of Hosts, who is wonderful in counsel, and excellent in working."—Isaiah xxviii. 29.

MUCH more pleasing task now devolves upon us than that we have just completed. A prospect opens upon us, beautiful and exhilarating, as a morning without clouds after a night of blackness, and darkness, and tempest. The islands that have just passed under review present little or nothing to relieve the gloom which, as the shadow of death, envelopes them. Let us take heart, however. One thing is set over against another. The set time to favour them will come; of this we have an earnest in the adjacent islands. But a few years have passed since these were in a state sufficiently discouraging. Indeed, the time was when we looked with far more sanguine hopes to New Caledonia and the Isle of Pines, than to either Maré or Lifu. But "His ways are not our ways, nor His thoughts our thoughts." He has made the last first and the first last.

The following extract from Captain Erskine's work will appropriately introduce what we have to say about Maré. "The discovery of Maré has been claimed for a Captain Butler, of the ship *Walpole*, in 1800, and by others for the *Britannia*, in 1803, which latter name appears first on any chart as attached to one of the larger islands of the group. M. d'Urville states that in 1827, although the 'uncertain group of Loyalty Islands' appeared on a chart of Arrowsmith's, M. Rossel, his hydrographer, doubted their existence; and their extent was certainly first ascertained by M. d'Urville, who connected his work (on the northern sides) with that of M. d'Entrecasteau at Isle Beupré, retaining the name of Britannia for Maré, and giving those of Chabrol and Halgan to Lifu and Uea."

The island is called Nengone by its own people, and Maré by the neighbouring islanders. Among foreigners it is now generally known by the name of Maré, and this is likely to continue to be its designation. It is estimated at from sixty to eighty miles in circumference, and has a population of seven or eight thousand. It is a low, flat island, of coral formation, and presents rather an uninviting appearance from the sea. On some parts clumps of pines, and on others immense blocks of coral, resembling artificial fortifications diversify the scene, and give it something of a picturesque appearance. One of these, from its resemblance to an old military castle, is named Castle Point; and others, both on Maré and Lifu, might with equal propriety bear the same name. Occasionally, also, instead of the bold shore and barren coast, there are tracks of low land, sloping down to the sea and terminating in a sandy beach. The island is not well watered. Neither running stream nor fresh water fountain is found in it. There is indeed abundance of water, such as it is, but it is all brackish. To the natives, however, it is neither disagreeable nor unwholesome; and the same is true with regard to foreigners who have resided any considerable time on the island. The greatest disadvantage connected with the island, as regards foreign intercourse, is the lack of a harbour. The only anchorage is in a wide bay which opens to the north, and affords no shelter, except from the prevailing trade winds.

Among the vegetable productions of the island, the most valuable are yams, cocoa-nuts, bread-fruit, bananas, and sugar-cane. Yams are the main dependence of the natives, "the staff of life," and are produced in great abundance and of very fine quality. Oranges, pineapples, and some other fruits have been introduced since the island was brought under Christian culture. No quadrupeds were found on the island when we first visited it. Hogs, sheep, and horned cattle have since been introduced. As regards the people of Maré, incidental notices will be found in this and the chapter on Lifu; and all that has been said of the natives of New Caledonia and the Isle of Pines is more or less applicable to them.

The first missionary visit to Maré was made by the writer, in the brig *Camden*, in 1841. It was then called by the name of Britannia Island, and so little was known of it, that we were in doubt as to whether the small island of Toka, which we made first, and with whose people we had intercourse, was not the island of which we were in search. The following morning scattered our doubts, by revealing to us the island which, according to our chart, was ascertained to be really Britannia Island. We lay off the island the whole forenoon, anxiously looking out for canoes, or something on shore that might indicate the presence of human beings. At length, tired with waiting, and almost despairing as to the accomplishment of our object, a boat was lowered, and Captain Morgan and myself went in close to the shore. Still nothing hopeful appeared. A rugged, repulsive-looking coast stretched away before us, as far as we could see, without any trace of human beings. We pulled slowly along the coast, eagerly looking out for something that might encourage hope.

At length a canoe was descried in the distance, making towards us, which filled us with joy. We felt as if our object was gained. We were soon within hail; and how were we surprised and delighted to be accosted with the following language: "I know the true God!" Who could this be in this land of darkness who knew the true God, and who could speak a language intelligible to us? The mystery was soon solved. Our new friend turned out to be a native of Niuataputapu, one of the Tonga, or Friendly Islands, who, with seven others, had lost their way at sea, and had been by a merciful Providence brought to Maré. Taufa and his companions had been on the island for about seven years. Thus he was just the man we wanted—an interpreter provided to our hand. We had lowered our boat at a venture, and pulled into the part of the island that we happened to be off; but had we been at any other part of the coast, we should in all probability have been able to accomplish nothing. Thus we were led in a way that we knew not. Thus had we, as we have so often had since, to mark the hand of God in our Polynesian missions.

To a guide thus marvellously provided for us we did not hesitate to give ourselves up; and we were led by him to a place named Eoche, in the bay of Waeko, which has ever since been occupied as one of our mission stations. Here we found Jeiue, the principal chief of one side of the island. He did not usually reside here, but was on a visit at the time; and this also was an important providential coincidence, as he was the only man on the side of the island where Taufa lived, and had influence, with whom the teachers could be left.

The chief and one or two attendants went with us on board, and Taufa and the teachers designed for the island slept on shore. All was satisfactorily arranged with the chief and his attendants; the teachers were much pleased with all they saw on shore, and the important step was taken which has led to all the subsequent changes which have transpired on the Loyalty Islands. What mighty consequences are suspended on incidents in themselves trifling and apparently fortuitous!

It was on the 9th of April, 1841, that Christian teachers were landed on Maré. The teachers were two in number; they were both Samoans. The one, Tataio, was from Savaii; the other, Taniela, was from Tutuila. All passed off encouragingly. One or two acts of theft were attempted as we were landing the teachers, but in such a simple and artless manner as to amuse rather than anything else. One man was detected walking off with a sailor's jacket, and another with the boat-hook. Without much difficulty we got them brought back. The thieves themselves came and laid them down in the boat, with as much simplicity as if they hardly knew that they had been doing wrong. On the whole, the impression made on our mind was, that the natives were a remarkably harmless people. Thus we were greatly surprised, when massacre upon massacre took place on the island in after years. It is altogether probable, that had they not been most cruelly and outrageously wronged by foreigners, the bloody deeds which they perpetrated would never have taken place.

Shortly after our visit to the island it was noised abroad that sandal-wood was to be found on it. Parties in search of that article flocked to it; and after a short time a series of deeds commenced which, happily, has had few parallels in any single island of the Pacific. We cannot give the particulars of the numerous affrays that took place; most of them have already been made public.

We cannot minutely trace the history of our operations on the island; the teachers passed through many sufferings and trials, and were often in great danger; the old chief, however, was their staunch friend, and a gracious Providence watched over them. With commendable perseverance they continued at their post through several most discouraging years. An unusually long time passed before any decided impression appeared to be made, and Maré was long regarded by us as one of the most unpromising of all our outstations.

It was not until 1849, when it was visited by the Rev. C. Hardie, in connection with the writer, that it was ascertained that a change had commenced, and that decided indications of success were apparent. There is reason to believe, however, that the causes which led to it had been silently operating for a length of time. The chief who received the teachers, and continued their faithful friend and protector till his death, was not favourable to Christianity; and his authority, which was wellnigh absolute, was employed to prevent its spread. "Don't worship the God of the foreigners, but do as I do," he was wont to say. From what took place after his death, which happened about the close of 1848, it is manifest that a deep impression had been made, and a great change effected in the views and feelings of the people before that occurred, though it was prevented from developing itself. No sooner was the obstruction removed, than the most satisfactory evidence of this appeared. The sons of the deceased chief led the way. "Now," said they, "our father, who led us astray, is dead; let us abandon our old system, and throw away our evil practices, and receive the new religion, and learn and obey the Word of God." From the ready response given by the people, and the decided and permanent character of the change which followed, it is evident that they were as much disposed to embrace the new religion as the chiefs. They responded in the most cordial manner, and a change of the most gratifying and astonishing character took place throughout a large part of the island.

In June, 1852, it was the writer's privilege, in conjunction with an esteemed brother, the Rev. J. P. Sunderland, again to visit the island. We had learned that a change was in progress before we reached the island, but had formed no adequate idea of the actual state of things. Indeed, we could not do that, for "the half had not been told us." We made the island on Saturday, June 5, and had the privilege of spending a Sabbath at Waeko, one of the stations—and *such* a Sabbath! We were anchored nearly opposite the village where the teachers are located. When we went on deck in the morning (we came to anchor during the night), the objects that met our eye were two neat plastered cottages, a large white chapel, and the natives flocking together from all quarters to engage in the hallowed services of the Sabbath. How such sights affected us may be conceived, when it is remembered that for years Maré had been associated in our minds with scenes of cruelty and blood, and that we had been wont to approach its shores with a feeling of horror.

We went on shore at the very spot where, eleven years before, we landed the teachers. What a change since then! Instead of a rude, disorderly rabble of naked savages, we found a company of people—about six or seven hundred—all seated in a circle, all more or less clothed, all quiet, mild, and kind. We proceeded to the chapel. The scene there, and the emotions to which it

SOCIETY ISLANDS.

gave rise, baffle description. The chapel is 72 feet long, and 24 broad. It was densely crowded with evidently deeply-interested worshippers. There is a Sabbath-school at noon, attended by about 200, who apply themselves to learning to read with the utmost vigour. Another general service is held in the afternoon. There are thirty-one good readers, 200 members of a select Bible class, and fifty-one candidates for baptism and the Lord's Supper. Hitherto there have been two teachers at this station, Fili and Mika, both Samoans. Fili was taken suddenly ill, and died a few days before our arrival; so that now there is only one. Fili died as it becomes a Christian to die. The poor people made great lamentation over him, and appeared as if they could hardly part with his widow and children. The state of things at Guahma, our other station on this island, is rather in advance of what it is here. Guahma is the principal station. It is the centre whence the astonishing movement now in progress took its rise. There is a chapel there, 120 feet by 30, which, the teachers say, is filled every Sabbath. There are fifty good readers at the station; and the people, old and young, are striving to learn. A large number at both stations have abandoned polygamy and other works of darkness. The Sabbath is universally observed throughout the Christian district. There are upwards of seventy candidates for baptism and church membership, and altogether a most marvellous change has taken place. The change began to appear about three years ago. There is reason to believe, however, that it was silently going forward for some time before; but its external development was prevented by Jeiue, the old chief who received and protected the teachers, but who was, nevertheless, decidedly unfriendly to Christianity. After his death, his sons, who were well disposed, encouraged the people to embrace Christianity, themselves leading the way.

A large part of the island, about one-half, still remains heathen. The principal chief and people of that district tried to engage the Christian party in a war, shortly after they began to take a decided stand in favour of Christianity. They assembled at the boundary, where they had been accustomed to fight in former years, and sent them a challenge. One of the principal chiefs and one of the teachers went and met the assembled warriors. They told them that they were not afraid of them, but they were afraid of God, and desired to obey His Word, and would not fight. The heathen were disarmed by their admonitions and exhortations, returned quietly to their own homes; and there has been no war on Maré from that day to this. Shortly after the above occurrence, the chapel already mentioned was erected; and from that time the work spread with amazing rapidity. The chapel was built in an astonishingly short space. The teachers say it was not longer than one month in hand. It is plastered, seated, and furnished with a pulpit and reading-desk. Men, women, and children, all lent a hand. After leaving Waeko we visited this station. All we saw fully bore out what we had heard; indeed, our expectations were greatly exceeded. We found upwards of a thousand people assembled to welcome us in the same manner as at Waeko. A meeting was held in the chapel, which was crowded. After the meeting the people requested us to receive a present. This consisted chiefly of yams. Every individual—man, woman, and child—came, bringing a yam or a piece of sugar-cane. When all was collected, one of the chiefs made a short speech, telling us that their present was an expression of their love to us, and their joy at meeting us. We replied; and all passed off in a most orderly and peaceful manner. Beside two good plastered dwelling-houses belonging to the teachers, we counted eight or nine similar to these, most of which we visited and inspected. They belong to the chiefs and principal people. We returned on board greatly surprised and delighted at what we had witnessed, and feeling that if ever there were a field prepared of the Lord, surely that field is Maré. It is painful to have to add, that, while these delightful movements were in progress, others occurred of a very different character.

Three natives were barbarously murdered in the Christian district by an Englishman, the master of a sandalwood vessel. They swam off to his vessel to talk to him about the disposal of some sandal-wood, and were murdered in cold blood on the deck. Two died on the spot; the third, though wounded, was able to leap into the sea. Two wretches fired upon him from the ship, and put an end to his life. The individuals thus cruelly murdered belonged to the Christian party. They were related, however, to parties in the heathen districts. These took up the matter, and the sad result was, that they took the *Lucy Ann* cutter, in December of the same year, and killed all hands, seven in number, including the master of the vessel. Who has the larger share of the guilt of the murder of these seven men, the poor ignorant natives of Maré, or the fiendlike Englishman, who wantonly murdered the three unoffending natives?

The island was again visited by the same parties in November, 1853. Of that visit the report is as follows:—

"We got sufficiently near Guahma, the principal station on Maré, on Thursday, the 3rd, to allow of one of the teachers coming off to us. We were not taken by surprise on reaching this and the neighbouring island of Lifu on the present occasion, as we were last visit, and so were in more favourable circumstances for forming a dispassionate judgment of the state of things. And we rejoice to be able to state that our former impressions have been fully sustained by all we have seen and heard. During the sixteen months that have passed since we were last here, there has been steady progress, and the state of things is certainly such as has never before been witnessed in similar circumstances, either in Eastern or Western Polynesia.

"As regards external matters, everything is much the same as it was last visit. One new object, indeed, met our eye on going on shore at Guahma, and greatly interested us—a large, well-built, commodious dwelling-house. But what was there so wonderful about the said house? Well; it struck us as a deeply-interesting and significant fact, that a people circumstanced as these are should build a house 54 feet by 30, containing six rooms, the walls 13 or 14 feet high, with a spacious verandah in front, Venetian windows, and panel doors, for the reception of a missionary or missionaries, when they should arrive. Surely this is a speaking fact, and should powerfully appeal to those on whom it devolves to send missionaries to these most interesting people. How could they give stronger expression to their desires, or more forcibly and affectingly strengthen their appeal? The teachers informed us that the people had done all the work (under their direction, of course) except the doors and windows, which were made by them.

"Services, schools, and classes continue to be attended as formerly; and progress is being made in the acquisition of knowledge, and the formation of character and habits in keeping with the requirements of Scripture. Hundreds can already read well, and hundreds more are learning. Large numbers profess to be anxiously seeking the salvation of their souls, and are desirous of professing their faith in Christ, and attachment to Him, whenever they may have an opportunity of so doing. A complete revolution has taken place throughout the entire framework of society, and externally, at least, there is a most striking fulfilment of the prophetic declaration, 'Behold, I make all things new.' Even the heathen party are being influenced by the mighty change that is in progress. They say they wish no more war, and highly approve of the new religion; but there is one difficulty in the way of their embracing it which they cannot yet get over, namely, that it requires them to put away their wives. This, they profess, is their sole reason for standing aloof. It is not likely that they will continue long in their present state. A fire is already kindled in their midst, which will doubtless spread till the entire system of heathenism is consumed. One village has embraced Christianity, and is regularly visited, and services conducted in it every Sabbath; and a teacher will probably be settled in it shortly, agreeably to the wishes of the people.

"On the morning of Saturday, the 5th, we got to the

anchorage at Waeko, our other station on Maré. There is no anchorage at Guahma. On this account our visits to it are very hurried, and much less satisfactory than they might otherwise be. We spent the Sabbath at Waeko. All that has been said respecting Guahma is applicable to Waeko. The work is steadily and rapidly progressing; there is the same earnest desire for missionaries as at the other station; a house has been built in anticipation of their arrival; and, on the part of the people, 'all things are ready.' Alas! how long will it be ere the same be true with regard to us? How long shall the imploring and most deeply affecting appeal of these poor people fail to meet with an appropriate response?

"At both stations the people made liberal collections of food for the vessel, and all our intercourse with them was of a most delightful character. Only one thing tended to damp their joy and ours, namely, that we had no missionaries to leave amongst them. It would seem as if the old and usual order in such matters were reversed in the case of this people—instead of our going to them to compel them to come in, they have to use their utmost effort to compel us to go to them, and teach them the way of life and salvation. We reinforced the mission by adding a teacher to each of the stations. There are still but four, however, on the island, as it was necessary to remove one of the old ones, on the ground of some reports detrimental to his character, and another died before last visit. There are now three Rarotongans and one Samoan; and they are assisted by a numerous body of the most advanced among the natives."

The above extracts indicate very plainly that the mission had now reached a critical juncture. The Samoan and Rarotongan teachers had done their work. They had reached a limit beyond which they could not much advance. The way was prepared for a more effective agency; and, unless such an agency could be procured, reaction and retrogression must soon take place. So we, who were eyewitnesses of the state of things, deeply felt at the time; and fervent were our longings, and earnest our prayers to the Lord of the harvest that He would send forth labourers into His harvest. Happily the answer was not long deferred. In 1853 the claims of Western Polynesia were brought before the friends of Christian missions in Australia, and an appeal was made to them for help. Among the results of this appeal was the occupation of Maré by English missionaries. The church, then under the care of the Rev. Dr. Ross, made a proposal to the directors of the London Missionary Society to take upon themselves the support of two missionaries, to be employed on some island of Western Polynesia. To this proposal the directors of the London Missionary Society acceded, and with great promptitude they sent forth two missionaries, the Rev. S. M. Creagh and the Rev. J. Jones. These brethren reached Samoa, on their way to their destination, in June, 1854, and sailed thence in the *John Williams* in September of the same year. They were accompanied by Messrs. Hardie and Sunderland, of the Samoan mission. Maré was selected as having the first claim, and as being, all things considered, the most eligible field for them to occupy.

An extract from Mr. Hardie's account of the introduction of the brethren to their sphere of labour, and embracing other important matters, will interest the reader. The party reached Maré on the 23rd of October. They went to the principal station, and finding appearances all that could be desired, they intimated to the teachers their wish "to have a meeting with the chiefs and people. Very soon a large number eagerly assembled in the space before the house erected for the missionaries. We then asked them if they still held the desire, repeatedly expressed, for missionaries to come and live among them; whether it was their wish that Messrs. Jones and Creagh should do so; and, if they did, whether they would protect them and their wives, and treat them kindly, and

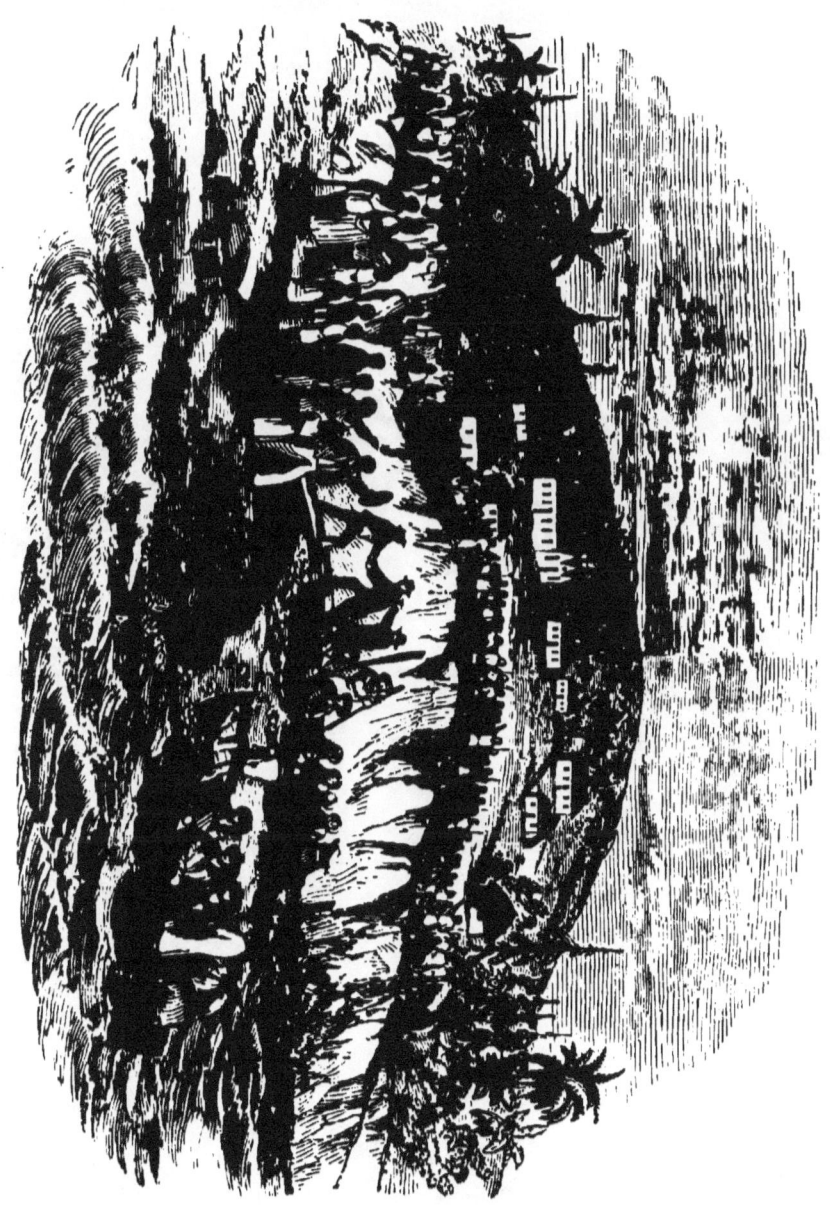

attend to their instructions. To all these questions the chiefs promptly answered in the affirmative. We then told them that, in case of political differences, or of war breaking out, the missionaries could take no part; that their aim would be to promote peace and friendship among all parties, and to labour for the present welfare and everlasting happiness of all.

"All being thus satisfactorily arranged, the next thing was to get houses, as temporary residences for our newly-arrived friends, and Mr. and Mrs. Sunderland, who were appointed to remain with them for a time, to assist them in commencing their labours. As there were three families to be accommodated, we wished to know what houses they might have, and were told they might have any they liked. We soon fixed on three convenient plastered cottages, which their owners gave up most cheerfully. Having thus got the way fully prepared for the landing of our friends and their property, we returned to the vessel, which was soon brought to anchor about two miles from the settlement. Early in the afternoon of the 25th October the landing of the goods and cattle was completed, and our dear friends took up their residence at this most interesting station. Seldom or ever has it been the lot of missionaries to commence their labours under circumstances so favourable, among a people so prepared to receive them, and to benefit by their instructions. More than one half of the island have abandoned heathenism, and are thirsting for instruction; and in those parts where the people are still heathen the teachers are well received, so that there is every reason to hope that the whole island will very soon profess Christianity.

"At Neche, the station at which the missionaries now are, and throughout the district of Guahma, the whole population with the exception of the very aged and the very young, can read, and about forty can write. About one hundred persons are candidates for Gospel ordinances, and there is every reason to hope that the missionaries will soon have the happiness of forming a Christian church. Each of the chiefs has put away all his wives but one; twelve plastered houses have been built; and, since last voyage, in place of a large plastered chapel which a storm had blown down, a strong stone chapel has been built, 80 feet long by 50 feet wide, which is filled to overflowing every Sabbath with attentive hearers.

"Having completed our work so auspiciously at this station, we left—Mr. and Mrs. Sunderland accompanying us—on the afternoon of the 25th, to visit the district of Waeko, our other station on this island.

"We came to anchor at that station on the morning of the 26th. Here we found things in a state of prosperity similar to that at Guahma. Heathenism and polygamy are entirely abandoned; the people are equally desirous of missionaries, and thirsting for knowledge. They very much wished that one of the missionaries should live among them. We told them it was likely that this would be the case; and that, in the meantime, the missionaries would visit them till further arrangements could be made. At this station, sixteen plastered houses have been built; and, since last visit, their plastered chapel, blown down by a storm, has been replaced by another 90 feet long by 30 feet wide, which is crowded every Sabbath. Two hundred and fifty persons have learnt to read well, and a large number, in different stages of progress, are learning. Nearly forty have learnt to write. There are eighty-five candidates for church fellowship; and here, too, it is likely a church will soon be formed. We had a deeply interesting service with the people. It was most encouraging and refreshing to hear them join in the song of praise to God, and to see them listen with so much attention to the word of life.

"The teachers at both stations are highly respected and esteemed, and treated with great kindness. They have gained great influence, which they have used to good account, as appears from the large measure of success with which, under the blessing of God, their labours have been crowned.

"We left three more teachers from Samoa on the island, two of them married, who, with the four there before, will greatly aid the missionaries in carrying forward the good work which has already been so successful."

Thus our brethren had a very encouraging reception, and their labours were commenced under circumstances singularly favourable and promising. A morning almost without clouds was the morning of their missionary life. Their sky, however, was soon overcast. The motto of one of the most esteemed and beloved of the missionary brotherhood, Henry Martyn, "They that will do good must themselves suffer," might be adopted by all, since it has its verification in all. In the case of our esteemed friends it found a speedy fulfilment. Only a few months had passed, when one who seemed to promise not less fair than any of the party for a life of prolonged and distinguished usefulness, was suddenly called away from the sufferings and toils of earth to the repose of the better land. Grievous did the blow seem to us, and with stunning weight did it fall on the bereaved husband in his circumstances of solitude and desolation. But doubtless all was right. He was sustained and enabled to weather the storm, and the cause in which she fell will not ultimately be a loser. To her we may apply, with some alteration, words which have been touchingly applied to another loved servant of Christ,* who fell in a very different cause :—

> "Go to thy grave! At noon from labour cease,
> Rest from thy toils, thy brief career is run;
> Come from the field of conflict, and in peace,
> Sister, go home! with thee the fight is done."

The following extract from the *Samoan Reporter*, for January, 1856, contains the first intelligence that reached us after the commencement of the mission. From that it

* Hedley Vicars.

appears that Mrs. Creagh died in March, 1855, little more than four months from the time of reaching Maré.

"From Maré our brethren, Sunderland, Creagh, and Jones, report marked and delightful progress. Two churches have been formed, embracing an aggregate of nearly eighty members; the desire for instruction is great; the Gospel of Mark has been printed; and although many on the island are still in heathenism, the kingdom of Satan has there received a blow which it will never recover. One of the teachers, Tataio, who landed among them in their heathenism in 1841, and who subsequently returned to Samoa for further instruction, on going back lately, thus speaks of his treatment at a village where he is located:—'Now the people respect and reverence me; formerly they were constantly talking and scheming as to how they might kill me. They rejoice, and thank God that I have lived to return to them, that they may recompense me for their former ill-treatment. Great indeed is their kindness to me. It was not so of old.'* Having given valuable aid to the brethren Creagh and Jones in commencing their mission, Mr. and Mrs. Sunderland left Maré in August, to return to their station on Samoa, by way of Sydney.

"Connected with the mission to Maré, we have been deeply grieved to hear of *the death of Mrs. Creagh*, in March last, just at the outset of her missionary career. We had hoped that God had many days of usefulness in reserve for her on earth, in company with her devoted husband; but she has thus early been removed to a better world, where her love to her Saviour, and intense desire to be devoted to His service, will find ampler scope for development, and shine with brighter lustre."

Mr. and Mrs. Jones were also tried. Heavy domestic

---

* The other teacher, Taniela, who was landed in 1841, died at an early stage of the mission. After enduring many trials in connection with Tataio, and maintaining a consistent and exemplary course, he rested from his labours and entered, as we trust, into the joy of his Lord some time in 1844.

affliction overtook them. The nature of their trials and other important matters are embraced in the following account of Messrs. Harbutt and Drummond's visit to the island in June, 1857.

"On Saturday morning, the 20th June, Maré lay full in view, but baffling winds prevented us getting near the anchorage before Monday. On that afternoon we went on shore in a boat, with the captain, at Waeko, Mr. Jones's station. A messenger was sent to Guahma for Mr. Creagh, and he and his little boy arrived on the forenoon of the following day. On the same evening the vessel came to anchor in the large bay, and we all landed.

"Three months previous to our visit, Mr. and Mrs. Jones had been called to pass through the deep waters of affliction. Two of their dear children, their eldest boy and a little girl, had been severely afflicted. The latter had recovered, but the former had been removed from this world of sorrow to the land of unfading joy. The afflicted parents were sorrowing, but not as those that have no hope.

"On this island the good cause continues to prosper, but not many additional converts have been made to the number of professing Christians from the heathen party since last report. The missionaries have been obliged to desist sending teachers to preach to the heathen, as formerly; the latter having several times threatened to kill the teachers if they did not cease their visits. They declared, on the last visit to them, that if they returned they would eat them. Nor would they allow them to sleep in the place whither they had gone, although it was late on Saturday night when they arrived. One chief shook his spear, and threatened to run a teacher through with it; but the teacher spoke so kindly to him that he was afraid to hurt him. The missionries have been all round the island and they suppose the population to amount to 8,000.

"The number of hose who have given up heathenism and desire religious nstruction, amounts to about 3,000.

At Waeko, Mr. Jones's station, the number of church members is eighty, and the number of candidates for church fellowship about one hundred. He is assisted in his work by two Samoan teachers. Mrs. Jones has a school for teaching reading and writing, at which from twenty to one hundred and fifty attend. She has also a select class, which numbers fourteen.

"At Guahma, Mr. Creagh's station, the number of church members is seventy, and candidates for admission, 300. Mr. Creagh is assisted in his work by two Rarotongan teachers, one Samoan, and one native. He has a select school three times a week, at which from fifty to ninety attend. Nearly the whole population attend the day school. Mr. Creagh is about to visit his native land, but he intends, before he leaves Polynesia, to print at the Samoan press one or more of the Gospels in the language of Maré."

When the island was next visited, in July, 1858, the state of things was still encouraging. Progress was making among the Christian party, but the heathen continued to cleave tenaciously to their delusions. The number of church members at the two stations had risen to 180; and the number of candidates was 400. A missionary meeting had been held in the month of May of that year, and five pounds in cash raised by the natives in aid of the funds of the London Missionary Society. An interesting incident this, as being the first movement of the kind, not only on Maré, but on the group to which it belongs, and the first of a series of similar movements which will be continued and extended till the "knowledge of the Lord shall cover the earth as the waters cover the sea." Mr. Jones had erected a new stone dwelling; and a new chapel, 54 feet by 21 feet, had been built at his outstation. On this occasion Mr. Creagh returned to his labours, having formed a connection which promises much for the good of the cause in which he is engaged. The last visit of the *John Williams* was in October, 1860; of that visit Dr. Turner writes as follows:—

"Sabbath, Oct. 23.—Anchored at 9 A.M. in the roadstead off Waeko, the station of Mr. Jones, on the northwest side of Maré. Soon after the anchor was down, Mr. Jones came off in a canoe. The canoe was leaky, and the crew could hardly keep her afloat; but they got safe on board, and we were glad to find that Mr. Jones and his fellow-labourers on the island were well. About 4,000 people on the other side of the island still cleave obstinately to their heathenism; but all in the districts occupied by the brethren Jones and Creagh are professedly Christian. The number is about 3,000. Of these, 224 are church members, and 220 are candidates for admission to church fellowship. There are eight teachers also, and a number of assistant teachers. After our English and Samoan services on board, Captain Williams, Mr. Macfarlane, Mr. Baker, and I accompanied Mr. Jones to the shore, and there we had an afternoon's service with the natives. About 250 were present. Mr. Macfarlane and I addressed them through Mr. Jones. What a change, as I told them in my address, the Gospel has effected at Maré. Instead of seeing them armed savages, as they were when I first saw them fourteen years ago, with their bodies whitewashed from head to foot, and without a rag of clothing, there they were—men, women, and children—clean and clothed, most of them with books in their hands, singing God's praises, following the words read, bowing the head in prayer, and listening with deep interest to every word we said.

"The contrast, however, between this side of the island and the other is still great and affecting. There a cloud of the darkest heathenism still hangs over the people. There they still worship the gods of their forefathers, fight with each other, eat the bodies of the slain, and delight in all manner of wickedness. Two of the Christian party, who went to preach the Gospel to them some time ago, were killed by these heathen. This, however, was not so much a blow at Christianity as an outburst of political revenge on two men who belonged by birth to the tribe with whom that party were then at war. They were advised not to go; but, in the heat of their zeal and devotedness to the good cause, they with some others went. They were recognised, waylaid, and killed, and their bodies dragged off to the oven. The rest of the party were spared. Once a month select parties of teachers and church members, headed occasionally by the missionary, visit that side of the island. God's hammer will yet break the rock. Light will yet penetrate the darkness."

Such is a brief sketch of this interesting mission. We will not indulge in any lengthened reflections in closing our notice. One cannot reflect upon the history of the mission, from the hour when a guide was so remarkably and unexpectedly provided to lead us to the spot to which it was needful we should go in order to effect an entrance, without being struck with the fact that the providence of God has in a very marked manner been over the Maré mission. Through all the long dreary night of apparently hopeless toil the pioneers were sustained, and not seldom were safe, though they were " in deaths oft," and in great destitution, and without any reliable friend except the Friend who never faileth. And in how remarkable a manner did the blessing come at last! When hope was almost gone, when visit after visit had been made by the anxious missionary, and the island was still a valley of dry bones—still a wintry scene, cheerless, desolate, dead—how marked was the change! How manifest the cause, when

> " Dry bones were raised and clothed afresh,
> And hearts of stone were turned to flesh."

Ah! how grateful was the blessed change to those who had so long waited and watched for its appearance!

CHAPTER XII.

LIFU.

"*The wilderness and the solitary place shall be glad for them; and the desert shall rejoice, and blossom as the rose.*"—*Isaiah* xxxv. 1.

THE important island of Lifu next claims our notice. Lifu is the largest and most populous island of the Loyalty group. It is about thirty or thirty-five miles distant from Maré, and about sixty from New Caledonia. We are not aware that anything like a complete survey of the island has been made, but a considerable amount of information respecting it may be obtained from Captain Erskine's work. It may be about eighty or one hundred miles in circumference. It is a low, coral island, resembling in its general appearance the adjacent island of Maré. Captain Erskine remarks:—"The appearance of the land differs from that of Uea, and we may add from that of Maré also, in being much higher, the bluff point being between 200 and 300 feet in height, and its western side a steep wall, on which were seen two or three rows of very distinct lines resembling tide marks, the lowest being not less than 60 feet above the level of the sea. Shoal patches lie at intervals along the shore, but there is neither a fringing nor a barrier reef, and on the summit of the cliffs the lofty pine seems to grow out of the bare coral reef rock."

Captain Erskine's description of the natives agrees with our own knowledge of them, obtained from personal observation, and from our teachers who have resided among them. They are very similar in appearance, character, and habits to their neighbours on Maré, though their language is different. All that has been said of the people of Maré in their heathen state may be applied, without qualification, to the natives of Lifu. We found them in a state of the lowest barbarism. Both sexes wore nothing worth the name of clothing, and they seemed utterly devoid of any idea of decency—a rare thing even among savages. The island was divided into two parties, who lived in a state of perpetual strife—hateful, and hating one another; each party being on the watch to surprise victims, which, when found, were cooked and

ISLAND OF LIFU.

devoured. No more inveterate cannibals, I suppose, have been found anywhere than were the Lifuans. We will not, however, dwell on what they were, but proceed to the more pleasing task of narrating the commencement and progress of the change which has issued in their becoming what they now are.

The introduction of the Gospel to Lifu dates as far back as 1842; but it was not until 1845 that the island was visited by the missionary ship.

In 1842, Messrs. Buzacott and Slatyer left two teachers on Maré, to wait for an opening to Lifu, and proceed thither in case of their being able to do so. After a while these teachers obtained a footing on Lifu. The Maré teachers accompanied them to their field of labour, and assisted them in effecting an entrance. A long and deeply trying struggle followed the introduction of the Gospel to Lifu. For many years scarcely any impression was made, and, when the circumstances are considered, it does seem a wonder of wonders that the little light was not quenched in the blood of the solitary man who was God's witness in that dark and savage land. We say solitary man, for so it was. One of the two teachers that were placed on the island apostatized, and sank into a state of savagism almost, if not quite, equal to that of the Lifuans themselves. And how this must have stumbled them may be readily conceived. Nor was this the only stumbling-block in their way. There was another equally great, perhaps greater—an Englishman! A man from the land of Christian light—whence the teachers themselves had received the religion they came to teach—was in the way! It was the writer's lot to meet this man on his visit to the island in 1845, and a more appalling and humiliating instance of reckless depravity is hardly on record than this case furnishes. Perhaps the most awful feature was the absence of any proper sense of the fearful condition into which he had sunk. He came on board the *John Williams* among the natives, apparently as destitute of shame as they; and talked with indifference, possibly feigned, of his state and conduct, expressing himself to the effect that the course of life he was leading—that of a savage and a *cannibal*—was as good as any other. And this young man, "Cannibal Charley," as he was called by traders visiting the island, had had the advantages of a Christian education, and was the son, we believe, of highly respectable parents. What was the end of the wretched man we are not aware.

But to return: notwithstanding the deeply discouraging circumstances in which Paoo, the teacher who remained steadfast, was placed, he stuck to his post; and eventually, by God's blessing, succeeded. But how forlorn a situation was his; and how apparently hopeless the undertaking in which, single-handed, he was embarked. But all things are possible with God. He hath chosen the weak things of the world to confound those that are mighty. A powerful friend was provided for Paoo in Bula, an influential chief, who continued his uniform and staunch supporter until his death, which did not occur till the mission had passed the most critical stage of its history. Bula was an interesting character. He was blind, but his influence did not appear to be lessened on that account. He was the principal chief of half the island, and appeared to be very much respected. He seemed quite in earnest in his efforts to induce his people to abandon heathenism and embrace Christianity; yet it is remarkable that a very small number complied with his wishes—an interesting fact, as it evinces that nothing beyond moral influence had been employed. When Dr. Turner and myself visited the island in May, 1845, some thirty or forty people were accustomed to attend the services on Sabbath. Bula, who had been an inveterate cannibal in former days, had abandoned that revolting practice, and had been for some time attached to the teacher and the truths he taught. Great was his joy and that of the little Christian party, and especially that of the teacher, to have the mission reinforced by the addition of two teachers. The next visit was in 1846, when things were found progressing a little. The number of the Christians had increased; services, both on Sabbaths and week-days, were well attended; and a few individuals had begun to worship God in their families. Thus the prospects of the mission were brighter than they had ever been. But trials were at hand. A storm, fierce and long-continued, was about to burst, which nearly led to its extinction. The following extract from the report of the next deputation, Messrs. Turner and Nisbet, who visited the island in 1848, shows the critical state in which they found the mission, and in which it had been for a length of time.

"The teachers left at Lifu we found at Maré. Owing to a war which scattered the tribes among whom they laboured, they fled to Maré about twelve months ago. Up to the time they left, schools and services on the Sabbath were kept up and attended. They wait at Maré for a favourable issue of the war, when they will return. The blind chief Bula is dead. He died, we fear, a heathen; yet he evinced a pleasing concern on his death-bed for the safety and protection of the teachers after his death. There are rival claims for the chieftainship; and these have led to and prolong the war.

"Many of the people, including some of the chiefs of Lifu, were cut off by an epidemic, towards the end of 1846. As it broke out soon after the arrival of new teachers, they were blamed as having brought it. Many were determined to kill them, but some were raised up to defend them. 'Kill them,' said their enemies, 'and there will be an end to the sickness.' 'No,' was the reply, 'we are dead men if we do; their God will avenge their death!' 'Then banish them from the island,' said they. 'That will also expose us to the Divine judgments,' their friends replied. 'Let them alone, they have come among us for good, and not for evil!' A chief from the Isle of Pines, who was there at the time, was then consulted. 'Spare the teachers,' said he; 'we on our island foolishly killed our teachers, thinking it would remove disease; but after their death their God punished us, and disease and death raged among us more than ever. Spare them, lest it be the same here.' While this heathen council was being held, the teachers were assembled in their own house, spending the day in prayer and preparation for their end. They thought that day was to be their last. They cast themselves on the arms of Him who has said, 'Lo, I am with you alway;' and He delivered them from death. The chiefs Bula and Gaisone were on this occasion mainly instrumental in saving them. But soon after this Bula died; and then again they were in great peril. It is a custom, on the death of a chief, to impute his death to human agency; and on these occasions the friends, like so many avengers of blood, are up in arms, and rest not until they have spread desolation and death somewhere in the land. Malice at such times is at work, pointing out some parties as having caused the death through their incantations. When Bula died the cry was again raised, 'Kill the teachers!' Gaisone was firm on their side, and told the people they must kill him first. Some talked of killing him to get at the teachers; but on this another party was blamed, and revenge sought that very night in the blood of a family of eight individuals in another part of the district."

It is painful to read the opinion expressed, or at least implied above, that "Bula died a heathen." A *virtual* heathen, the brethren mean, as he had long renounced heathenism in name. Perhaps there may be too much reason to fear that the opinion is correct, though there is much in the case to encourage hope. To abandon all he had been accustomed to regard as sacred, and rise above the superstitious fears by which all around were enslaved; to break off the cherished practices of heathenism—cannibalism, polygamy, and other abominations; to do all this in advanced life, supported b yonly a mere handful of his people, and to continue steadfast in his attachment and adherence to the little light he had for a number of years, and "on his death-bed to evince a pleasing concern for the safety and protection of the teachers;" all this shows the operation of a powerful influence on his mind, and, in the absence of positive evidence to the contrary, would seem to encourage the hope that he himself was made a partaker of the blessings of the Gospel. It is worthy of notice that one of his dying requests was that he should be buried in a Christian manner; and that that was effected, notwithstanding the strenuous efforts of the heathen to have it otherwise. Bula's successor was a heathen; but having received a solemn charge from the dying chief that the teachers should be protected, he stood their friend, telling his people that "Bula had not died as their fathers, he had died a worshipper of Jehovah." The teachers seem, under God, to have owed their safety to the determined interference of Gaisone, who had been the friend and counsellor of Bula, and was a man of great influence. Hence the feeling of the heathen, that while he was in the way they could not get their will upon the teachers. He seemed a sort of prime minister to the chief. The death of Bula evidently brought matters to a crisis; and, as we have seen, the teachers considered it right to retire before the storm. In 1849, a few months after their retirement from the island, they determined to visit it, in order to ascertain the state of affairs. At this time the prospects of the Maré mission had begun to brighten, and the teachers were accompanied by a number of influential people from that island, who were prepared to bear effective testimony to the excellence of the new religion, from what they themselves had witnessed and experienced. This was a matter of vast importance to the teachers and their cause, in their somewhat hazardous experiment. They had a rough reception, but were allowed to land in safety. They found a small party still desirous of Christian instruction, and by these they were joyfully welcomed. From all that appears, they might have remained and at once recommenced their work. They had not come prepared to stay, however, so they returned to Maré, the object of their visit having been answered. The existence of a party attached to Christianity and desirous of the return of the teachers was ascertained, and the only question was as to the time of reoccupying the island—whether that should be attempted at once, or whether it was advisable to wait for a season. The latter plan was adopted, but it was soon manifest that the time to resume the mission had arrived. The storm had expended itself, and peace was restored shortly after the visit of the teachers. The seed which had been sown in former years, and which had seemed to be hopelessly lost, began to spring up and bear fruit. For a long season it had lain dormant under the repressing influence of a dreary winter. Vitality, however, was there; and it required but the return of spring to develop the hidden life, and transform dreary, desolate Lifu, into a garden of the Lord. Most marvellous was the change which came over the island, all the more so, as it was so sudden and rapid. In the course of a few months the island seemed to pass from darkness to light. Hence the joyful surprise felt by the writer and the Rev. J. P. Sunderland, when they visited the island in May, 1852. The teachers had returned to Maré but a short time when they were followed by messengers from Lifu, entreating them to resume their labours there without delay. The way being thus clear, preparations were at once made, and the teachers returned to their field of labour, and re-entered upon their work in circumstances of high promise. As already intimated, the labours and sufferings of bygone years had not been in vain; the miseries the people had endured from war and kindred evils, and the wonderful reports that had reached them from Maré—all these had, by the blessing of God, prepared them to hail the return of those " who preached good tidings, who published peace." The teachers threw themselves into their work with an ardour and heartiness befitting the circumstances, and everything progressed apace. They had now a willing people among whom to labour; the way was prepared, and nothing remained but to improve to the utmost the facilities that were afforded. Temporary buildings were at once erected for school-houses and chapels: and in these instruction was imparted, and services conducted, till better could be obtained. The reader will now be prepared for the following extract from the report of our voyage, to which allusion has been made.

"At this island we found the most cheering indications that this for so many years unproductive field has at length begun to yield its increase. The external appearance of the natives was proof sufficient that a great change had taken place. But other and more decisive evidence soon met us. A large substantial stone building, 100 feet long by 40 feet wide, was the most prominent object at the mission station. It would not be easy to describe the feelings of grateful surprise with which we surveyed this interesting object. The walls are about nine or ten feet high, and three feet thick. It has a good pulpit and reading desk, doors, and Venetian windows, and it is being furnished with seats. It had been only four months in hand at the time of our visit. Probably in another month it will be completed. The boards which have been used about it were sawn by the natives on the island of Maré, which is fully thirty miles distant, and brought from thence in canoes. A foreigner who resides on the island kindly lent them a pit-saw; but he would not have it brought to Lifu. There are only two teachers on the island, the one a Rarotongan, the other a Samoan; so that the great body of the work has been done by the natives. The dwelling-house of the teachers is quite in keeping with the chapel. It is a comfortable plastered house, enclosed, and having a neat gate and gravel walk in front, which gives it quite a civilised appearance. When the group to which this island belongs was last visited, it had been abandoned on account of the war which had broken out. It is only about two years since the teachers returned; and during that short space the change which has taken place has been effected. The great body of the people have embraced Christianity. Heathenism, including war, cannibalism, etc., has been abandoned. Polygamy, one of the most difficult things to get a people to abandon, has been in many cases discontinued. Probably as many as 150 have abandoned this evil. There is a select class, which numbers 300, the members of which are pledged to outward conformity to the requirements of Christianity. The teachers say the large chapel is filled every Sabbath. It is quite likely that there is a congregation of 600 or 700. The people are rapidly availing themselves of what few facilities they possess for learning to read. A number can read fluently, and multitudes are learning. The teachers are obliged to employ some of the most advanced in teaching their countrymen, and even in conducting religious services. The desires of the people for teachers and missionaries are so great, that it is quite painful to hear them expressed, while one has not the means of meeting them. When an intelligent young chief was making inquiries as to the probability of their soon getting a missionary, it was replied, that they would get one some day. 'Say not *some* day!' he replied, 'I do not like to hear that word *some day!* Why not say, *to-day?* Why not one of you stay?'"

The above extract, as the reader will perceive, indicates an astonishing state of things. We doubt whether the history of missions furnishes a parallel case. The change on Maré was equally remarkable as far as it went, but it was confined to a part of the island; and the instrumentality also by means of which the change was effected there, bore something more like a proportion to the extent of the change than was the case on Lifu. On that island there were but two teachers at the time of our visit, yet the mighty change in progress had extended to every part; the people as a body had abandoned heathenism and embraced Christianity, and were stretching out their hands towards God with an eagerness which it was most affecting to behold. Never will the writer forget his emotions when surveying the wondrous scenes in question, and especially when listening to the touching pleadings of the people for missionaries. Sad is it to think that so long a time passed before these were forthcoming.

It was again the writer's privilege, in company with the same esteemed brother, Mr. Sunderland, to visit the island in November, 1853. On that occasion we were not able to have much intercourse with the people. What we had, however, was altogether satisfactory, as the following extract from our report will show.

"We found that the teachers, pursuant to instructions given them last visit, had separated, and taken up a second station. Unhappily, both stations are on the windward

A MISSIONARY MEETING IN POLYNESIA.

side of the island, and very difficult of access from the sea. We went first to Anerewede, the old station; but finding that unapproachable, we were obliged to stand off for the other. Here we succeeded with much difficulty, and risk to the vessel, in communicating with the teacher. It is about fourteen months since the station was commenced, and during that time the most gratifying progress has been made. A good dwelling has been erected for the teacher, 42 feet by 30; and an excellent and spacious chapel is in progress. There is the same earnest spirit here as elsewhere throughout this group, and the same astonishing change is in progress. Hundreds of people met us on the beach, and manifested their joy in every possible way. Had we been able to remain sufficiently long, hundreds more would speedily have assembled. It had been arranged, that when the *John Williams* arrived, a collection of yams, etc., should be made; and, as we went off to the ship, we saw the people flocking together from the distant villages. The vessel being in danger, however, we were compelled to forego the pleasure of remaining longer among them. We left our only remaining teacher at this station, with directions that a new station should be taken up as soon as possible, at another part of the island, where there is a harbour. This will doubtless be done; so that, when the island is again visited, it will be advisable to go direct to the harbour, and thence communicate with the other stations. In this there would be little difficulty; the vessel would be safe, and the business would be accomplished in a greatly more satisfactory manner than it can otherwise be."

The next visit was by Messrs. Hardie and Sunderland, in October, 1854. On that occasion the state of the mission was found much as described above. The deputation remark as follows:—"At this station more than 3,000 persons assembled to welcome us;" and again, "With very trifling exceptions, the entire population of the island have embraced Christianity, and the call for missionaries is becoming louder and louder." Alas! there were no missionaries for them, but the next best thing that could be done, was done; the mission was reinforced by the addition of two teachers. The island was not visited again until June, 1857; still, notwithstanding the urgency of the case, we had not been able to obtain missionaries to occupy the island, nor were they obtained till two years more had passed, and till the patience of the people was tried almost beyond endurance. It is a marvel indeed that they bore the repeated and prolonged disappointments as they did; and it supplies a very strong proof that the wonderful movement which has taken place among them was of God. This is one advantage to place over against the manifold disadvantages, and the very great hazard incident to the long delay. It is matter for shame and humiliation that such cases should occur as that before us, and shows the existence of a wrong state of things somewhere. "Go ye out into the highways and hedges, and compel them to come in," is the Master's command. Here the order is reversed, and they of the highways and hedges have to compel us to go to their help! But where lies the blame? As regards the Directors of the London Missionary Society, we suppose they regret the delay as much as ourselves, and that it was wholly unavoidable in as far as they were concerned. They can only apportion to the best of their judgment the resources placed at their disposal by the churches; and that, no doubt, they conscientiously do. We must therefore exonerate them. Augmented resources must be furnished; the churches must bestir themselves; the various sections of the Protestant Church must consider and respond to the claims which the great cause of Christian missions has upon them; and how blessed would be the reflex influence, and how precious the reward! "He that giveth unto the poor shall not lack." "He that hath pity upon the poor lendeth unto the Lord, and that which he hath given will He pay him again." Where, oh! where is there poverty to be compared with that of those who know not the Lord Jesus? And where is there charity to be compared with that of those who minister to perishing man the bread of life?

Messrs. Harbutt and Drummond were the next visitors of Lifu. Their visit was in June, 1857. They reported as follows:—

"We reached this island on the 26th June. We stood in for Anerewede, the station of Tui and Kakorua. The house of Kakorua stands on the opposite side of the bay to that on which Tui resides, at a place called Mu. But the people of Anerewede and Mu assemble in the same chapel. Kakorua had gone to another station; but Tui and Isaaka, of Thubenata, came off to the vessel in a canoe; and we were glad to learn that the mission continued to progress. The vessel stood off and on whilst we went ashore with the teachers' supplies. As we approached the shore, we saw the natives in great numbers coming along the beach towards Tui's house; most of them were more or less clothed, and they were delighted to see us. After the teachers' supplies were put ashore, we had a meeting with the people, in their large stone chapel at Anerewede. The chapel is 114 feet by 38; and the walls are 3 feet thick. The chapel is all seated, and has a respectable pulpit and reading desk, and holds a thousand people; it is filled every Sabbath. As the people could not all be informed of our meeting, only two-thirds of the chapel were occupied. We spoke to the people in the Samoan language, which Tui interpreted. We encouraged them to hope for missionaries. In doing so, did we do right?

"Isaaka, who came from Thubenata to meet us at this station, has only been a month on the island. His place is some miles distant from Anerewede; and a chapel is there in course of building. The services are at present well attended, in a large house where the chiefs hold their assemblies. We had here an interview with the principal chief of half of the island. He and his friends pressed us very hard for missionaries. The people here are in a delightful state. What a pity we had no missionary for them! Anerewede would make a good missionary station.

"After bidding the people farewell, we returned to the vessel, impressed with a deep sense of the responsibility under which the Directors of the London Missionary Society have brought themselves to supply their spiritual wants. On Saturday morning, the 27th, we reached the great bay on the south side of the island, the south point of which is called Gaicha, and the north point Ngara. We came to anchor on the north side of the bay, near Hepenehe, the place where the teacher Apolo resides. Wainya, the chief of the place, and Apolo, were soon on board. Wainya is a fine-looking young man, and he speaks a little English. 'Me want missionary,' was one of his first sentences. He was very respectably dressed, and he conducted himself in a very gentlemanly manner.

"The information communicated to us by Apolo was of a nature no less encouraging than that communicated by Tui, the teacher at Anerewede. Nearly the whole of the population have turned from heathenism, and greatly desire missionaries. We arranged with Apolo to have the ordinance of the Lord's Supper ashore on the following Sabbath, and he engaged to inform the other teachers.

"On Sabbath morning, the 28th, we all went ashore, accompanied by the captain and first officer of the *John Williams*, and as many of the ship's company as could leave the vessel, and the Maré and Rarotongan teachers. We were welcomed on shore by a large crowd of natives, who were waiting to receive us. Men, women, and children crowded around us, that they might welcome us with a cordial shake of the hand. This process was gone through all the way up to the teachers' house, which stands on an eminence near the chapel, and commands a beautiful view of the large bay. After our arrival at the teachers' house the native bell was rung, to summon the people to the house of God. Thither we proceeded, and found a large congregation assembled. The chapel is large, and, if crowded, will hold a thousand people. There were about 700 inside, and there might have been another hundred crowded around the doors and windows outside; many of these belonged to the few remaining heathen. Tui preached in the native language from John i. 6, 7. The congregation listened with intense interest to his sermon, and at its close they sung with all their might, in their native tongue, to the praise of Him who died to redeem a lost world. The melody was well fitted to make angels weep for joy. At the close of the service, Mr. Harbutt baptised the wife of Apolo, and a child of another of the teachers. The former was not a member of the church when she left Samoa, and that day for the first time she sat down at the table of the Lord. We conversed with her, and were satisfied with her conversation. She was also well recommended by all the teachers on the island. After the ordinance of baptism was administered, there assembled around the table of the Lord members of the family of Christ belonging to eight different nations, namely, Britain, Sweden, Samoa, Maré, Savage Island, Rarotonga, Tonga, and Aneiteum. Addresses were delivered to the communicants in English, Samoan, and Aneiteumese. The Lifu congregation looked on with wondering interest. No church has yet been formed among the natives, but the meaning of the service was explained to them by one of the teachers. After the service was over we dined at the teachers' house, and then returned to the *John Williams*, where Mr. Inglis preached in the evening from Psalm cxxxii. This closed the public services of one of the most delightful Sabbaths we ever spent on earth. But ours was not unmixed joy, for it was sad to think that the *John Williams* had come to visit a people so desirous to have missionaries to put the Word of God into their hands, and to tell them more about Jesus, and not one to leave with them!

"On Monday morning, the teachers came on board. We filled the jolly-boat with their supplies from England, Samoa, and the Hervey Islands, and then went ashore with them, whilst Captain Williams surveyed the large beautiful bay. We had notice given us that the people at Wetch, belonging to the chief Ukeneso, on the other side of the island, where Sepetaio is stationed, and also the people at Apolo's station, were going to bring a present of yams for the vessel, so we were not surprised to see a large assembly on the beach ready to receive us and welcome us ashore. Shortly after we reached the teachers' house the people of Wetch approached, walking in regular procession, and each carrying a yam or fish. They marched first in single file, and formed a circle round the teachers' land, lessening the interior space as they gathered in, until they were four or five men deep; they laid down their yams and fish in order, which made one large heap. They then retired and made room for the approach of the people of Hepenehe, where we were. These came with their fish and yams in the same regular order, and laid them down in another great heap. They made no speech, as is the custom on such an occasion in Samoa, but quietly retired, and sat down a short distance off. Mr. Harbutt addressed them in the Samoan language, his address was interpreted by Apolo, and the people listened to it with great interest. We pledged ourselves to do all we could to get them a missionary and a printer, to translate and print for them the Word of God, that they might read in their own language those great truths the teachers have been telling them for the last ten years. There were present, we thought, no less than a thousand people, among whom were some of the remaining heathen. The latter are very easily known from the Christian population.

"The teachers say the people are very kind to them, giving them food in abundance, of which there is no scarcity on the island, and helping them to build their dwelling-houses and chapels. When we arrived, the teachers were living at six stations, at some of these there were two teachers; but they all agreed to live for the future each at a separate station, and as there are nine teachers on the island, there will be henceforth nine separate stations, which will occupy fully the whole island. They had not taken a census of the population, but they say the inhabitants are much more numerous than they are on Maré. What is wanted now for Lifu is missionaries and a printing press. The teachers candidly say they can make no further progress until they get the Word of God to put into the hands of the people; and this they never can get till missionaries come and dwell among them, master the language, and translate it into the Lifu tongue. When the day will come is known only to Him who knows the end from the beginning. But the responsibility which rests upon those who sent them teachers to send them missionaries is very great. It was delightful to witness the conduct of the people on the Sabbath. Not one of them, either Christian or heathen, visited the vessel on that day. This people used formerly to worship the nail of a man's toe, or a finger nail, or a tuft of human hair put into a basket, and also stones of a peculiar shape; and so fond were they of eating human flesh, that they would go at night and steal a corpse from its last resting-place, and cook and eat it. How great the change through which they have passed! War has ceased on the island, and cannibalism is seldom heard of. A few years ago they all went in a state of nudity, now there are very few who do not wear some kind of clothing, and many of them are very respectably dressed. Let us hope the printing press will be at work here before long."

What an interesting state of things does the above extract exhibit! Was ever a people more remarkably prepared of the Lord? But how manifest was it that the mission had reached a stage when to leave it longer without a more effective agency was to expose it to imminent peril; and still more painfully manifest was this when the island was again visited, about twelve months later, and yet no missionaries had been obtained. The deputation, Messrs. Stallworthy and Gill, who visited the island on that occasion, were placed in most painful circumstances. Repeated disappointments had so exhausted the patience of the people, that they hardly knew how to brook further delay; and they were almost ready to feel as if they were being deceived or trifled with. Nor were the pain and disappointment felt by the teachers less than what was manifested by the people. But we will not dwell upon this painful subject. The long desired boon was granted at length; the disappointment now referred to was the last the people were called to endure. And while they were ready to despair of ever obtaining the object of their desire, God was preparing to turn their grief into joy. In September, 1859, Messrs. Macfarlane and Baker, appointed by the directors of the London Missionary Society to labour on Lifu, reached Samoa on their way to their appointed field. On the 27th of September these brethren sailed in the *John Williams* from Samoa, for Lifu, accompanied by the Rev. G. Turner, as a deputation from the Samoan mission. The following is Dr. Turner's account of the introduction of the brethren to their sphere of labour, and other important matters connected with Lifu.

"As the wind was strong and fair, we made all sail for Lifu, and by 4 P.M. were off Mu, on the south-east side of the island, where we had arranged to place Mr. and Mrs. Baker and family, and three of the Samoan teachers. There being no anchorage, Captain Williams, Mr. Jones, and I again left the ship in the boats, together with Messrs. Baker and Macfarlane, and the new teachers. A crowd of natives on the beach awaited our arrival, and among them we were glad to find the young chief, Bula, his brother, and two of our teachers. The first words after the shake of the hands were, 'Have you brought us our missionaries?' Their joy was unbounded when we pointed to the brethren, Macfarlane and Baker, and said, 'Yes, there they are; Mr. Baker to live here, and Mr. Macfarlane on the other side of the island.'

"Mr. Jones and I remained on shore for the night to converse with the teachers, arrange for a meeting with the people, the landing of the goods, etc.; and Captain Williams, with Messrs. Baker and Macfarlane, returned to the ship. While conversing with the teachers in the course of the evening, they related, among other things, a remarkable escape which two of our Samoans, and the wife and two children of a third, lately had from a watery grave. While crossing to Maré, their canoe was struck by a sea, and went down, leaving them all swimming. A native tub floated from the canoe, and in that one of them, a teacher named Isaaka, placed the two children, steadied the tub with one hand, and swam with the other. Three Lifu men who were with them soon became exhausted, and sank. For hours, the two teachers and the women struggled on, and at last they were carried by the current to a little island. But it was a bold shore, and they could not see any way of getting a footing on it. Here they thought they must perish. At length Isaaka, who was still swimming with the tub and the children of his fellow-teacher, said, 'Taniela, come here; you steady the tub, and let me throw myself on to the next great roller. If I perish, I perish; but perhaps God will lift me on to that shelving rock up there.' He threw himself on the next wave, and was borne aloft in safety on to the rock. But, on looking down, he saw that the tub was upset, and the children in the sea. Again he courageously jumped over, dashed down among them, seized one of the children, clasped it to his left breast, threw himself on another roller, and was lifted up, child and all, on to a ridge of rock. He threw the child up higher, and climbed after it. It seemed dead. He shook the little fellow by the heels, sucked his mouth and nostrils, and life returned. He then ran off in search of natives, got ropes, and all were soon safe up with himself; and there they sat down and wept, and thanked God for their marvellous preservation. Isaaka deserves a gold medal.

"Friday, October 28th.—Captain Williams stood in again with the ship, manned three boats, and proceeded to land the goods. Mr. and Mrs. Baker and family, and Mr. and Mrs. Macfarlane, came on shore with the first boats, and soon after we had a meeting in the chapel. The chapel is a strong stone building, erected some years ago by the teachers and people, 114 feet by 38 feet.

LAUNCHING A MISSIONARY BOAT.

About 600 people were present. The brethren, Jones, Baker, Macfarlane, and I, all spoke. In my address, which was interpreted by Isaaka, I referred to the time when the *John Williams* first came to their shores; of our intercourse with their old blind chief, Bula; of his promise to be kind to the teachers, and to listen to their instructions; of the hope Mr. Murray and I held out of their getting missionaries at a future time to teach them the way of the Lord more perfectly; and then I added, 'This day the promise is fulfilled. You have done your part, we have done ours. Mr. and Mrs. Baker are now your missionaries; and may God bless you all!'

"Visitors continued to arrive every hour, from various parts of the district, to pay their respects and express their joy. By 11 A.M. on Saturday, everything was on shore. Mr. and Mrs. Baker were comfortably lodged in a neat plastered six-roomed cottage, which the teacher gave up for their residence; we bowed the knee, committed our dear friends to God, left them, and pulled out to the ship. Mr. Baker has under his care six Samoan and Rarotongan teachers, and a district containing a population of about 4,000 people, the most of whom have abandoned heathenism, and become professedly Christian.

"Sabbath, October 30th.—At noon we anchored off a place called Hepenehe, in the wide bay on the north-west side of Lifu, where we had arranged to locate Mr. and Mrs. Macfarlane. Our arrival here, as on the other side, was the occasion of great joy. We were in good time for the afternoon service, which was held out of doors, in front of the teachers' house. The chapel was blown down in a gale, in March last; but the people have raised the stone walls of a new one, which is ready for a roof.

"On the following day the teachers and, I should think, 1,000 people assembled from the neighbouring villages; and here, as at Mr. Baker's station, they brought us a present of yams for the ship. In the short speech which accompanied their present, they said, 'We are greatly pleased that we have at length got a missionary. We do not know what may spring up in our hearts some other day; but at present there is nothing there but joy.' Mr. Macfarlane's goods were soon landed. The willing crowd picked the things from the boat as soon as it touched the beach; and trunks, casks, and cases flew up to the teachers' house, and were laid down in whichever of the seven rooms Mr. Macfarlane pleased to direct. So rapidly did everything go on, that by evening all was landed, and Mr. Jones and I had a cup of tea from Mrs. Macfarlane in her new abode, at the close of her first day of actual missionary life.

"In the division of the island assigned to Mr. Macfarlane he has under his care six Samoan and Rarotongan teachers, a number of Lifu assistant teachers, and a scattered population of probably from three to four thousand souls. War and cannibalism have for many years been laid aside; the most of the people are professedly Christian; our teachers and chapels encircle the island; and never, probably, were *first* missionaries located under more favourable circumstances. But, although these people are nominally Christian, they are but a step removed from heathenism—the merest babes in Christian knowledge; and, although our brethren Macfarlane and Baker have had 'an abundant entrance,' they have still the great work to do of translating the Bible, of explaining its meaning, and of raising up men qualified to be the future pastors and teachers there, and in the regions beyond.

"The four natives of Lifu, to whom I have already referred as being on board our vessel, now rejoiced to find themselves on their native shores. There is a tale connected with these four young men which makes us ashamed of our country. They say that they were decoyed from their island by a sandal-wood vessel from Sydney, upwards of three years ago. They had gone on board to sell some things, were battened down in the hold, and let up on deck next day, when their island was all but out of sight. They were nearly a year on Espiritu Santo, cutting and cleaning sandal-wood, and were then taken to the Island of Ascension, and sold for pigs, yams and firewood. They were rated according to age, etc., and fetched from two to five pigs, and a proportionable quantity of yams and firewood, for each man. There were ten of them in all. After a time six managed to run away, and escaped to Hong Kong, where five of them died. The remaining four might still have been in slavery on Ascension, but for the kind help of the American missionaries there, together with Captain Thompson, of the whaling ship *China*. The captain bought off two of them, and the other two were redeemed, partly by their own earnings, and partly by the missionary. They were then taken to Honolulu. The Rev. S. C. Damon and others kindly attended to them at that place, until another generous American captain took them to Rarotonga, there to await the arrival of the *John Williams*. One of them speaks English well. In the course of our voyage we have traced the name of the Sydney vessel, and also that of her captain and super-cargo. The Lifu people had long given up these four young men as dead; and their restoration was no small addition to the joy occasioned by the arrival of the missionaries. Two of them are of high rank in the bay where we anchored, and it was affecting to see how the people clung to them, listening to their tale, and following them wherever they went."

Here we must take our leave of the Lifu mission. We have traced its interesting story as fully perhaps as is desirable in the present stage of its history. We take our leave of it in circumstances that promises fair as regards the future. As Dr. Turner remarks, "a vast work remains to be done;" but, as far as man can see, there is no ground for apprehension as regards the doing of that work. In all likelihood the most critical period in the history of the mission is past, though it is not improbable that after a time a reaction may take place, and a struggle more or less prolonged be the consequence. There is no doubt, however, as to ultimate success; the mission will live, and the glorious work advance, whoever or whatever may oppose. "He that is for us is greater than all that can be against us." May a large measure of His presence and blessing be vouchsafed to those whose honour and privilege it is to labour for Him on Lifu! May the beauty of the Lord their God be upon them; may He establish the work of their hands upon them; yea, the work of their hands, may He establish it!

There is yet one more island, or rather group, connected with the Loyalty Islands, to which we must allude, to give completeness to our sketches, namely, Uea. This group we have not seen. It has but recently been brought under Christian culture, and one of the most interesting considerations connected with it is the manner in which this has been effected. Christian teachers were introduced to it some two or three years ago by the brethren labouring on the adjacent island of Maré, and these teachers are *natives of Maré*. The following interesting notice from Dr. Turner's report embraces all we have to communicate respecting the island and the work in progress on it, and with it we close our notice of the New Caledonia group.

"Tuesday, Nov. 1, 1860.—We parted with Mr. and Mrs. Macfarlane at 10 A.M., and were immediately off with a fair wind for Uea. About dusk we dropped anchor again in the lagoon off the teachers' house, in the settlement of King Whenegay, as he is called. This is one of the loveliest coraline groups which I have seen. Hnie is the name of the principal island, a long curved strip of land, thirty miles in length, three miles wide in some places, and about 150 feet high. Whakaia, not half so long, is separated from it by a narrow strait; and then there are upwards of twenty islets dotting the surface of the ocean all around, and forming a circular lagoon of about thirty miles in diameter, with anchorage throughout.

"The population may amount to 4,000. They are settled principally on the large island, and divided into two parties; the one in the district called Vekinie, under a king named Pasil and six tribal chiefs; and the other, in the division of the island called Fazaue, under King Whenegay and seven tribal chiefs. Whenegay and his people call the group not Uea, but Iai (Eaye). These two parties have not fought for some time, and are on speaking terms. They keep up two distinct dialects, but understand each other. They are a shade or two lighter than the Lifu people; but in most of their manners and customs are akin to them. They subsist on yams, taro, cocoa-nuts, fish, fowls, and pigs.

"Wednesday, Nov. 2.—After having met with the teachers on board, heard their report, and given them their annual supplies, Captain Williams, Mr. Jones, and I proceeded to the shore, and had a meeting with about 200 of the people, in the large council-house at Whenegay's house, which is at present used as a chapel. The size and general appearance of this house struck me as one of the best specimens of ancient Polynesian royalty which I have seen. It is 130 feet long and 30 feet wide. The posts round the sides of the house, close to the eaves, are only five feet high, but they are about *nine feet* in circumference, and from them run up the rafters, which are great beams, four feet round. The ridge-pole is supported by a row of central pillars. The roof is thatched with grass. The back and ends and two-thirds of the front are wattled and plastered. The remaining third is open in front, and decorated on the outside of each post with five carved boards, each having at the top a human face painted red, and as if grinning at an enemy. Two additional figures project a few feet in front on either side, as the guardian spirits of the place, with a Herculean wooden spear over their heads pointed to the entrance through the high palisade, a little way in front of the building.

"The house was built by Jokuie, with whom I met at sea, in company with Captain C——, in 1845. He is dead, but his son is now king. In my address to those assembled in the great house, I reminded them of the earnestness with which Jokuie entreated us to send teachers to their group of islands; and expressed our joy in knowing that many of them had abandoned heathenism and commenced to worship the true God, and seek salvation through Jesus Christ. Mr. Jones, in his address, told them that he had brought them a new teacher from Maré, and likewise exhorted them to give heed to the Word of Life. We have now five teachers at Uea, and five preaching stations, at which an aggregate of 1,300 people worship God and listen to His Word every Lord's day.

"Here, and also at Lifu, Maré, and Aneiteum, I had presented to me as many as eighty-six of the castaway idol gods of heathen times—gods of the sea, gods of the land, gods of the plantation, war gods, disease-making gods, storm and rain-making gods, etc. etc. I have also received twenty-six more to be taken to some of my brother missionaries, making in all 112 of these unmistakable trophies of the power of the Gospel of Jesus to overturn idolatry of every name, and triumph in every place."

CHAPTER XIII.

NIUE; OR, SAVAGE ISLAND.

> "Lions and beasts of savage name
> Put on the nature of the lamb."

> "Not unto us, O Lord, not unto us, but unto Thy name give glory."
> *Psalm* cxv. 1.

THE island whose name stands at the head of this chapter has no connection with Western Polynesia. Being one of the offshoots, however, of the mission with which the writer has been identified during the whole of his missionary life, and having been under missionary culture simultaneously and in connection with the islands which form the subject of these sketches, it may appropriately find a place among them. This island does not possess any very special claims to an extended notice as regards extent, population, and other matters of general interest; but, in a missionary point of view, it has of late years become possessed of great attractions, from the fact that a work has been accomplished upon it, through the instrumentality of Christian teachers, such as has few parallels in the history of missions.

A low, unpretending looking spot is Savage Island, as the voyager approaches it in its isolation amid the surrounding waste of waters; and in former times it was as uninviting as it looks. It lies in south latitude, between eighteen and nineteen degrees, and in west longitude about one hundred and seventy degrees; about 300 miles to the south of Samoa. It is about forty miles in circumference, and has a population numbering 4,300. It is of coral formation, and in its general appearance resembles more some of the islands of Western Polynesia than those in its own neighbourhood.

The Savage Islanders belong to the Eastern Polynesian race. They are a fine, robust, noble-looking people, but in their heathen state they were the wildest and rudest of all the tribes of uncivilized men with whom it has been my lot to come into contact. This was doubtless owing in a great measure to the fact that they had been almost entirely cut off from intercourse with the world from time immemorial. When strangers visited them their excite-

A CHAPEL AT TAHA.

ment knew no bounds, and broke through all restraint. They realized most fully the idea one is accustomed to form of the savage—wild, fierce, ungovernable. Many of them wore long hair, which hung down upon their shoulders in the most disorderly manner. Clothing they dispensed with as an unnecessary incumbrance. Ornaments, consisting of feathers of various colours, and prepared in different fashions, were worn. A profusion of war weapons appeared on all occasions, and altogether they presented a finished specimen of the untamed barbarian. Such they were, and such they continued to be until within a few years, just what they were when the island was discovered by Cook about ninety years ago. Captain Cook gave it the unenviable designation it still bears on account of the peculiarly fierce character of the people. He says they rushed upon him like wild boars; they commenced an attack on him and his party immediately on their landing; and had he not been a humane man, it is probable that they would have paid dearly for their barbarous conduct. He was disposed, however, to make the allowance that should always be made for a people so circumstanced; and as the island presented no attractions to him compared with his other discoveries, he at once abandoned it, and its savage inhabitants were left to their own uninterrupted solitude for another half century. Their next visitors were a party of Tongans, Friendly Islanders. Whether they received them as they did Cook, we do not know. However that may have been, the Tongans drove back the inhabitants of the district where they landed, and established themselves in their place. I am not aware whether there were any women among the Tongans. Some of these, however, we know formed alliances with native women, and their descendants are found on the island at the present day. When the natives who had been driven from their lands had sufficiently recovered themselves, they came down upon the intruders and repossessed themselves of their ancient homes.

The arrival of the Tongans was followed by another interval, during which the Savage Islanders were again left to their wonted solitude. How long this lasted we do not know, as we are ignorant of the date of its commencement. It was interrupted by an event from which dates a new era in the little island's history. In the month of June, 1830, Mr. Williams, then on his way to Samoa, called at

Savage Island, and made an attempt to place Christian teachers upon it. The teachers were landed, but they found it impossible to remain; the savages rushed upon them and tore their clothes to fragments, and seemed as if they would serve themselves in a similar manner; they were glad to make their escape with their lives. Mr. Williams brought away two natives whom he took to Raiatea, and after a time they were taken back to their native isle. One was killed by his barbarous countrymen, and the other, probably fearing a similar fate, left in some vessel that touched at the island.

The natives had a great dread of disease, and they had an idea that if foreigners were admitted among them they would introduce disease; and when any of themselves left the island and returned, they were regarded in much the same light as foreigners, and in consequence were in nearly as much danger. From the existence of this notion arose the greatest difficulties with which we had to contend in our efforts to introduce the Gospel to the island. The second attempt, which was also planned by Mr. Williams, was made after his death, in 1840. In June of that year a party went from Samoa in a small schooner, and tried their utmost to obtain a footing on the island: the attempt again failed, and the party were exposed to great dangers from the savages and the roughness of the weather; they were mercifully preserved, however, and returned to Samoa, bringing with them three natives and an immense quantity of war weapons, which they were glad to purchase, in order to disarm the noisy and ungovernable barbarians, who surrounded their little craft in numbers that made them feel anything but secure. One of the natives who accompanied them to Samoa was afterwards of some service in the accomplishment of our object. Of the other two, one died shortly after their arrival, and the other left in a ship and was never heard of more.

It was not until 1846 that a positive hold was gained

upon the island. In October of that year the Rev. W. Gill, of Rarotonga, and the Rev. H. Nisbet, of Samoa, visited the island, and succeeded in placing on it Peniamina,* a native who had been several years on Samoa, and who, it was hoped, was really a Christian. He had been a member of a church in Samoa, and had been some time in our institution at Malua. He was allowed to land, and thus we obtained a hold on this peculiarly intractable race. How blind and infatuated is man? We had been pursuing them all these years that we might confer upon them the highest boon, while they, in their ignorance, apprehended only evil from contact with us, and resisted to the utmost our efforts.

The next visit to the island was made by Messrs. Turner and Nisbet, in 1848; they found Peniamina alive and well, but thought they perceived indications that he was not doing much good. He had had a narrow escape from falling a sacrifice to the superstitious notions entertained by his countrymen. "He was in great danger," the brethren write, "when he first landed. The first day crowds assembled—armed, and wishing to kill him. The Samoan canoe given him, together with his chest and property, they wanted to send back to the vessel as soon as they were landed, saying that the foreign wood would cause disease among them. He reasoned with them, told them to examine the wood; it was the very same as grew on their own island. And as to himself, he said, 'you know this

* Peniamina was brought to Samoa in an American whaler, by Captain Simpson. Captain Simpson had touched at Savage Island, and Peniamina had gone on board his vessel and refused to return to the shore. He had heard wonderful tales respecting Samoa, and had conceived an earnest desire to go and see for himself. The captain, who appears to have been a kind and well-disposed man, allowed him to remain, and took him, as he desired, to Samoa. He anchored at Apia, and took an early opportunity of introducing his Savage Island friend to Mr. Mills, the missionary at that place. Mr. Mills took immediate steps towards turning Peniamina's visit to Samoa to account. He got him introduced to the institution at Malua, and there he was brought under those influences which, as we trust, led by the Divine blessing to his conversion to God, and fitted him to return to his own land to become the pioneer of Christian teachers and Christian missionaries.

is my country; I am not a god, I am just like yourselves, and have no control over disease.' Then he told them of the new religion, immortality, heaven, hell, and salvation through Christ. He also prayed with them, and for them. The hearts of many were touched, and they wished to spare him. Others still insisted on his being put to death. 'Let us do it now,' said they; 'let us do it now, while he is alone, and before disease breaks out; by and by others will join him, and then it will be a hard matter.' Night came on, and he had no place to lay his head. The people, fearing pollution, were afraid to let him sleep in their houses. They told him to sleep under a tree for the night. Then they thought of an old fortification, and said he had better go there. Thither he went; but rain came on, and as there was no shelter, he got up and wandered about the settlement. He was asked into one house and there had a morsel of food; and in another he at last found a resting-place. Next day he had to open his chest and show his property; some things were stolen, others he gave them at their urgent request, and he was left with all but an empty box." How truly was poor Peniamina an alien and a stranger in his own land and among his own kindred!

In October, 1849, the writer, in company with Mr. Sunderland, visited the island, and the suspicions that had been awakened respecting Peniamina's conduct were confirmed; he had not acted consistently, still a few had attached themselves to him, and professed to receive Christianity. By these a teacher whom we had reserved for the island was very cordially received, and from that time the evangelization of Savage Island really dates. Paulo, the teacher now introduced to the island, and his wife, were altogether suitable. They had been several years at Malua, and so were tried characters, and were also pretty well furnished for their work. Another step taken during this voyage has also had important consequences. Two natives, a father and son, who were very desirous of learning the Word of God, and seeing what it had done for Samoa, went with us. The reports of Peniamina and others who had been to Samoa had awakened this desire, and also inspired them with confidence in us and our object.

In June, 1852, when Mr. Sunderland and the writer again visited the island, it was found that not only had the teacher and his family been preserved, but very considerable progress had been made. The Gospel had proved itself adequate to the work of taming this otherwise untameable people. The teacher and his worthy wife had been steadfast and faithful in circumstances eminently trying and often perilous; and the Master whom they served had shielded them in the hour of danger, and cheered their hearts by causing His work and power to appear before them. Between two and three hundred had renounced heathenism and embraced Christianity. These had stood nobly by the teacher and his family, making common cause with him, and declaring their determination to stand by him and defend him at all hazards. They had assisted him in procuring the necessaries of life, and in the erection of a dwelling-house. They had also built a chapel which is forty-two feet by thirty. Both this and the teacher's house are weather-boarded. It would be extremely difficult, perhaps impossible, with the means at their command, to procure any considerable quantity of lime at the part of the island where the teacher is stationed, that being surrounded by a bold shore. No small amount of labour must have been required to procure the boards, as they were all cut out with hatchets; there being at that time no such thing as a pit-saw on Savage Island. They had a more formidable obstacle, however, to encounter in building the chapel than anything connected with the mere labour could present. The heathen, who were still a vast majority, had been regarding the movements of the teacher and the Christian party in a jealous, apprehensive spirit, from the beginning. As matters assumed a more and more decided and aggressive bearing, their apprehensions increased; and when the

A GROUP OF NATIVES.

erection of a chapel was proposed, it was considered time to take some active measures. The leading men on the little isle of the sea "wondered whereunto this would grow," and determined on imposing a check. The building of the chapel was forbidden, and war was declared against the Christian party, in case of their persisting in their purpose to build. The teacher was consulted. He referred the matter back to the people; and after full consideration they determined to go forward, whatever the consequences might be. The heathen grumbled and threatened, and on one occasion a party assembled with a view to fall upon the teacher, whom they regarded as the arch evil-doer. The Christian party had gone to a distance to cut wood for the chapel, so they had him and his family quite in their power; they departed, however, without injuring them. Dread of the God of the Christians probably operated chiefly in restraining them; as fear of their own gods influenced them, on the other hand, to oppose what they believed would be displeasing to them. The erection of a place of worship to the God of the strangers must, they seemed to think, be peculiarly provoking to their gods, and expose them to their indignation.

The chapel was finished, and none of the apprehended evil consequences followed. Had it been otherwise, the teacher and the Christian party would have been in most imminent peril. All ended well, however, and a very important step was gained. The influence of the Gospel continued to increase, the leaven continued to spread, and at the time of our visit a sprinkling of Christians was found in various parts of the island, though up to that time we had but one missionary station. In hope of being able to commence a second, we had reserved two teachers. We were in peculiarly favourable circumstances for doing this, as we had with us the two natives taken to Samoa on the former visit, and two others who had been under missionary instruction and influence for several years in Samoa. The name of the old station is Mutalau, and we succeeded in commencing a second at another part of the island named Alofi. We had great difficulty, owing to the outrageous wildness and rudeness of the natives, but all ended well. At the time referred to the state of things was decidedly encouraging. All who professed themselves Christians, and were within reach of the chapel, attended the services steadily. Some walked a considerable distance to attend them every Sabbath. The Christian party generally had worship in their families, and some were accustomed to retire into the bush for private prayer; they had abandoned most of their heathen practices, and broken through the restraints of their ancient superstition, such as regarding sacred places, sacred food, &c. Spots formerly esteemed sacred were being cultivated or built upon, as the case might be. All who professed to have received Christianity wore some article of clothing. Theft, which was very common among the heathen, had quite ceased among the Christians. There had been no war upon the island since the location of the teacher in 1849, and among the Christian party only two instances of polygamy remained.

In some things the customs and practices of this people differed from those of all the tribes of Eastern Polynesia. Suicide, which is rare on the other islands, was rather common on Savage Island. The people were of a very proud and haughty spirit, and rather than submit to things of a humiliating and mortifying character, they would put an end to their lives. Bodily deformity, quarrels, disappointments in love, and the like, led to this step. Lovers, when their desires were opposed, would sometimes commit suicide together.

Illegitimate children were put to death, the parents and relatives of such being ashamed to own them. The teachers had succeeded in saving one of these shortly before our visit. The treatment of the sick was very barbarous. They were removed into the bush and placed in a temporary hut, where they were left until they might recover or die. Their relatives took food to them, but no one remained with them; this practice was owing to the great horror they had of disease. There is a remarkable peculiarity in their disposal of the dead; instead of burying them, or throwing them into the sea, as is done on other islands, they deposited them in natural caves, which abound in the interior of the island. Cannibalism was unknown. They had a vague idea of a future state. Prayers were addressed to Tangaloa, the great deity of Eastern Polynesia, but no sacrifices were offered; the chiefs have very little influence, the man who renders himself most formidable by warlike deeds being the man of greatest consideration.

From the time at which we have now arrived the mission made steady progress, notwithstanding the many and great difficulties with which the teachers had still to contend. The stand taken by the Christian party with reference to the building of the chapel seemed to be the turning point. At the time that stand was taken the heathen interest was on the wane, and the influence of Christianity was being deepened and extended. For a length of time, indeed, the progress was slow, as will be seen from the following extract from the report of the next visit, which was also made by Mr. Sunderland and the writer.

"Owing to a succession of unfavourable winds and calms, we did not reach this island till the 1st of January, 1854. We made the island early on the morning of that day.

"Tidings had reached Samoa which had led us to expect that we should find Alofi, the station we took up last voyage, abandoned. We were happy to find, however, that the teachers had been enabled to remain at their posts, and that some little progress had been made. It will be recollected that the prospects were far from bright when the station was commenced; and shortly after that occurrences took place which occasioned great danger to the teachers, and gave rise to difficulties which will not soon be wholly overcome. Still, they were safe; and the infant mission has lived, and to some extent prospered. A large number have embraced Christianity, and, in consequence, are somewhat improved in external appearance, and attend steadily upon the services conducted by the teachers. A dwelling-house has been erected, and a chapel is about to be built. They have a house which they occupy at present as a temporary place of worship, which answers tolerably well. The usual congregation is about one hundred. From twenty to thirty children are under instruction, and everything encourages the hope that there will be continued progress.

"At the old station, Mutalau, the state of things continues highly encouraging. There has been steady advancement since last visit. The chief, Laumahina, has exerted a most favourable influence. So far he has fully realized our expectations. The people treat the teacher most kindly, and are very attentive to his instructions. A spelling-book and hymn-book have been prepared by the teachers in the native language, with a view to their being printed in Samoa. In the meantime Samoan spelling-books are used. The language spoken on Savage Island is so closely allied to the Samoan that the natives readily learn that. The desire for teachers is now universal, and we hope very shortly to occupy the island fully."

The difficulties referred to as having placed the teachers and the mission in danger at Alofi, arose from the conduct of foreign visitors who had touched at the island. The particulars were made public shortly after the occurrences referred to, and as all is now forgotten, and similar things are not likely to take place again, we forbear reproducing them here.

The report of the next visitor, Mr. Hardie, shows continued and increasingly rapid progress. Mr. Hardie wrote as follows:—

"We reached this island in the afternoon of the 24th of November, just three weeks after we left Mraé. One of the teachers came off and remained on board all night; and on the following day we saw all the teachers, and got their reports. We were happy to find that the hostilities and bad feeling, occasioned by the difficulties referred to in the report of last voyage, had subsided; and that, with with very trifling exceptions, heathenism had been abandoned throughout the whole island. The people now go from land to land without fear, and the teachers can pursue their work everywhere without interruption, and are kindly treated by the people. The desire for instruction is becoming general. To use the words of one of the teachers, 'The mountains of difficulty are now all removed; the Word of God is growing, and will grow rapidly in this land.' The desire of the people for clothing and useful articles, such as hatchets and knives, is very great, and we were pleased to see so much improvement in the covering of their bodies.

"At Mutalau, the first formed station, considerable progress has been made in the work of instruction and moral improvement. About fifty persons have learnt to read well, and many, in different degrees of progress, are learning. The desire for scriptural knowledge is increasing, and upwards of twenty of the most hopeful inquirers have been formed into a select class.

"At Alofi a few have learnt to read, and the desire for instruction is great. More would have been effected here, had not circumstances led to the suspension of the teacher who laboured at this station. We left a new teacher and his wife, from Samoa, at this place; and we have now every reason to hope that the work will progress more rapidly.

"At the new station, formed by the teacher that was taken to the island last voyage, things are very encouraging. He has acquired the language, and preaches among the people very acceptably. He has a good house erected for himself, and also a good chapel, which is filled to overflowing with attentive hearers. He has also two outstations, at which he preaches regularly. The teachers are highly respected, and have gained great influence and are doing much good. Their labours are much hindered for want of suitable school apparatus. We hope this want will be supplied when they are next visited. It was our happiness to convey to them 1,000 copies of an elementary school book, containing select portions of the Old and New-Testaments, and also a small collection of hymns. It will be a great boon to the people, and will be highly

PAPEETE BAY, TAHITI.

prized by them. This book was translated by the teachers into the native language, and printed at Samoa.

"The desire for teachers is great, and we ought as soon as possible to send two more efficient men, who, with those already there, will fully supply the island."

The words of the teacher quoted above have had an emphatic fulfilment. The Word of God has grown rapidly in this land. From this time the Word of God had free course and was glorified. Mountains sank to plains, and hell in vain opposed. To this the report of the next deputation, Messrs. Harbutt and Drummond, bears decisive and delightful testimony. They write as follows:—

"We sighted this island on the morning of Saturday, August 1st, and at evening stood close in to Tamahatava, the station of Paula. He came off to the vessel in a canoe, and from him we learned that the work of the Lord continued to make rapid progress on the island. We intimated through him to the people that we should spend the Sabbath ashore, and requested that the teachers should be invited to meet us at his station, that we might have the ordinance of the Lord's Supper together; and on Sabbath morning we perceived, from the crowds of natives assembled near the road leading to the teacher's house and the chapel, that our request had been attended to. So, immediately after morning prayer, Mr. Turpie, the first officer, took us ashore in a boat, whilst the vessel stood off and on. We were accompanied by Mr. Creagh and his little boy, and Mrs. Harbutt and children. We proceeded at once to the teacher's house, amidst a crowd of natives sitting on each side of the path. They did not interrupt us in our walk by their usual salutation, as they had been instructed by the teachers not to do so before the close of the services. It was a happy thing for us that they attended to their instructions, as we had found shaking hands with such concourses of people to be rather a formidable affair. After arriving at the teacher's house, we learnt that so many of the people had arrived from different places that it would be impossible for them to get into the chapel, and it was proposed to hold the meeting at a place near, under the shade of bread-fruit and banana trees. To this we agreed, and had the native bell rung to call the people together. We were quite surprised to find an assemblage of at least 2,000 congregated. The services were commenced by Paulo, the teacher placed at Mutalau. He first gave out a hymn in the native tongue, which was sung by the assembled multitude, in strains not over refined, but sweet and melodious to a missionary's ear, and, we have no doubt, also to the ears of those ministering spirits who are sent forth to minister to those who shall be the heirs of salvation. After the hymn was sung, Paulo prayed in the native language; then followed our addresses in the Samoan language, which were translated by Paulo. The people listened to the words spoken with intense interest. Mr. Harbutt next baptised some children belonging to the teachers, after which the ordinance of the Lord's Supper was administered to the teachers and other church members present. This ordinance was accompanied with addresses in the Samoan language suitable to their circumstances. We retired to the shore, and returned in our boat to the vessel, with hearts filled with gratitude to God for what He had done for this once savage land through the instrumentality of native agency.

" On Monday morning we again went ashore, to receive from the teacher of this station some arrowroot belonging to the London Missionary Society, obtained in exchange for the edition of the elementary school books brought to the island last voyage of the *John Williams*, every copy of which had been sold without half supplying the wants of the people; and also to receive a present from the people in the shape of supplies for the vessel. This was another deeply interesting day. The number of people present was not less than on the previous day; and their joy and delight on our approach seemed to know no bounds. We gave the teachers their supplies, and conversed with them about the state of the people and the progress of their work. Their reports were of a highly satisfactory nature. Heathenism is completely subverted, and on that savage island, which only a few years ago was the scene of ceaseless strife and savage warfare, Peace has established her reign, and men live together in unity and love beneath the sway of her golden sceptre. The teachers expressed a strong desire for additional help, and we left with them Amosa and Sakaio, two Samoan teachers, who had laboured many years on Aneiteum. These teachers will occupy two additional stations, which will increase their number on the island to five. We left them two works (1,000 copies each), a sketch of Scripture History and a Doctrinal Catechism; these had been translated by the teachers here, and printed at Samoa; also a few copies of the New Testament in the Samoan language, which some of the natives understand and others are attempting to learn. The teachers took a census of the island a short time ago, and they report that it contains a population of 4,276. The entire population capable of instruction attend the schools of the teachers.

"At Mutalau, Paulo's district, the number of catechumens is 240; at Tamahatava, Paula's district, the number is 153; and at Avatele, the district of Samuela, 284.

"Captain Williams was employed all day carrying off to the vessel the arrowroot above referred to, and supplies for the vessel presented by the teachers and people. And in the evening, highly pleased with our visit, we proceeded to the beach amidst a crowd so dense, that we found some difficulty in making our way through it. After getting into our boat we soon reached the vessel, which was waiting for us at a little distance, being highly favoured by the wind, which was blowing off the land. We then bore down for Avatele, Samuela's station, where we had promised to call for more arrowroot belonging to the Society, and supplies for the vessel, which the people promised to have all ready for us as soon as we went ashore. This place we reached on the following morning, and without delay went ashore. Here we received the same kind of welcome that we had at Paulo's station the previous day; indeed, many of the people whom we saw at the latter place had followed us thither, and were as ready for a shake of the hand as ever. Captain Williams had the boats loaded immediately with arrowroot and returned to the vessel, and we proceeded to the teacher's house. All around it were piled up heaps of yams, taro, bananas, &c. We examined the teacher's house; it is, like Paula's at Tamahatava, an excellent boarded house, with three or four rooms. The wood is of superior quality. Every board in the house was cut out with a hatchet, one tree yielding two boards. What immense labour must have been expended on it by the hewers of wood! We also visited the chapel adjoining the teacher's house. It is a very excellent piece of workmanship, with doors, Venetian blinds, and a good pulpit. It will seat a congregation of 400 people; but it is too small, as one-half of the Sabbath congregation have to sit outside. All the pillars are made of excellent wood, and beautifully hewn. The Savage Islanders must be a very ingenious and industrious people. After inspecting the chapel we returned to the teacher's house; and after a short time took a stroll through part of the settlement, to look at the soil which so abundantly supplies the wants of the people. This island is entirely of coral formation, very much resembling that of Maré, but much more fertile. Captain Williams was busy all the day with his boats, carrying off to the vessel what the natives carried to the shore; and now he approached the shore for the last time, which was a sufficient warning for us to prepare to leave; and at last we left the teacher's house and proceeded towards the sea, amidst an immense crowd of people of all ages, from the grey-headed great-grandfather down to the little urchin only beginning to chatter. The process of shaking hands and bidding adieu went on without intermission till we reached the boat, into which we were tumbled with some difficulty from the shoulders of those who picked us up and carried us through the rising tide to the rocks which bound its approach.

"The Savage Islanders are a remarkably mild and intelligent looking people. How marked the difference between them now and the portrait drawn of them by Williams, when he visited the island in the year 1830!"

RECEPTION BY SAVAGE ISLANDERS.

Marked indeed was the difference between the Savage Islanders of 1857 and 1830—and, indeed, of 1853. Here is an extract from Williams's description of the first they succeeded in inducing to come on board the *Messenger of Peace*:—" An old chieftain was at length induced to venture into the boat, and with him they hastened to the ship. His appearance was truly terrific. His whole body was smeared with charcoal, his hair and beard were both long and grey, and the latter, plaited and twisted together, hung from his mouth like so many rats' tails. He wore no clothing, except a narrow strip of cloth round his loins for the purpose of passing a spear through, or any other article he might wish to carry. On reaching the deck the old man was most frantic in his gesticulations, leaping about from place to place, and using the most vociferous exclamations at everthing he saw. All attempts at conversation with him were entirely useless; we could not persuade him to stand still even for a single second. Our natives attempted to clothe him, by fastening around his person a piece of native cloth; but, tearing it off in a rage, he threw it upon deck, and stamping upon it, exclaimed, 'Am I a woman, that I should be encumbered with that stuff?'" Let the reader imagine that instead of one such "child of nature" as is here described, there are some forty or fifty assembled on the deck, all equally fierce and ungovernable, with perhaps thirty or forty canoes surrounding the ship, each carrying two, three, or more savages not less wild and formidable, and he will have before him a scene such as was often witnessed on board the *John Williams* off Savage Island a few years ago. Mr. Williams concludes his notice of the Savage Islanders as follows:—" They are certainly the most wretched and degraded of any natives I have ever seen, except the aborigines of New Holland." Such *were* the Savage Islanders. How altered *now!* How marvellous the change! Who after this will dream of doubting the adaptation of the Gospel to man in his most degraded state, and its power to subdue and tame the wildest and most fierce of the race of Adam? Had philosophy achieved any such triumph as the Gospel has accomplished, not only on Savage Island, but on several other islands which have passed under review in these pages, its praises would have been sounded to the world's end. But seeing it is only the Gospel that has done it, it attracts but little notice, and excites but little interest or inquiry. A different estimate, however, is formed in that world where things are viewed and estimated according to their true character. "Likewise, I say unto you, there is joy in the presence of the angels of God over one sinner that repenteth."

The report of the next deputation, Mr. Stallworthy and Mr. G. Gill, is not less encouraging than that of Messrs. Drummond and Harbutt. It is as follows:—

"We have now five Samoan teachers there (on Savage Island) who reside at so many villages, namely, Samuela, at Avatele; Paula, at Tamahatava; Sakaio, at Makefu; Paulo, at Mutalau; and Amosa, at Hakapu. By this arrangement the means of instruction are placed within a convenient distance of the whole population. God has graciously and wonderfully assisted and prospered the teachers in their work. The whole population, with the exception of thirty or forty individuals, are nominally Christian, and regularly attend worship.

"Early on Sabbath morning our vessel was close in to the land, at the station of Samuela. A canoe came off to us, and we learned that Samuela and all the teachers were at the next station, Tamahatava, where they had assembled on account of the dangerous illness of the wife of Paula, the teacher there. We accordingly proceeded to that place, which is not more than eight miles distant. The teachers received early notice of our approach, and delayed their morning service so as to allow us time to land.

"After a short rest in the teacher's house, the beating of two 'longos,' or hollowed trees, summoned the people to worship. The chapel has been erected during the past year. It is a thoroughly good one, and neatly ornamented; built and floored with wood, light, airy, and comfortable in appearance. It was well filled with a congregation, we judged, of about 600 persons, and many posted themselves around outside. As the language was foreign to us, and we desired to see the service as usually conducted, we left the whole proceedings in the hands of the teachers. Paulo officiated. He gave out the hymns, read a psalm, one of the few portions of Scripture printed in the language, and preached very energetically. The singing, which was led by a Samoan, was very good. The behaviour of the people was most becoming, and their attention unwavering. We were exceedingly interested, and could not but magnify the grace of God, which had given such efficacy to the humble instrumentality of the teachers. A similar service, equally well attended, was conducted by Sakaio in the afternoon. We slept on shore the two nights of our stay.

"During a great part of Monday, and till breakfast-time on Tuesday, we were occupied in conversing, one by one, through the teachers as interpreters, with the class of candidates for church fellowship, which had been formed in accordance with the instructions of last year's deputation.

"Most of those received to that class had for a long time maintained an irreproachable standing in the preparatory classes of the teachers. As might be expected, we found among them great diversity of attainment in knowledge and religious experience; but there were only four of those presented to us whose admission we thought it desirable to postpone. On Tuesday forenoon we met the accepted candidates, consisting of forty men and twelve women, in the chapel, when some words of instruction and exhortation were addressed to them, and we admitted them to the church by the divinely instituted ordinance of baptism. One fallen Samoan Church member, who resides on the island, was restored to communion. The total number of church members now on Niue, including teachers, their wives, and Niueans admitted in Samoa, is sixty-five. The names of all were entered in a book, which is left in the hands of the teachers for their reference, and for future deputations. May the little one become a thousand, and the Christians on Niue continue to show forth the praises of Him who has called them out of darkness into His marvellous light, until the Saviour shall appear a second time on the earth!"

The above visit was made in August, 1858; and in December, 1859, the last visit which we have to record was made. The report of that visit, which was by Dr. Turner, is a deeply interesting record. It furnishes most delightful evidence of the reality and extent of the work that has been accomplished on the island, and touches on a variety of incidental matters which will interest the reader. It is as follows:—

"Monday, Dec. 12.—Sighted Savage Island at 9 A.M. Instead of approaching it as I did eleven years ago, half expecting to hear that the teacher was killed, it was delightful now to look upon it as a Christian land, and to draw near to it anticipating a happy meeting with a Christian people. For a period of sixteen years the powers of darkness resisted every effort to obtain an entrance for Christianity. It is eleven years now since the Savage Islanders were induced to receive a Samoan teacher, and from year to year the good work has gone on and prospered.

"By two P.M. we were off the station of our teacher Samuela, on the south side of the island, and Captain Williams, Mr. Inglis, and I proceeded in the boats to the shore. Although the sea ran high, no fewer than seventeen canoes were launched and off to meet us; and, accompanied by this fleet and its happy band of natives, we pulled to the landing-place. The first glance at the people in their canoes, from the ship's deck, showed a marked change since I was here before. Instead of nudity, and long dishevelled hair flying in the wind or fast in a coil between the teeth, all have their hair cut short, and at least a wrapper or a kilt of some sort from the waist down below the knee. We found the teacher Samuela and his family well, and living in one of the best teacher's houses I have ever seen—quite a *palace* of a place: eighty feet by thirty feet, divided into seven apartments, well plastered, finished with doors and Venetians, and furnished

REV. J. GREEN'S ISLAND HOME.

with tables, chairs, sofas, and bedsteads. We were delighted also with the size and unusually fine workmanship of the chapel. It is ninety feet by twenty-four feet, and holds 500 people; but it is too small, and the people are about to build a larger one. After spending an hour or two here, Captain Williams and Mr. Inglis returned to the ship; I remained on shore, and arranged to meet them on the following day at Alofi, eight miles farther on, round towards the west.

"The teacher Amosa soon arrived from his station at Hakapu, on the south side, and with him and Samuela I spent the evening, talking over the affairs of the mission, and arranging for the services of the coming day. Retired to rest on a nice muslin curtained bedstead, which they kindly spread for me with blankets and sheets; but I had too much to think about to get more than a two hours' nap. Soon after midnight, the natives were all on the move, church members, candidates, and others going to the meeting, and others catching pigs and fowls to take off for sale to the vessel.

"Had family prayer early with the teachers, and was off by 4 A.M., in the moonlight, to walk to Alofi. It was heart-stirring to hear at daylight the voice of prayer and praise proceeding from the cottages of the natives as we passed along the road. Some had family worship over, and were out, eager to get a shake of the hand as I passed. Some were not content with the hand or arm, but they must seize the *leg* too, and give it a hearty national *snuff* or *smell*. I was thus brought to a hard and fast standstill at times, but after a *smiling* wrestle with the warm-hearted people I got clear, and on along the road again.

"The natives have completed a good six feet road all round the island. It has been partly made and kept in repair by convict labour. For theft and other crimes the chiefs sentence offenders to two, five, ten, or even fifty fathoms of road-making. They fill up the spaces between the uneven coral with small stones, and level all with a layer of earth or sand. They are raising a row of cocoa-nuts on either side of the road for a shade. A missionary will find this road a great facility to his labours, as it will enable him to take a horse all round the island, a distance of from forty to fifty miles perhaps.

"The island is well wooded. Of the cultivated places

along the road, I was especially struck with some large sugar-cane plantations, and the canes standing erect as high as thirty feet. They support them with long poles, which keep them erect and separate the clumps from each other. I observed also that the cocoa-nuts of the island are unusually large. Eighteen inches in circumference is the common average of the nut after the husk has been taken off.

"About half way, I looked in as I passed at a school-house just finished, fifty feet by twenty feet, and in the finest style of their workmanship. They have five more of these school-houses at regular distances round the island, between the five large chapels.

"I was at Alofi by 7 A.M. Here I met with some of the natives who had been with us at Samoa, and was besieged again by the hand-shakers, but soon got into the teacher's house—a fine building that is too, even more so than the one I saw the day before. Here I met with the other three teachers, namely, Paulo, Paula, and Sakaio, and commenced the important, but very difficult, work of examining candidates for admission to the church. The teachers had evidently been careful in the selection of them, and out of those proposed from the five stations we decided on receiving thirty-one men and nineteen women. Those who were formed into a church last year have all remained steadfast, and, with the addition of those just named, there is an aggregate of 102 of the Savage Islanders in church fellowship. After baptising the newly-admitted members, we all united in commemorating the death of Christ.

"After the communion I met again with the five teachers, gave them their annual supplies, and talked over a variety of matters; arranged that Paula, whose wife died some time ago, and who is aged and inefficient, should return to Samoa, and that the Samoan teacher Elia should take his place; supplied them with copies of the commentary on the Gospel of Matthew in the Samoan dialect, and left 4,000 copies of a revised Hymn and Scripture Lesson Book in the Savage Island dialect, the paper for which was kindly furnished by the Religious Tract Society in London.

"The teacher handed me a manuscript of a translation of the Gospel of Mark in the dialect of Savage Island, with a request to print it at Samoa, if approved of by us. It was translated by Paulo, who has been ten years on the island; and subsequently all the teachers met in committee and revised the MS. I said they might go on with Matthew next. Of course they translate from the Samoan version. They will exert themselves, I have no doubt, to do it well; and, although a translation from a translation, and by native teachers, the MS. may be of much service to missionaries who, I trust, will ere long be sent forth to the island.

"The population may be set down at 4,300. All are now Christian, with the exception of some ten, who still stand aloof. The opinion is universal all over the island that there is now an increase of the population. The women are more numerous than the men, and we were all struck with the number of children to be seen, compared with many other islands. There was a fearful destruction of children in the days of heathenism, principally *before* birth. The climate is remarkably healthy. We have found this universal with the *coral* formations. It is on the *volcanic* islands where our teachers and missionaries have suffered so much from fever and ague.

"The teachers said the chiefs wished to know how they could obtain a protectorate from the British Government. I said it was not likely that Britain would grant their request; still it could do no harm to make known their wishes, only they must do it, not through the missionaries, but through some of H.B.M.'s official representatives—say the British Consul at Samoa, or the commander of any of H.B.M.'s ships which may touch at the island.

"The *John Williams* was off the settlement of Alofi all

day, and the boats made five trips to the shore, taking off arrowroot, pigs, fowls, yams, teachers' parcels, etc. The arrowroot amounted to about 2,240 lbs., and is the proceeds of sales of books; 1,540 yams, 10 pigs, and 40 fowls were a present from the people to the *John Williams*, and, in addition, Mr. Griffin bought about 50 pigs and 120 fowls for the vessel. I was glad to find that the demand was not for tobacco, but exclusively for such useful articles as calico, shirts, knives, hatchets, etc.

"In the afternoon we had a public meeting in the

QUEEN POMARE'S PALACE, TAHITI.

chapel. It is 100 feet long by 35, and is one of the finest chapels I have seen in the South Seas. It was closely packed with a clean, decently clothed, and attentive audience. Captain Williams, Mr. and Mrs Inglis, the Misses Geddie, and others from the ship were also present. Including those on the verandahs on either side of the chapel, there were at least 1,100 present. Mr. Inglis and I addressed them through the teachers as interpreters and they also conducted the singing and devotional parts of the service. Such a sight, and in such a place, made it a season of joy to all of us which we shall never forget.

"We were again on board ship and off for Samoa before dark. I have repeatedly wished in the course of this voyage that I had another body to dispose of, and give up to labour in the cause of Christ; but I never felt this to such an extent as I did on leaving that shore of Savage Island, covered with loving, grateful people, all eager for a shake of the hand, and to express, as best they could, their unfeigned respect. And these are the children of the men who rushed out upon our great navigator Cook, 'like wild boars,' and who, for sixty years after his time, kept to the determination that no stranger should ever live upon their island. They repeatedly rushed out upon parties of white men, as they did upon Captain Cook, and were occasionally fired upon. Natives of other islands who were drifted there in distress, whether from Tonga, or Samoa, or elsewhere, were invariably killed. Any of their own people who went away in a ship, and came back, were killed; and all this was occasioned by a dread of the introduction of disease. For years, too, after they began to venture out to ships, they would not immediately use anything obtained, but hung it up in the bush in quarantine for weeks.

"Eleven years ago the exclusive system, against which we had so long been struggling, gave way, and the wish was formally made known to us that Samoan teachers should be sent to them; and that now nothing would be more grateful than the arrival of white missionaries. God soon granted to them the desire of their hearts. Nor is the great change confined to their reception of Christianity as a religious system, but, as is manifest from what I have already said, the whole framework of their political and social life is changed. Their wars and more clandestine lurking for each other's blood are ended. Old grievances are laid aside, and free intercourse is the rule all over the island. The pig-sty dwellings are fast giving way to the Samoan model of large houses, well spread with mats. Instead of destroying all the plantations and fruit-trees of a person who dies, that they might go with him, all is now spared, and the consequence is an abundance of food, such as they never had in heathenism. Instead of living in single families, and migrating here and there in the bush, the five teachers' stations are fast becoming the nuclei of settled villages, with magistrates and laws; and the change in the whole state of affairs is as amazing to the people themselves as it is to a stranger. I have never seen a more inviting field of missionary labour. Happy the men who may be privileged to cultivate it!"

What a picture does the above report present! What a wonderful picture! We can only exclaim, "What hath God wrought!"

Our last tidings from Savage Island are contained in a letter from Paulo, the senior teacher on the island, dated July 1st, 1860. It is addressed to Mr. Stallworthy. It is a touching consideration that Mr. Stallworthy had rested from his labours many months before the letter was written. The island is so seldom touched at by vessels that, though in our immediate neighbourhood, more than twelve months often pass without any intelligence reaching us. Paulo's letter furnishes an interesting comment on the above report. He writes as follows:—" We are all living happily with the people. Nothing untoward is occurring these days. The work of God is prospering, indeed. There are a great many candidates. The laws also are obeyed, and the ordinances of religion are respected by those who are irreligious, and do not incline to the Word of God. The remaining heathen are of small account; perhaps not ten remain. Of the church members admitted by you, three have fallen on account of theft, and one has died; all the rest have remained steadfast. So also is it with those who were admitted by

Dr. Turner; the forty-nine remain steadfast, but one has fallen, having been guilty of stealing food."

In closing our notice of Savage Island, we will not indulge in general reflections. The record speaks for itself in language which needs no interpreter. "In due time ye *shall* reap if ye faint not." What a delightful comment does it furnish on these words of Divine encouragement! And those other cheering words, "Your

THE ISLAND OF FOTUNA.

labour is not in vain in the Lord." Let the friends of Christian missions be stimulated to put forth their utmost efforts in the high and holy enterprise in which they are embarked, seeing that the cause in which they are engaged is the cause of God; and that success—ultimate and complete success—is just as sure as are the promises and the oath of the Most High.

POSTSCRIPT.

THE present special edition of Mr. Murray's deeply interesting volume takes the place of one now out of print, and brings the memorable details of his work in the Islands down to the year 1862; since then, Mr. Murray has been zealously working for his Divine Master, and has accumulated further illustrations of successful labour in various islands, and especially of his pioneering work in *New Guinea*, whither he has gone to introduce among that people the all-conquering Gospel of the Grace of God; and these further details of Mission Life in Polynesia may possibly be given to the Christian public ere long in another volume, by Mr. Murray.